GLOBAL BEST PRACTICE

# Managing Successful Programmes

London: TSO

Published by TSO (The Stationery Office) and available from:

**Online**
**www.tsoshop.co.uk**

**Mail, Telephone, Fax & E-mail**
TSO
PO Box 29, Norwich, NR3 1GN
Telephone orders/General enquiries: 0870 600 5522
Fax orders: 0870 600 5533
E-mail: customer.services@tso.co.uk
Textphone: 0870 240 3701

**TSO@Blackwell and other Accredited Agents**

First edition Crown copyright 1999
Second edition Crown copyright 2003
Third edition Crown copyright 2007
Fourth edition Crown copyright 2011
Third impression 2014

ISBN 9780113313273

Printed in the United Kingdom for The Stationery Office
Material is FSC certified and produced using ECF pulp, sourced from fully sustainable forests.

# Contents

# List of figures

# List of tables

# Foreword

Change has joined death and taxes as one of the certainties in life, or so it seems. Organizations need to select, introduce and implement important changes to their businesses in a structured way so that the right changes are introduced in an orderly way. The Best Management Practice portfolio sets out what 'good' looks like for portfolio, programme and project management by drawing on and sharing the knowledge and experience of experts, academics and, most importantly, practitioners. It supports a consistent approach to introducing transformational change and promotes a common language both within and between organizations.

This latest edition of *Managing Successful Programmes* (MSP®) has rightly concentrated on the need to achieve high-quality outcomes, and the majority of the updates have therefore focused on three key elements:

- The identification and delivery of benefits that were anticipated when the programme was authorized
- Quality and assurance to ensure that the programme is well run and will deliver change effectively and produce the desired outcomes
- The active management of risk.

The report 'Assurance for High Risk Projects' (National Audit Office, 2010) called for a mandatory and integrated approach to assurance for high-risk projects. The same increased focus on assurance is reflected in this edition of MSP, which is consistent with, but not limited to, the approach being taken by the UK government for high-risk projects. For example, MSP focuses on the generic principles and shows the specifics of the approach employed by the UK's Major Projects Authority.

The latest changes to MSP make the guidance more straightforward to use, strengthening the links to desired outcomes, outlining the risks to achieving them, and adding value throughout the process. At the same time, MSP retains its focus on the underpinning principles of programme management as described in the previous edition. These principles flow throughout the governance themes and the MSP framework to deliver the transformational change. MSP helps to ensure that organizations are introducing changes that are aligned with corporate strategy, and that the reasons behind the changes and the vision for a better future are effectively communicated.

I am confident that this new edition, along with the associated accredited training and qualification scheme that supports it, will help current and aspiring programme managers and their support teams to successfully deliver transformational change for their organizations.

David Pitchford

*Executive Director*
*Major Projects Authority, Cabinet Office*

# Acknowledgements

This edition of *Managing Successful Programmes* updates the 2007 edition following a review of the changes proposed through the Best Management Practice change control system. The Cabinet Office and publishers are grateful to the following for their contribution in developing the update, as well as those who worked on the 2007 edition.

## 2011 EDITION

### Authoring team

Rod Sowden, Aspire Europe Ltd
                                   Overall lead author and mentor
Martin Wolf, Echolot Ltd     Principal change author
Garry Ingram, Tanner James                         Author

Geof Leigh of Goaldart Ltd helped with drafting the change control and configuration management sections.

### Project governance

The update project management team comprised:

| | |
|---|---|
| Mike Acaster, Cabinet Office | Project executive |
| Eddie Borup, ibp | Senior user |
| Janine Eves, TSO | Senior supplier |
| Neil Glover, TSO | Project manager |
| Richard Pharro, APM Group | Senior supplier |

### Reference and design review group

The mandate and product description for the new edition were developed with the help of:

Stephen Barney, Core IS; Colin Bartle-Tubbs, cbt Programme Solutions Ltd; Ian Bush, Ministry of Defence; Anne-Marie Byrne, independent consultant; Professor Darren Dalcher, Middlesex University; Dr Bill Egginton, Cranfield Defence & Security; Alan Ferguson, AFA; Alan Harpham, APM Group; Adrian Hicks, Kalamunda Consulting Ltd; Chris Hobson, CITI Ltd; Adrian Kent, NSG; Julia Lawrence, FSA (interim consultant); Geof Leigh, Goaldart Ltd; Robert Owen, University of Salford; Julian Parkin, Barclays; Tim Porter, Standard Chartered Bank; Paul Rayner, ex Logica plc; Andrew Schuster, King's Health Partners; Carole Sullivan, Civil Service Learning; Andy Taylor, Aquila Business Services Ltd; Lia de Zoete, Capgemini Netherlands

### Change control panel

The following people helped with the assessment of change requests and reviewed drafts throughout the development process:

John Brinkworth, Solution Identification Ltd; Rubina Faber, Regal Training and Consultancy Ltd; Tim Reeks, HMRC; Graham Williams, GSW Consulting Ltd

### Reviewers

We are very grateful to the following for the time and effort put into reviewing drafts of the new edition:

Carol Bartlett, Amicar Consulting Ltd; Colin Bartle-Tubbs, cbt Programme Solutions Ltd; Colin Bentley, author of the early PRINCE2 manuals; Anne-Marie Byrne, independent consultant; Alison Cesaro, Adaptive Frameworks; Robert Cole, Centre for Change Management; Alistair Cranmer, Oppidum BV; Terry Dailey, Deliverables LLP; Kenn Dolan, FPMS; Dr Bill Egginton, Cranfield Defence & Security; Alan Ferguson, AFA; Chris Ferguson, Novare Consulting; Daniel Fisher, Cambiel Consulting; Anne Gibb, Agba; Peter Glynne, Deloitte; Piotr Górny, Infovide-Matrix; Alan Harpham, APM Group; Adrian Hicks, Kalamunda Consulting Ltd; David S. Hinley, Enodatum Ltd; Chris Hobson, CITI Ltd; Adam Humphrey, Effective Projects Ltd; Stephen Jenner, Portfolio Solutions; Peter Johnson, independent consultant; Phil Kemp, Cabinet Office; Julia Lawrence, FSA (interim consultant); Geof Leigh, Goaldart Ltd; Vincent Marsi, Hilogic; Ruth Murray-Webster, Lucidus Consulting; Garth Newboult, Pentagon Professional Development; Robert Owen, University of Salford; Julian Parkin, Barclays; Brian Phillips, Yellowhouse; Jens Pind, EPM Group; Tim Porter, Standard Chartered Bank; Geoff Rankins, Goal Professional Services Pty Ltd; Paul Rayner, ex Logica plc; Michelle Rowland, A&J Project Management Ltd; Stelios Sapountzis, University of Salford; Noel Scott, Symantec Corporation; Claire Skuse, VOSA; Joseph A. Sopko, Siemens; Jennifer Stapleton, independent consultant; Andy Taylor, Aquila Business Services Ltd; Steve Tremblay, Excelsa Technologies Consulting Inc; Lorraine

Trenchard, UK Transformational Consulting; Shelagh Turnbull, Scottish Borders Council; David Waller, goalmodelling.com; David Whelbourn, Government of New Brunswick, Canada; Stephen Wierzbicki, Bristol Management Centre; Lia de Zoete, Capgemini Netherlands

## 2007 EDITION

The 2011 edition has left much of the 2007 edition unchanged and Best Management Practice is grateful to the team that developed the earlier work.

### Authoring team

| | |
|---|---|
| Rod Sowden, Aspire Europe | Lead author |
| Geof Leigh, Goaldart Ltd | Author |
| Patrick Mayfield, pearcemayfield | Author |
| Chris Venning, Henley Change Management Ltd | Author |

### Mentors

Gerald Bradley and Andrew Schuster

### MSP reference group

In order to maintain MSP's reflection of current best practice and to produce guidance with lasting value, the Office of Government Commerce (OGC) consulted widely with key stakeholders at every stage in the process. OGC would like to thank the following individuals and their organizations for their contributions to refreshing the MSP guidance:

Pippa Bass, OGC; Graham Bird, GCHQ; Mark Fensome, DfES; Nick Meadham, National School for Government; Siobhan O'Connell, OGC; David Partington, Cranfield School of Management; Andrew Richards, Holos Consulting; Andrew Schuster, Department of Health; Andy Taylor, APMG chief examiner for MSP; Martin Wickes, KPMG

### Additional support

Anne-Marie Byrne, as OGC project executive, is grateful for the additional support to the authoring team provided by Ian Stanbury and Graham Williams.

Colin Bartle-Tubbs, Pieter deWet, Anne Middleton and Dez West provided additional quality assurance as members of the change control panel.

### Reviewers

John Bartlett, Great Stave; Denise Blunn, OGC; John Brinkworth, Serco Consulting; Terry Dailey, Deliverables Management Consultants; Alan Ferguson, AFA; Charles Fox, Core IS; Melanie Franklin, Maven Training; Peter Glynne, Northern Ireland Department of Finance and Personnel; Alan Harpham, APM Group; Bert Hedeman, Insights International BV; David Hillson, Risk Doctor & Partners; Peter Johnson, OGC; Hosam Mostafa, Olympic Programme Support Unit; Ruth Murray-Webster, Lucidus Consulting; Keith Norton, Serco; Nita Patel, NHS; Geoff Reiss, Geoff Reiss Ltd; Michelle Rowland, A&J Project Management Ltd; Magnus Schoeman, Xansa; Graham Tanfield, Department for Children, Schools and Families; Sue Vowler, Project Angels; Nick Walker, National Policing Improvement Agency; Peter Weaver, The PSO

# PART 1

## Introduction and programme management principles

# Introduction

1

# 1  Introduction

## 1.1  PURPOSE OF THIS GUIDE

Today's organizations are subject to continual change. There are often many, dynamic and contradictory drivers for change, including innovations in technology, working practices (for example, outsourcing and partnerships), mergers, increased demands from regulation and, for the public sector, delivery of policy driven by changing political parties and/or ministers. Whatever the organization, wherever it is located and however it is structured, the rate of change is increasing.

Organizations that have learned how to transform themselves through effective leadership and strategic control are more likely to survive and prosper. Programme management is increasingly being recognized as a key tool to enable organizations to deliver their strategy and manage that transformation.

*Managing Successful Programmes* (MSP) represents proven good practice in programme management in successfully delivering transformational change, drawn from the experiences of both public and private sector organizations.

This guide provides:

- An adaptable route map for programme management, bringing together key principles, governance themes and a set of interrelated processes to facilitate the delivery of business transformation
- Advice on how these programme management principles, themes and flow processes can be embedded, reviewed and applied, to gain measurable benefits from business change.

The MSP framework is based on three core concepts as shown in Figure 1.1. These are:

- **MSP principles** (outer ring)  Derived from lessons learned in programmes that had both positive and negative results. They represent common factors that underpin the success of any programme of transformational change.
- **MSP governance themes** (second ring)  An organization's approach to programme management needs to be defined, measured and controlled. The governance themes

allow organizations to put in place the right leadership, delivery team, robust organization structures, controls and control information (e.g. blueprint, business case, quality and assurance strategy), giving the best chance of delivering the planned outcomes and realizing the desired benefits.

- **MSP transformational flow** (inner circle)  The flow provides a route through the lifecycle of a programme from its conception through to delivering the new capability, transitioning to the desired outcomes, realizing the benefits and finally on to the close of the programme.

This guide is intended primarily for those who are involved in the direction, management, support and delivery of programmes. It is presented as a guide for programme managers, business change managers (BCMs) and programme office staff. It also provides guidance for leaders and programme sponsors who are also known as the senior responsible owners (SROs) of programmes of change.

## 1.2  WHAT IS A PROGRAMME?

In MSP, a programme is defined as a temporary, flexible organization created to coordinate, direct and oversee the implementation of a set of related projects and activities in order to deliver outcomes and benefits related to the organization's strategic objectives. A programme is likely to have a life that spans several years.

A project is also a temporary organization, usually existing for a much shorter duration, which will deliver one or more outputs in accordance with an agreed business case. A particular project may or may not be part of a programme.

Programmes deal with outcomes; projects deal with outputs. Programme management and project management are complementary approaches. During a programme lifecycle, projects are initiated, run and closed. Programmes provide an umbrella under which these projects can be coordinated.

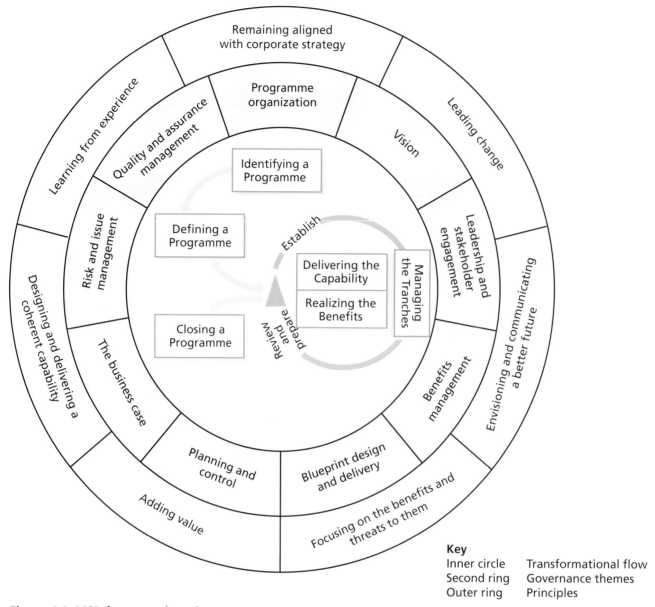

*Figure 1.1 MSP framework and concepts*

Programme management does not replace the need for competent project direction and management. Programmes must be underpinned by a controlled project environment of effective direction, management, delivery and reporting disciplines that are common to all projects within a programme.

## 1.3 WHAT IS PROGRAMME MANAGEMENT?

MSP defines programme management as the action of carrying out the coordinated organization, direction and implementation of a dossier of projects and transformation activities

(i.e. the programme) to achieve outcomes and realize benefits of strategic importance to the business.

Programme management aligns three critical organizational elements:

- Corporate strategy
- Delivery mechanisms for change
- Business-as-usual environment.

It manages the natural tension that exists between these elements to deliver transformational change that meets the needs of the organization and its stakeholders. It also manages the transition of the solutions developed and delivered by projects into the organization's operations, whilst maintaining performance and effectiveness. It does this by breaking things into manageable chunks (tranches) with review points for monitoring progress and assessing performance and benefits realization to date.

Programme management provides a framework that integrates and reconciles competing demands for resources, providing a context and control framework for the projects of the programme. It often involves changes to the culture, style and character of organizations. The people aspects of change must be recognized and accommodated if the programme is to succeed.

## 1.4 WHY USE PROGRAMME MANAGEMENT?

Where there is major change there will be complexity and risk, many interdependencies to manage and conflicting priorities to resolve. Experience shows that organizations are likely to fail to deliver change successfully where:

- There is insufficient board-level support
- Leadership is weak
- There are unrealistic expectations of the organizational capacity and ability to change
- There is insufficient focus on benefits
- There is no real picture (blueprint) of the future capability
- There is a poorly defined or poorly communicated vision
- The organization fails to change its culture
- There is insufficient engagement of stakeholders.

Adopting a programme management approach such as MSP provides a structured framework that can help organizations avoid these pitfalls and achieve their goals.

Organizations make choices as to how they will manage their activities and need to decide on the most appropriate approach to successfully deliver their business goals. In particular they need to ask:

- Is this a portfolio of change programmes and projects that needs to be coordinated corporately?
- Is this a single programme of business change implemented through the coordination of several projects and business activities?

Understanding the nature and scale of the proposed change activities, and also the context of the organization(s) owning the benefits, will be essential for making this decision.

For example, building a new school may be a straightforward project for the construction company carrying out the work, with the output being the completed building. However, for the education authority, it may be part of a programme, where the building is merely one of several different interdependent outputs, which together will ensure the longer-term benefits of providing improved education and recreation in a particular community.

In this example, the portfolio would be held by the government department responsible for education, and would be aimed at delivering a strategic objective to raise standards of education nationally.

Appendix B looks at the key differences between portfolios, programmes and projects in more detail.

## 1.5 THE PROGRAMME MANAGEMENT ENVIRONMENT

A programme is a major undertaking for most organizations, meaning significant funding and substantial change for the organizations and individuals involved. Figure 1.2 shows a typical environment for programme management.

The organization's corporate strategies, initiatives and policies are influenced and shaped by both the internal and the external environment. Programmes are then defined, scoped and prioritized to implement and deliver the outcomes required. Programmes in turn initiate, monitor and align the projects and related activities that are needed to create new products or service capabilities to effect changes in business operations. The projects will deliver the required outputs and capability and transition them into operations to achieve the outcomes. Finally, the full benefits of the programme can be realized and business transformation will have been achieved.

Even as programmes are in the process of implementing changes and improvements to the target operations, they may need to respond to changes in corporate strategies or accommodate new initiatives or policies. A continual process of realignment is required to ensure that the programme remains linked to strategic objectives.

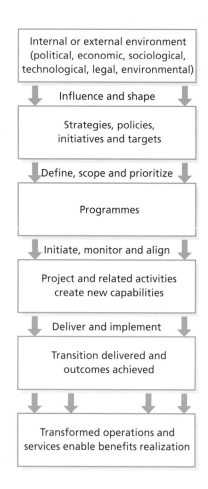

**Figure 1.2 Programme management environments**

Figure 1.3 shows some of the drivers for change and the areas that may be affected by change, and Appendix B looks in more detail at the drivers for change that are likely to contribute to the initiation of a transformational change programme.

## 1.6 TYPES OF PROGRAMME

A programme can be triggered in a number of ways:

- Vision-led programme:
  - Has come into existence to deliver a clearly defined vision that has been created and is sponsored by the top of the organization
  - Tends to be top down in approach, with cross-functional implications for the organization's operations
  - Entrepreneurial programmes developing new products and services, that focus on innovation or strategic opportunity offered by the business environment
  - In the public sector, this could be the translation of political priorities into a programme which will refine and deliver the desired changes
- Emergent programme:

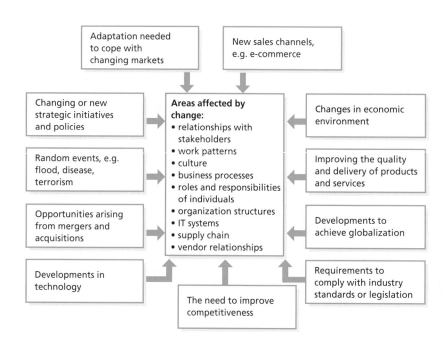

**Figure 1.3 Drivers for change**

- Evolves from concurrent, individual projects that have grown within an organization. There is now recognition that coordination of the projects is necessary to deliver the changes and the desired benefits
- Is transitory, as it becomes a planned programme when its vision, context and direction have been defined and established
- Compliance programme:
  - May also be referred to as a 'must do' programme
  - The organization has no choice but to change as a result of an external event, such as legislative change
  - Benefits may be expressed in terms of compliance, achievement and avoidance of negative implications rather than measurable improvements in performance.

In reality, most programmes have a mix of these characteristics, but it is helpful to understand the dominant characteristics of a programme as it will help to develop and optimize the priorities and approach. For example, the benefits for a compliance programme may focus on the avoidance of penalties.

## 1.7 PROGRAMME IMPACT

Programmes may be set up to deliver change in parts of an organization, across the entire organization, across more than one organization, or in the environment in which the organization operates. In deciding on the best approach to managing a programme it is useful to assess its likely impact on the organization, and this can be done by looking at the nature of the change a programme is expected to deliver. The impact matrix in Figure 1.4 shows how different types of programme have different impacts on the environment, and provides some examples of the changes they may deliver.

Some programmes will be highly complex in nature, but have a reasonably well-defined expectation, i.e. there will be high levels of predictability in terms of outcome even though the journey may be costly and complex. On the other hand, change to societal behaviours over a long period, driven by policy and legislation, will have low levels of predictability due to the long timescales, and the cause and effects may not be fully anticipated as other societal trends develop. The programme impact matrix, together with the

| Focus of the change | Predictability of outcome | | |
|---|---|---|---|
| | High | Medium | Low |
| Specification-led | Major engineering programmes, e.g. Olympic park; Complex products based on known design; Large-scale technology replacements | Globalization of technology services; Adoption of technology that is new to the organization, e.g. ERP; Multi-organization delivery | Pioneering engineering techniques; Unproven technology implementation; Specification-led organizational change |
| Business transformation | Implementation of approaches used in similar organizations, e.g. ISO adoption; Process change affecting technology and structures | New products or services to existing market place; Changing historical working practices, values and structures; Supply chain changes, e.g. outsourcing of services | Diversification of new products into new markets; Internal external and customer behaviour; Radical restructuring of supply chains |
| Political and societal change | Change to current legislation or policies; Increases or decreases to investment programmes; Predictable or clear stakeholder base | New legislation reacting to societal trends; Legislative change to affect socio-economic behaviour; Changes to public service delivery models, e.g. health provision | Changes to societal values and behaviour, e.g. criminality; Incentive-driven change to lifestyles and economic behaviour; Long-term societal effects, e.g. health |

**Figure 1.4 Programme impact matrix**

explanations below, can be used to decide whether an MSP approach is required or, if not, which programme management techniques could be useful in those circumstances.

The impacts can be:

- **Specification-led** Where the change being delivered is based on the making and delivering of new facilities, the programme will tend to be led by the specification of the outputs required – for example, a major capital construction programme. There will be relatively low levels of ambiguity about what the programme is to deliver but there may be high levels of complexity and risk in the delivery. The scope will be reasonably well defined and adjusted according to circumstances. MSP's approach can be used in this type of programme but may need to be scaled down, as some of its elements may not be required.

- **Business transformation** Where the change is more focused on transforming the way the business functions (for example, implementing a new service partnership or moving into a new market) the programme will tend to be vision-led with desired outcomes and associated benefits. There is likely to be ambiguity about the overall implication of the changes; for instance, it may not be known how some parts of the organization will react. The greater the impact on customers and the markets, the greater are the levels of ambiguity and risk. MSP is designed to provide structure for such programmes.

- **Political and societal change** Where the change is focused on improvements in society, the level of predictability will be reduced, as there will be many uncontrollable external factors also at play. For example, a change that aims to improve the early education of pre-school-age children in order to increase their likelihood of making a more meaningful contribution to society when they leave full-time education will not only take time to design and introduce but the implications for the students and the economy will not necessarily be controllable or predictable in the long term. The scope may need to be adjusted as ambiguities are clarified and the changes are delivered in steps (tranches) over a number of years. MSP is highly suitable for programmes with a high level of complexity, ambiguity and risk. The programme

management framework of MSP is primarily designed to cater for leading and managing transformational change.

## 1.8 WHEN TO USE MSP

MSP is highly suitable for business transformation and political/societal change, being an approach designed to accommodate high levels of complexity, ambiguity and risk. Adopting a programme approach is not necessary where something new is delivered within the existing business model. Incremental improvements to an existing product or service would not normally warrant a programme approach, nor is a programme relevant in organizing all the projects within an enterprise solely for prioritizing and allocating resources. Organizations have successfully used MSP, or elements of it, in such situations; however, the programme management framework of MSP is primarily designed to cater for leading and managing transformational change.

Programme management principles may be applied to any change, whatever the level of its focus or the nature of its outcomes, and can provide structure and process to support all types of change. However, it is important to remember that using programme management requires significant resourcing (including the provision of appropriately skilled and experienced individuals) with relatively high levels of funding. Therefore it is less likely such an approach will be needed in full for the specification-led programmes.

A programme is always planned and managed with an end in mind. Programmes are designed as temporary management environments that are expected to end. Changes to the drivers of the programme may mean the programme having to change its boundaries (e.g. re-plan an end date further into the future). This could happen several times during the life of a programme but it will always be managed as if it will end one day. However, if a programme drifts into becoming never-ending, then it is no longer a true programme but becomes another expression of operational management and is part of business as usual. In such cases, although elements of programme management may be employed, much of this programme management framework in MSP becomes less appropriate.

**Example**

The London 2012 Olympics is a good example of a programme designed to change its impact and focus as it moves from one tranche to another. In simple terms the programme can be viewed as three tranches:

■ The first tranche is largely specification-led, with the focus being on the construction of the Olympic facilities in east London.
■ The second tranche started when much of the construction was completed and the focus moved to business readiness for the Games, designing the complex operational model that would be needed to manage the Games. This tranche completes before the Games will be held.
■ The third tranche begins after the Games, with the focus on the Olympic legacy and the achievement of sustainable socio-economic change and benefits as a result of the Games.

## 1.9 BEST MANAGEMENT PRACTICE GUIDANCE

MSP is part of a portfolio of best-practice publications (known collectively as Best Management Practice or BMP) aimed at helping organizations and individuals manage projects, programmes and services consistently and effectively (see Figure 1.5). MSP can be used in harmony with other BMP products, and international or internal organization standards. Where appropriate, BMP guidance is supported by a qualification scheme and accredited training and consultancy services. All BMP guidance is intended to be tailored for use by individual organizations.

BMP publications include:

■ ***Management of Portfolios* (MoP™)** Portfolio management concerns the twin issues of how to do the 'right' projects and programmes in the context of the organization's strategic objectives, and how to do them 'correctly' in terms of achieving delivery and benefits at a collective level. MoP encompasses consideration of the principles upon which effective portfolio management is based; the key practices in the portfolio definition and delivery cycles, including examples of how they have been

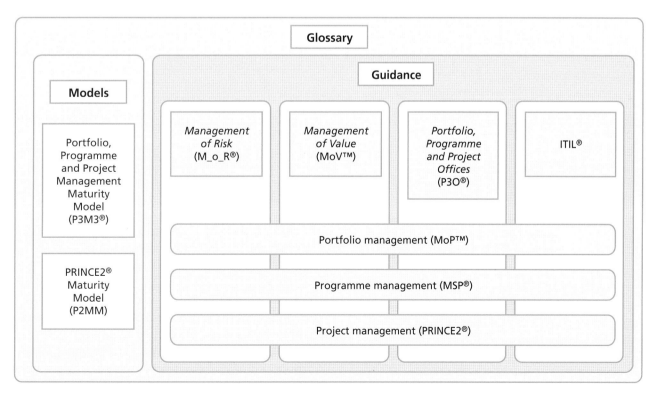

*Figure 1.5 MSP's relationship with other Best Management Practice guides*

applied in real life; and guidance on how to implement portfolio management and sustain progress in a wide variety of organizations.

Office of Government Commerce (2011). *Management of Portfolios*. TSO, London.

■ *Management of Risk* (**M_o_R®**) M_o_R offers an effective framework for taking informed decisions about the risks that affect performance objectives. The framework allows organizations to assess risk accurately (selecting the correct responses to threats and opportunities created by uncertainty) and thereby improve their service delivery.

Office of Government Commerce (2010). *Management of Risk: Guidance for Practitioners*. TSO, London.

■ *Management of Value* (**MoV™**) MoV provides a cross-sector and universally applicable guide on how to maximize value in a way that takes account of organizations' priorities, differing stakeholders' needs and, at the same time, uses resources as efficiently and effectively as possible. It will help organizations to put in place effective methods to deliver enhanced value across their portfolio, programmes, projects and operational activities to meet the challenges of ever-more competitive and resource-constrained environments.

Office of Government Commerce (2010). *Management of Value*. TSO, London.

■ *Managing Successful Projects with PRINCE2®* PRINCE2 (PRojects IN Controlled Environments, V2) is a structured method to help effective project management via clearly defined products. Key themes that feature throughout PRINCE2 are the dependence on a viable business case confirming the delivery of measurable benefits that are aligned to an organization's objectives and strategy, while ensuring the management of risks, costs and quality.

Office of Government Commerce (2009). *Managing Successful Projects with PRINCE2*. TSO, London.

■ *Portfolio, Programme and Project Offices* (**P3O®**) P3O provides universally applicable guidance, including principles, processes and techniques, to successfully establish, develop and maintain appropriate support structures. These structures will facilitate delivery of business objectives (portfolios), programmes and projects within time, cost, quality and other organizational constraints.

Office of Government Commerce (2008). *Portfolio, Programme and Project Offices*. TSO, London.

■ **ITIL® service management publications** ITIL provides a systematic and professional approach to IT service management (ITSM). Because ITSM is driven both by technology and the many different organizational environments in which it operates, it is in a state of continual evolution and derives enormous benefits from a best-practice-driven approach. ITIL is based on a lifecycle approach and the core guidance consists of five publications, each representing a stage in the ITIL service lifecycle.

For more information on ITIL and the ITSM publications, visit: www.itil-officialsite.com

BMP models include:

■ **Portfolio, Programme and Project Management Maturity Model (P3M3®)** P3M3 is a tool for assessing an organization's current capabilities for managing its portfolios, programmes and projects. It helps the organization to implement change and improvements in a structured way. P3M3 consists of a hierarchical collection of elements describing the characteristics of effective processes. It uses a five-level maturity framework and focuses on seven process perspectives, which exist in all three models and can be assessed at all five maturity levels. P3M3 allows organizations to review all seven process perspectives across portfolio, programme and project management or across only one or two of them.

■ **PRINCE2 Maturity Model (P2MM)** The PRINCE2 Maturity Model uses the same structure as the P3M3 from which it is derived, but specifically applies to project management under PRINCE2.

For more information on both P3M3 and P2MM, visit: www.p3m3-officialsite.com

## 1.10 SOME MSP TERMINOLOGY

The glossary provides explanations of all the terms commonly used in this guide that have a specific meaning in a programme context. However, throughout MSP, there are four key terms used that have a hierarchical relationship that it is important to understand from the start:

- **Corporate strategy** defines the organization's approach to achieving its corporate objectives in any given area of its business
- **Corporate policy** arises as a result of corporate strategy (e.g. the risk management policy described in M_o_R) and lays out the rules for all parts of the organization to follow when implementing that particular aspect of management
- **Programme governance strategies** are developed during the course of implementing an MSP programme and describe why and how something will be undertaken within the programme
- **Programme plans** describe the explicit activities, including their timing and resourcing, that are required to implement the programme governance strategies.

## 1.11 HOW TO USE THIS GUIDE

This guide is not intended to be read from cover to cover. It is a reference guide designed to help those involved in programmes to understand how business transformation should be delivered and their roles in this.

In addition to this introduction it is recommended that all readers familiarize themselves as a minimum with the programme management principles in Chapter 2, the governance themes overview in Chapter 3, and the transformational flow described in Chapter 13 to gain a good overview of MSP. These chapters provide an insight into the key principles that underpin all successful change programmes; explain how governance within a programme works; and describe the lifecycle of a programme and how it passes through the various stages of development and delivery to achieve the outcomes and benefits desired.

For people who have a role within a programme or who have responsibility for programme delivery, together with anyone wishing to gain a deeper understanding of programme management, the guide is navigated as follows:

- **Part 2** provides useful reading on the governance themes (the management controls that keep the programme on track). They are relevant throughout the lifecycle of the programme and should be adhered to throughout to maximize the likelihood of the successful achievement of the programme objectives.
- **Part 3** describes the iterations through which the programme passes on its journey. There are distinct states that it travels through, and it may require different skills and approaches depending on its state of evolution.
- **Part 4** (the appendices) provide more in-depth coverage of topics relevant to MSP that will be of interest to practitioners and people with management responsibilities within a programme environment:
  - **Appendix A: Programme information** To be read by programme managers and programme office staff
  - **Appendix B: Adopting MSP** To be read by those with responsibility for organizational standards, senior managers and programme managers
  - **Appendix C: Programme office** To be read by programme managers and programme office staff
  - **Appendix D: Health checks** Outlines the areas that should be regularly reviewed to ensure that the programme is being well run. To be read in conjunction with Appendix B
  - **Further information** Useful reading references that can supplement knowledge of MSP and provide practitioners with further research sources
  - **Glossary** Contains a list and explanation of the terms used in this guide.

# Programme
# management principles

2

# 2 Programme management principles

## 2.1 INTRODUCTION

It is possible to provide a common framework of understanding for all programmes. Managing Successful Programmes is such a framework, because it is principles-based. These principles are:

- Universal in that they apply to every programme
- Self-validating in that they have been proven in practice
- Empowering because they give practitioners of this framework some added ability or power to influence and shape transformational change towards success.

## 2.2 THE PRINCIPLES

The principles reflect the characteristics of successful programmes. If the following principles are observed when applying the rest of this guidance (covered in Parts 2 and 3 – the governance themes and the transformational flow), the programme will be more likely to achieve its objectives. These principles (shown in the outer ring of Figure 1.1) are:

- Remaining aligned with corporate strategy
- Leading change
- Envisioning and communicating a better future
- Focusing on the benefits and threats to them
- Adding value
- Designing and delivering a coherent capability
- Learning from experience.

### 2.2.1 Remaining aligned with corporate strategy

A programme is typically a large investment that should make a significant contribution towards achieving corporate performance targets. A well-managed programme maintains good links with a sometimes-volatile corporate strategy.

Programmes often have to prove or disprove strategic ideas. There needs to be effective feedback from programmes to the strategists, so that they can refine future strategies based on evidence from the programmes. As external drivers may cause frequent changes of direction, the programme must be durable yet adaptable enough to keep pace with strategy.

The programme must also ensure that the strategic drivers are extended downwards into the governance of its projects and business change activities. The programme must not allow projects to become detached from, or misaligned with, corporate strategy.

Thus, a programme needs to create a working environment that is both robust and flexible enough to be able to cope with frequent, and sometimes radical, changes of boundary.

The programme's business case must be robust, considering all the options, and once approved it should be reviewed regularly to ensure ongoing strategic alignment. The programme must have a flexible boundary and be able to cope with frequent changes to what is included within the programme and what is not; these changes must, however, be applied to the programme in a controlled and managed way. This adaptable approach does not apply to its projects, where a flexible, dynamic scope usually spells disaster. This is a major reason why effective programme management can never be codified into a rigid set of rules and procedures: it is necessarily agile and adaptive.

A law enforcement agency, with responsibility for vehicle regulation, identified some innovative hand-held recognition technology that could be used to scan vehicle registration numbers directly into a database and accelerate the processing of information and enforcement.

This original technology option was not available for general use from the suppliers, so an alternative technology was used that proved less robust. Staff were resistant to the change, as it threatened their jobs. The technology project overran by three years and costs escalated. Eventually, it went live but with a limited capacity and much resistance from users. The hardware and software were unreliable and it took more time to process than the old manual approach.

In the meantime, the organization's strategic focus moved towards intelligence-based enforcement, and other initiatives were developed that used a range of information to track vehicles using the rapidly expanding network of roadside cameras.

By the time the original programme was delivered, the information for enforcement was available from other sources. In effect, the new capability was already redundant when it went live and it should have been stopped two years earlier. The original programme had lost alignment with the organization's strategy and did not deliver a coherent capability.

## 2.2.2 Leading change

Seeing through change in a programme is a leadership challenge. In addition to the need to manage a large number of complex tasks, people have to be led. It is impossible to move to a better future without clear leadership. The kind of leadership that is required in programme management:

- Gives clear direction
- Engenders trust with consistent and transparent behaviours
- Actively engages stakeholders
- Appoints the right people at the right time
- Can live with a measure of uncertainty
- Solves problems and creates novel solutions

- Supports the transition until new methods are established and embedded.

Good leaders engender trust through leading with **consistency and transparency**. Programme management is most effective when issues are debated freely and risks evaluated openly. This requires personal courage and openness to challenge. Conversely, where there is lack of trust, stakeholder engagement and teamworking are so much harder. It is a sign of weak leadership to dismiss risks, issues and concerns by members of the team without appropriate examination and consideration.

A government agency decided to relocate its London base 200 miles away. Anticipating how tough the impact would be for all the staff in the agency, the senior management team decided that they would move first and would also forgo senior management perks and commit to the same relocation package as everyone else.

Moving plans of the senior team became part of the regular communications within the programme, as well as intelligence about housing, schools and other facilities in the new locality. The individual members of the senior team also agreed to be very open about how they felt about the move, so in personal presentations they referenced their own sadness at leaving their old neighbourhoods, their discomfort, struggles and surprises. This made a huge difference in influencing enough people to move with the agency.

Leading change means actively **engaging stakeholders**. In achieving transformational changes, programmes will alter the working practices, culture and style of organizations. The people aspects of change must be recognized and addressed if the programme is to succeed. A good programme actively engages stakeholders and takes seriously their perceptions of value and benefit. Programme management needs to be much more actively people-oriented than might be the case in a project.

A programme managed the merger of two large organizations. However, when the merger was complete, management realized that there remained two very different and sometimes conflicting cultures. Senior management recognized that this conflict was preventing the merger programme from realizing its stated vision. Transition to a common culture would take a long time, and this should have been recognized and included as part of the programme.

Leading change also means assembling the right people first. Evidence suggests that organizations which have succeeded in making breakthrough change have assembled the right team at the very beginning; assembling the leadership team early and with the right focus was a critical success factor. Some of the most successful strategic changes began with engaging key stakeholders as an early part of a visioning process (i.e. to build, establish and communicate a clear vision for the programme).

Well-led change focuses on people, using their strengths and abilities and bringing these people and their skills into play at the right time(s) in a programme. This can make a clear difference to the programme's progress and ultimate success. The people leading the change should look to early appointments of people with the experience and knowledge to design and implement the programme's frameworks and approaches.

Certain people may be more suited to working on different parts of the programme. For example, some may have excellent initial conceptual exploratory leadership skills, but be less effective in later periods of the programme where attention to logistics and the integrity of completed outcomes may be more vital.

An insurance company had to comply with new pension legislation through the products it offered to its customers. Very early in the programme, the managers realized that they needed to appoint 'change champions' in the six regional offices affected. These change champions would need to continue in their operational roles but also take on significant change management duties within their own offices.

By appointing the change champions early, people in the offices knew to whom they could put questions. Also, the change champions fed back early intelligence to the programme office. Regular videoconferences were organized that helped to identify where some individuals could develop their skills and understanding of their roles, and where others could offer valuable advice. Although the operational changes were scheduled for up to two years ahead in some cases, it proved vital that these people were appointed and involved early on.

Good change leaders can live with the uncertainty that inevitably comes with delivering programmes. Uncertainties can be made worse if:

- The path to achieving the vision is not clear at the start
- Plans have to deviate during the course of the programme
- The vision itself needs refining as work progresses.

Such leaders need to cope with complexity and ambiguity, particularly in the early parts of a programme. The early work of a programme may be more exploratory and uncertain about the detail of the eventual outcomes (and also about the route used to get there) than is the case later on. This is often the nature of engaging with transformational change, where the programme does not have examples or lifecycle templates to follow.

Change leaders are able to solve problems and create novel solutions, to see the big picture as well as identify and grasp critical detail. Competent programme management has a much more inclusive and adaptive view of its role and of its context than is the case with, say, a project management role. A programme role frequently requires mental agility and lateral thinking. Some programmes are created to meet a single objective, some to meet multiple objectives. Sometimes, two or more of these objectives can appear contradictory; sometimes stakeholders have competing and mixed agendas. These are some of the normal challenges of leading change in programmes, to which there is no routine correct solution.

Leading change also means supporting the change through the transition from the old to the new until the new ways of working are fully embedded. This area is often neglected or underestimated. It can result in excellent project outputs but the capability they offer not being exploited. The programme may then be branded a failure, when in fact it was a failure of change leadership, not the programme or any of its projects. Good leadership involves planning changes, preparing for their implementation, resourcing and then implementing them. The transition process should ensure business stability is maintained. Managing the transition involves leading people through change into an unfamiliar and probably uncomfortable new way of doing things.

All these aspects of change leadership can be provided by different individuals in a variety of roles throughout the programme's life and into transition. The important factor is that this leadership role is always visible and accounted for in the programme.

### 2.2.3 Envisioning and communicating a better future

A programme is relevant where there is a need to achieve transformational change, where there is some marked step change or break with the present required in the future capability. In order to achieve such a beneficial future state, the leaders of a programme must first describe a clear vision of that future.

A vision should be developed and refined in the early part of the programme. This should exist throughout the life of the programme and be one of the main tools for ensuring the ongoing strategic alignment of the programme. For example, if the vision statement is changed

significantly, it could indicate that the programme itself has altered significantly and needs to be reassessed against its original objectives.

Whilst creating a clear vision is necessary, it is insufficient without the clear and consistent communication of it towards gaining commitment and buy-in from a range of stakeholders. If the goal of a programme is a beneficial transformational change, then a clear picture or vision of what the future outcomes will look like is vital. Effectively communicating this message to stakeholders is part of the ongoing leadership task of engagement. A programme that continues without a clear vision will risk leaving stakeholders confused about the future intent, thereby reducing the likelihood of the programme's success.

#### Example

A faith community leader had a goal of setting up a day care centre for single mothers and other vulnerable groups within a city centre. This centre was such a departure from what his community had seen or experienced that the leader found it very difficult to explain his idea to them in a way that generated enthusiasm and essential commitment.

When he began to express the vision of the centre in terms of a story, for example 'a day in the life of Jane, a single mother', he found that this made the vision real, and people rallied to him. He also found he needed to create a short form of the vision story and repeat it regularly to the same stakeholders. He found that initially some did not quite get the picture, while others remained sceptical that this was nothing more than a fad. By repeating the same vision regularly, he was able to demonstrate his commitment to realizing this vision as well as to mobilize and sustain support from others.

### 2.2.4 Focusing on the benefits and threats to them

Best-practice programme management aligns everything towards satisfying strategic objectives by realizing the end benefits. Thus the programme's boundary, including the projects and activities that become part of the programme, is determined to enable the realization of these end benefits.

The ultimate success of a programme is judged by its ability to realize these benefits and the continuing relevance of these benefits to the strategic context. If the benefits are of strategic value, then effective risk management is crucial (see in particular Chapter 11).

It is common for programmes to focus on the day-to-day challenges of delivery and project issues but overlook the strategic and longer-term issues with the result that benefits fail to be realized. A useful technique to maintain focus is to put benefits management at the top of the programme board agenda to ensure that it maintains focus.

### Example

A medical organization embarked on several major changes to its service, integrated into one major programme. As part of this, it found that doctors, nurses and administrators all appreciated clear benefits maps, which showed them the big picture as well as their individual contributions to the overall programme. 'In terms of getting engagement, the [benefits mapping] exercise helped when people saw the benefits coming out,' said a member of the programme management team. The organization also found that the benefits maps helped to de-clutter the overall change by showing which projects did not contribute to any of the benefits and so could be removed.

## 2.2.5 Adding value

A programme only remains valid if it adds value to the sum of its constituent projects and major activities. If it is found to add nothing, then it is better to close the programme and allow the projects to proceed independently.

One confirmation of this synergy is the existence of programme benefits over and above individual project benefits – that is, benefits that the projects themselves are able to identify and claim. Related and dependent business change is often best managed at programme level so that these additional benefits can be identified and realized. For example, avoiding the double-counting of benefits by projects can be seen as a major value-adding activity from a programme.

## 2.2.6 Designing and delivering a coherent capability

The capability that the programme will deliver is defined in the blueprint. The programme will deliver a coherent organizational capability that is released into operational use according to a schedule that delivers maximum incremental improvements with minimal adverse operational impact.

Project scope and outputs need careful delineation; there should be rigorous identification and management of inter-project dependencies, and a clear understanding of programme versus project responsibilities. Drifting of scope and quality across a number of projects can aggregate into a major loss of coherence at the programme level.

The programme needs to focus on the bigger picture and should not take over the responsibilities of project management. However, clear direction should be given to the projects and regular reviews held to verify continual alignment to the programme blueprint and plans. This ensures that everything that can be done is done to facilitate a smooth transition of the project outputs into the operational part of the business.

The programme is focused on delivering a blueprint that meets the needs of the organization. During the programme these needs will probably change, and the programme's blueprint and resulting capabilities should evolve accordingly.

If the strategy of the business changes to the extent that the capability being delivered is no longer coherent or relevant, the programme's viability should be challenged and it may need to be stopped.

**Example**

A UK mobile networks organization adopted programme management as a management approach to ensure that it was investing in the right products. It wanted to address the problem of how to start, stop and change initiatives within its programmes to ensure that it did not waste money on projects that would be too late to the market to have an impact.

This enabled the organization to deploy its knowledge about technology, the markets and competitors to make early decisions about what products should be pursued and which ones should be stopped.

Using the MSP techniques, staff were able to identify which projects were significantly behind those of their competitors. This helped to identify where they should divest investment and reinvest in technologies that would gain the maximum advantage by earlier market entry with innovative products.

The benefits were a reduction in money wasted on unprofitable initiatives and competitive advantage gained from early delivery of products to the market.

## 2.2.7 Learning from experience

A programme is a learning organization in that it reflects upon and improves its performance during its life. Good governance requires approaches to managing the different themes that are regularly adjusted and adapted on the basis of experience and results to date. For example, good benefits management encourages stakeholders to identify new opportunities to realize benefits as their awareness and experience increases.

Programmes perform better where members of the management all assume the attitude of being learners. Such a reflective stance may require certain adjustments to be built into the programme, typically at major review points, so that the management team and the individuals within it can formally assimilate and express this learning as the programme progresses further.

An organization's ability to learn from experience often reflects its programme management maturity. P3M3 provides valuable insight into this and other characteristics of high-performing organizations. See Appendix B for more information.

# PART 2

# The governance themes

Governance themes overview

3

# 3  Governance themes overview

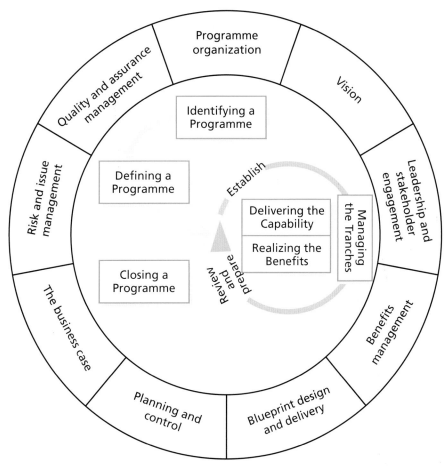

*Figure 3.1  The MSP governance themes overview*

Governance is the control framework through which programmes deliver their change objectives and remain within corporate visibility and control. A programme needs clear and open governance if it is to be successful. It will need to negotiate the resource it wants, manage the resources made available to it, and adjust to changing organizational contexts whilst delivering its agreed outcomes and benefits. The focus of this section is the core elements of an effective governance framework (Figure 3.1). The MSP governance themes are:

- Programme organization
- Vision
- Leadership and stakeholder engagement
- Benefits management
- Blueprint design and delivery
- Planning and control
- The business case
- Risk and issue management
- Quality and assurance management.

The need for governance over change is manifested in two ways:

- Control and direction of the transformation programme (in itself, and in relation to other change within the organization)
- The control and sustainability of the wider organization as a corporate entity.

The programme will need to integrate its control framework with the control framework of the organization. Given that MSP concentrates on programmes delivering transformational change, the programme will need to integrate with the corporate governance framework. Where they exist, the programme should ideally look to use the organization's existing governance and control frameworks, as these should provide the necessary structures and visibility.

This alignment should extend to (in terms of expression, unit of value, nature of analysis and minimum frequency of reporting) the corporate controls used in, for example:

- Finance and accounting
- Human resource management
- Risk management
- Quality systems
- Operations and performance
- Information technology
- Customer and stakeholder satisfaction
- Sourcing and procurement
- Corporate responsibility
- Health and safety
- Environment management
- Contract management
- Legislative compliance
- Information management.

To a greater or lesser extent, each of the governance themes provides guidance and tools to the transformational flow processes. More than one governance theme is likely to influence more than one of the transformational flow processes.

Governance themes are like a constant pattern in a fabric, and like a pattern should be woven into the programme; they are not one-off or occasional activities. For example, risk management should be central to every decision at each step and level in the programme; it is not a case of updating a risk register from time to time.

A number of governance themes have cycles associated with them that are continual; for example, with stakeholders, the identification, analysis, planning, delivery and review of effective engagement and communications should be cycling continually. The activities and work of the transformational flow are covered in Part 3.

## 3.1 EXPLANATION OF THE THEMES IN THIS GUIDE

Part 2 of this guide details the consistent controls needed to manage the programme. Each chapter in Part 2 contains information to help manage a particular aspect of the programme. There will be a full description of:

- Why the theme is important to the successful delivery of the programme
- Which programme management strategies and plans will need to be developed to ensure that the control framework and governance arrangements for the theme are in place and rigorous
- The tools and techniques that can be used to support the theme
- MSP documentation that is developed as part of the theme, bringing out context and/or providing control for the programme
- The cycle of activities that should be regularly undertaken to ensure that the theme is being applied to the programme
- Areas of focus for key roles on the application of the theme.

## 3.2 INTEGRATING PROGRAMME MANAGEMENT INTO THE ORGANIZATION CONTROL FRAMEWORK

Any programme delivery framework that is to be adopted or used by the organization will initially be seen as an add-on to the business-as-usual activities of the organization. While communications activities may raise the profile of the programmes, there is still a risk that the programmes are not fully accounted for by the organization. This means that the resources to be demanded and consumed, and the changes to be introduced by (and the possible impact of) the programmes may not be fully visible to the organizational hierarchy.

The keywords in achieving this understanding are **visibility** and **control**. To achieve these, organizations must understand the programme in terms of its business-as-usual controls, giving the visibility of the programme not only in terms of itself, but also in terms of its impacts on and constraints within the organization's policies, strategies, resources, assets, plans and activities.

Programmes that try to operate as an independent entity are unlikely to gain the organizational buy-in required to succeed. The programme management plans and strategies (see section 3.3) provide a vehicle for ensuring this integration.

For more information on integration with corporate frameworks, see Appendix B.

## 3.3 PROGRAMME MANAGEMENT STRATEGIES AND PLANS

As it is established, the programme will define a number of strategies and plans to implement the governance approach. These have a dual function:

■ The strategies set out the 'why' and 'how' of the approach that the programme will take to achieve its final (and intermediate) outcomes and benefits, including the policies, standards, cycles and responsibilities related to that particular governance theme. The programme strategies and controls are derived from, consistent with, and aligned to the organization's policies for managing that governance theme. This consistency should

extend to roles and responsibilities, approach, processes, units of measure and control, reporting etc.

■ The plans explain what activities will take place to deliver that element of governance, as well as where, when and by whom.

The appropriate sign-off and endorsement of these strategies and plans validates them as:

■ Addressing the organization's need for visibility and control

■ Ensuring that the programme has the right level of governance, visibility, control and detail for that governance theme.

Table 3.1 sets out the relationship between programme management strategies and their delivery mechanisms. For example, the quality and assurance strategy will describe the scope and control arrangements for the programme, whereas the quality and assurance plan would have an explicit schedule of events that ensures that the quality arrangements are implemented and managed.

**Table 3.1 Relationship between programme management strategies and delivery mechanisms**

| Programme management strategy | What the strategy covers | Delivery mechanism |
|---|---|---|
| Resource management | Resource to be consumed by the programme. Finances, people, systems, accommodation, facilities and specialisms will all be covered by this strategy | Resource management plan |
| Monitoring and control | How the programme will monitor progress in terms of expected and actual delivery of outputs, outcomes and key milestones | Programme plan |
| Information management | How programme information will be catalogued, filed, stored and retrieved, and how the programme will create and manage information | Information management plan |
| Quality and assurance management | How the delivery of quality activities will be incorporated into the management and delivery of the programme | Quality and assurance plan |
| Risk management | How the programme will establish the context in which risks will be identified and assessed, and responses planned and implemented | Risk register |
| Issue management | How issues will be managed consistently across the programme and how any resulting changes will be managed | Issue register |
| Stakeholder engagement | Who the stakeholders are, what their interests and influences are likely to be, and how the programme will engage with them | Stakeholder profiles and programme communications plan |
| Benefits management | The delivery framework for identifying, prioritizing and achieving benefits | Benefit profiles and benefits realization plan |

## 3.4 ILLUSTRATION OF THE RELATIONSHIP BETWEEN THE GOVERNANCE THEMES AND TRANSFORMATIONAL FLOW

If the transformational flow is the programme's time-based to-do list, then the governance themes can be seen as the reference manual. If the flow requires action, then the themes should provide guidance on how it should be done.

The analysis in Table 3.2 for the Identifying a Programme process will help to illustrate this.

The same interaction between the governance themes and transformational flow happens in each of the processes. If you have responsibility

**Table 3.2 Interaction between governance themes and transformational flow – Identifying a Programme**

| Transformation flow activity | Governance theme |
| --- | --- |
| Sponsoring the programme | **Leadership and stakeholder engagement** provides guidance on how to identify the critical stakeholders that need to be engaged.<br>**Programme organization** explains the roles, responsibilities and purpose of the sponsoring group. |
| Confirm programme mandate | The **programme mandate** explains the purpose and importance of the programme and of the sources of the information that is used to provide the mandate to the programme. Although not a theme, programme information (see Appendix A) advises what content to include. **Benefits management and risk and issue management** also provide guidance on what to consider when preparing the document justifying the programme. The **programme mandate** is the first stage of the **business case**, as it should set out the high-level expectations of the organization with regard to the costs and benefits of the change. The **programme mandate** should include a reference to the approach to assurance from the **quality and assurance strategy** and a summary of the 'as-is' state for developing the blueprint. |
| Appoint the SRO and programme board | **Programme organization** provides a description of the role of the SRO (senior responsible owner), the characteristics needed to fulfil the role, and who should be on the programme board.<br>**Risk and issue management** is also relevant, as poor selection of members may increase risk, and **leadership and stakeholder engagement** will help to identify appropriate members. |
| Develop the programme brief | Nearly all the themes are relevant when writing this document. Whilst the themes may be more relevant to the detailed work later in the flow (e.g. in Defining a Programme), in creating a robust programme brief it is necessary to anticipate work that takes place later in the programme.<br>**Vision** describes the purpose and types of content for the outline **vision statement** section.<br>**Risk and issue management** describes managing the risks and issues that the programme will face. The **business case** describes the cost-benefit balance for the programme, as well as different options to consider.<br>**Planning and control** develops timescales and estimates, showing how the programme will be controlled.<br>**Benefits management** provides guidance on describing, detailing and planning for expected benefits.<br>**Blueprint design and delivery** develops the vision statement and defines the 'to-be' goals and the 'as-is' state<br>(Appendix A provides guidance on content.) |
| Develop the programme preparation plan | **Programme organization** explains the roles and responsibilities of individuals during Defining a Programme; these should be reflected in the plan.<br>The **governance themes** overall provide input into what the plan should cover to enable effective governance and control during programme definition.<br>(Appendix A provides guidance on content.) |
| Review of programme brief and programme preparation plan | **Quality and assurance management** provides guidance on effective process and decision-making; this review meets those criteria.<br>**Programme organization** explains who should be involved with assurance and how it should be conducted. |
| Approval to proceed | **Programme organization** and **leadership and stakeholder engagement** provide guidance on who should be involved in this approval process and how they should be engaged to gain support. |

**Table 3.3 Governance and the key roles**

| Role | Areas of focus |
|------|----------------|
| Senior responsible owner (SRO) | The design, approval and compliance of the programme with:<br>■ Corporate controls<br>■ Governance strategies<br>■ Initiations of assurance reviews |
| Programme manager | Design and implementation of the programme governance strategies<br>Consultation with corporate governance bodies to ensure alignment<br>Initiation of stakeholder consultation<br>Supporting the SRO in implementation and control |
| Business change manager (BCM) | Review and contribution to governance development and control<br>Implementation of governance arrangements where they impact on operations<br>Monitoring performance information to assure the maintenance of business performance at acceptable levels of stable operation during transition<br>Input to programme assurance reviews<br>Specific focus on benefits and stakeholder governance |
| Programme office | Maintenance of records<br>Supporting governance assurance reviews<br>Application of governance arrangements on behalf of the programme manager as appropriate<br>Monitoring actions from assurance and audit reviews<br>Providing expertise to support assurance reviews on other programmes |

for implementing MSP in an organization, these interactions should be built into your process models wherever possible.

In each of the governance theme chapters there is specific guidance for the four key roles in a programme.

## 3.5 THE KEY ROLES

Table 3.3 is the checklist for each role in relation to governance.

There is no specific guidance for the two main control boards (the sponsoring group and programme board) because they are forums where decisions are made and direction is set with input from the four key roles. Therefore, guidance has been restricted to individuals rather than including groups.

This in no way weakens or undermines the roles of the sponsoring group or the programme board, which are essential for any essential programme. Their responsibilities are set out in Chapter 4.

# Programme organization 4

# 4   Programme organization

- Programme organization characteristics
- Programme leadership
- Programme structure
- Sponsoring group
- Senior responsible owner
- Programme board
- Programme manager
- Business change manager
- Business change team
- Programme office
- Programme assurance
- Additional governance roles
- Implementing and managing the programme organization
- Programme organization within the transformational flow

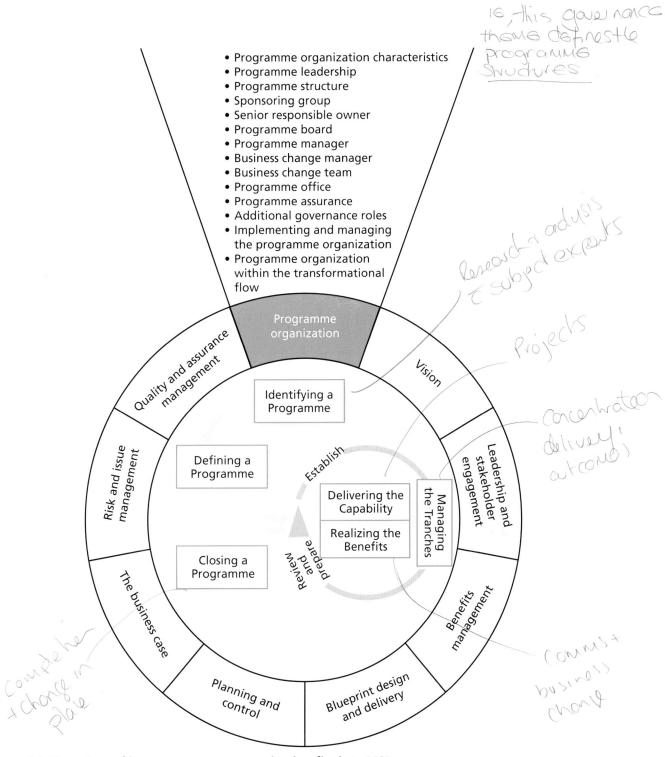

*Figure 4.1  Overview of how programme organization fits into MSP*

## 4.1 INTRODUCTION

Establishing a clear and effective organization is critical to programme success. Ensuring that the programme organization meets the needs of the programme in its context is an initial and ongoing task that cannot be avoided, dealt with lightly or done once and then forgotten.

Successful programme organization requires the effective combination of the following features to deliver the programme's desired outcomes:

- Defined roles
- Clear accountabilities and responsibilities of each of these roles
- Management structures and reporting arrangements.

The roles, responsibilities and structures discussed below provide the basis for effective programme management. They will need to be tailored to suit individual programmes.

## 4.2 PROGRAMME ORGANIZATION CHARACTERISTICS

However competent the personnel and however effective the procedures, some things will go wrong. The unexpected will arise, and major unplanned changes may be called for. Effective leadership of a programme can only be achieved through informed decision-making and a flexible management regime. Selecting a team with a good blend of personalities and skills and a structure that lets them carry out their roles effectively will support decision-making and management. Continuity and stability of the programme organization structure is also important to ensure that commitment to the programme is maintained.

Programme management is most effective when issues are debated freely and risks evaluated openly. This requires a leadership style and culture that encourages the flow of information between projects and the programme. Every opportunity to advance the programme towards its goals should be welcomed and converted into constructive progress.

## 4.3 PROGRAMME LEADERSHIP

Programmes take and combine strategic objectives by translating them into specific targets for individual projects. Leading and directing a programme provides the bridge between strategic objectives, business operations and project delivery.

The key principles for effective leadership of a programme (which fall primarily to the members of the programme board, including the senior responsible owner (SRO), programme manager and business change managers (BCMs)) are:

- Ability to create a compelling vision portraying a beneficial future and to communicate this future in inspirational ways to all kinds of stakeholders
- Empowered decision-making, giving individuals the autonomy to fulfil their roles effectively. Motivation, reward and appraisal systems are vital for fostering the attitudes and energy to drive the programme
- Visible commitment and authority, with enough seniority to:
  - Ensure that the correct resources are available to the programme
  - Influence and engage with stakeholders
  - Balance the programme's priorities with those of the ongoing business operations
  - Focus on realization of the business benefits
- Relevant skills and experience to provide active management of:
  - The cultural and people issues involved in change
  - The programme's finances and the inevitable conflicting demands on resources
  - The coordination of the projects within the programme to see through the transition to new operational services, while maintaining business operations
  - Risk identification, evaluation and management.

## 4.4 PROGRAMME STRUCTURE

Figure 4.2 shows the core programme layers and how they relate to each other. The following sections describe the generic responsibilities for each, together with the key roles and the skills that the individuals fulfilling them will need.

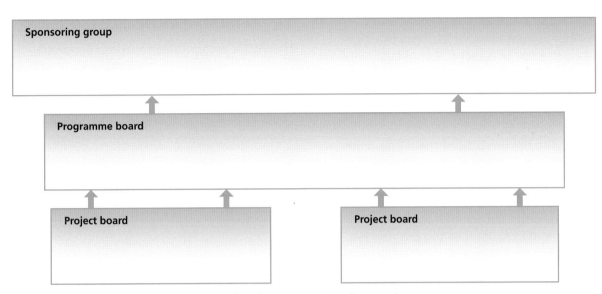

*Figure 4.2 Layering of programme organization, control and reporting*

## 4.5 SPONSORING GROUP

The sponsoring group represents those senior managers who are responsible for:

- The investment decision
- Defining the direction of the business
- Ensuring the ongoing overall alignment of the programme with the strategic direction of the organization.

The sponsoring group will appoint the SRO who, as part of the sponsoring group, is likely to be a peer of the other members. The role of the sponsoring group may well be performed by an existing executive committee, or other board of the organization.

### 4.5.1 Sponsoring group and multiple programmes

In a multi-programme environment – where the organization (or a part of it) is running more than one transformation programme at a time – it is necessary to coordinate across programmes to ensure cohesive strategic alignment and prioritization. Here, sponsorship means making the investment decision and providing top-level endorsement of the rationale and objectives for the programme in relation to other programmes and possible investments.

Championing the implementation of the new capabilities delivered by the programme must be balanced to ensure that expected benefits are realized and the desired outcomes achieved across the range of programmes, without undue or unbalanced focus on the delivery of the outcomes of one programme at the expense of another, i.e. ensuring the alignment of business priorities.

In a multiple programme environment the role of the sponsoring group may be performed by a 'corporate portfolio board'. This board would have the responsibility of ensuring ongoing strategic alignment and prioritization across all the programmes of the business portfolio. The *Management of Portfolios* guidance can offer further information on this topic.

### 4.5.2 Responsibilities of the sponsoring group

The sponsoring group have the overarching authority over the programme. They delegate much of this to the SRO, depending on the nature of the relationship that is established between the SRO and the sponsoring group, but they are likely to be formally involved with:

- Providing and ensuring the continuing organizational context for the programme
- Authorizing the programme mandate
- Authorizing programme definition
- Participating in end-of-tranche reviews and approving progression to the next tranche of the programme
- Authorizing funding for the programme

- Resolving strategic and directional issues between programmes, which need the input and agreement of senior stakeholders to ensure the progress of the change
- Authorizing the organization's strategic direction against which the programme is to deliver
- Authorizing the progress of the programme against the strategic objectives
- Leading by example to implement the values implied by the transformational change
- Providing continued commitment and endorsement in support of the programme objectives at executive and communications events
- Appointing, advising and supporting the SRO
- Authorizing the vision statement
- Authorizing delivery and sign-off at the closure of the programme.

### 4.5.3 Sponsoring group formality

Due to the nature of the sponsoring group, it may meet either on a formal and regular or ad hoc basis; much will depend on the nature of the programme and the relationship with the SRO. The greater the degree of transformational change predicated by the programme, the greater will be the need to have formal, visible control over the aggregate change. As a minimum, a sponsoring group will normally meet to give formal authorization for the programme at the end of Identifying a Programme and Defining a Programme, at the end of each tranche, and to approve closure.

Members of the sponsoring group must take the lead in establishing a style of leadership appropriate to the organization and the nature of the change. In most change situations there will need to be increased emphasis on motivation of staff, promotion of teamworking, empowerment at all levels, encouragement of initiatives and recognition of appropriate risk-taking.

The sponsoring group and the individual members should have terms of reference so that the expectations of them as individuals and as a group are transparent.

## 4.6 SENIOR RESPONSIBLE OWNER

The SRO is accountable for the programme, ensuring that it meets its objectives and realizes the expected benefits. The individual who fulfils this role should be able to lead the programme board with energy and drive, and must be empowered to direct the programme and take decisions. They must have enough seniority and authority to provide leadership to the programme team and take on accountability for delivery.

### 4.6.1 Responsibilities of the senior responsible owner

The SRO is accountable for the success of the programme and for enabling the organization to exploit the new environment resulting from the programme, meeting the new business needs and delivering new levels of performance, benefit, service delivery, value or market share.

The SRO's key responsibilities, which should be included in their terms of reference and objectives, include:

- Creating and communicating the vision for the programme
- Providing clear leadership and direction throughout its life
- Securing the investment required to set up and run the programme, and fund the transition activities so that the desired benefits are realized
- Ensuring that the programme delivers a coherent capability, achieves its strategic outcomes and realizes its benefits
- Establishing the programme's governance arrangements and ensuring appropriate assurance is in place
- Ensuring the viability of the business case
- Maintaining the interface with key senior stakeholders, keeping them engaged and informed
- Monitoring the key strategic risks facing the programme
- Maintaining alignment of the programme with the organization's strategic direction
- Commissioning assurance and audit reviews
- Ensuring the effectiveness and performance of the programme organization
- Appointing, chairing and setting priorities for the programme board.

### 4.6.2 Key attributes of a senior responsible owner

An SRO's key attributes are to:

- Have the seniority for the responsibilities and accountabilities the role involves
- Be proactive and visible as the driving force behind the programme
- Possess strong leadership and decision-making skills
- Have the experience, character and personality that are right for the programme
- Combine realism with openness and the clarity of expression to communicate the programme's vision effectively
- Be able to give purpose and direction to the programme and take strategic decisions
- Focus on delivery of the benefits and achievement of the end goal
- Build productive relationships across the programme team
- Have access to and credibility with key stakeholders.

Given the high level of personal responsibility that the SRO takes for the programme, this person will want to ensure that those selected to be on the programme board are able to contribute and support the programme with comparable levels of authority, commitment and ability.

## 4.7 PROGRAMME BOARD

Established by the SRO (and often coming into existence following approval of the programme mandate, or possibly the programme brief), the prime purpose of the programme board will be to drive the programme forward and deliver the outcomes and benefits. Members will provide resource and specific commitment to support the SRO, who is accountable for the successful delivery of the programme.

The programme board reports to the SRO (see Figure 4.3). Whilst the SRO may delegate responsibilities and action to members of the programme board, its existence does not dilute the SRO's accountabilities and decision-making authority.

Programme board members must take the lead in supporting the authority and control of the SRO over the programme as a whole, including ensuring the appropriate coordination across the projects and activities that comprise the programme.

### 4.7.1 Responsibilities of the programme board

Members of the programme board are individually answerable to the SRO for their areas of responsibility and delivery within the programme; these would normally include:

- Defining the acceptable risk profile and risk thresholds for the programme and its constituent projects
- Ensuring that the programme delivers within its agreed boundaries (e.g. cost, organizational impact and rate/scale adoption, expected/actual benefits realization etc.)
- Resolving strategic and directional issues between projects, which need the input and agreement of senior stakeholders to ensure the progress of the programmes

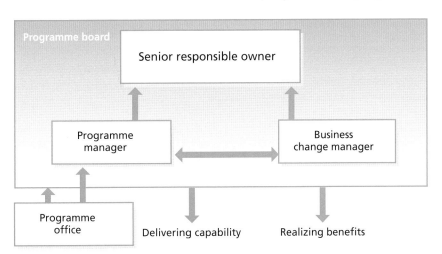

*Figure 4.3 Senior responsible owner and the programme board*

- Assuring the integrity of benefit profiles and realization plan
- Maintaining focus on the development, maintenance and achievement of the blueprint
- Providing assurance for operational stability and effectiveness through the programme delivery cycle.

Each member of the programme board will provide and commit support to the SRO for the areas that they represent. This may include:

- Understanding and managing the impact of change
- Monitoring the defined benefits achievement
- Resolving risks and issues relevant to their area
- Resolving dependencies with other pieces of work, whether change or business operations
- Ensuring the viability and integrity of the programme blueprint
- Representing local strategy as expressed in, for example, medium-term plans and operational blueprints
- Supporting the application of (and compliance with) standards, e.g. operating standards
- Making resources available for planning and delivery purposes.

### 4.7.2 Membership of the programme board

The SRO, programme manager and BCMs are mandatory members of the programme board. The following roles should be considered as optional attendees to provide advice and expertise, as required by the programme board:

- Project executives for current or relevant projects in the programme
- Representatives of corporate functions (e.g. finance, risk etc.)
- Lead supplier (if there are different senior suppliers across the projects of the programme, it may be advisable to appoint a lead supplier with whom the team will work at the programme level).

**Tip**

A number of UK public and private sector organizations have tailored the MSP organization to include the title of programme director. This is used where there is a need for a high-profile individual to support the SRO role. The day-to-day leadership of the programme is undertaken by the programme director, but it is not an alternative title to SRO. Where this has happened, care has been taken to ensure that tailoring of the MSP roles clearly identifies which accountabilities and responsibilities remain with the SRO and which are the remit of the programme director, and how this affects the programme manager and BCMs.

## 4.8 PROGRAMME MANAGER

The programme manager is responsible for leading and managing the setting-up of the programme through to delivery of the new capabilities, realization of benefits and programme closure. The programme manager has primary responsibility for successful delivery of the new capabilities and establishing governance. The BCM is responsible for benefits realization via the organizational adoption and usage of the capability and transition to the desired outcome.

The programme manager will normally be appointed as part of forming the team for Defining a Programme, though it is important that someone assumes the role of programme manager when the programme brief and plans for programme definition (programme preparation plan) are being developed in Identifying a Programme.

### 4.8.1 Responsibilities of the programme manager

The programme manager's responsibilities include the following, which may be integrated into individual terms of reference and objectives:

- Day-to-day management of the programme, including taking the programme forward from appointment (usually in Identifying a Programme or Defining a Programme), and supervising, controlling and closing the programme

- Being the day-to-day agent on behalf of the SRO, ensuring successful delivery of the new capability
- Planning and designing the programme and proactively monitoring its overall progress, resolving issues and initiating corrective action as appropriate
- Developing and implementing the programme's governance framework
- Effective coordination of the projects and their interdependencies
- Managing and resolving any risks and other issues that may arise
- Maintaining overall integrity and coherence of the programme, and developing and maintaining the programme environment to support each individual project within it
- Managing the programme's budget, monitoring the expenditures and costs against benefits as the programme progresses
- Facilitating the appointment of individuals to the project delivery teams
- Ensuring that the delivery of outputs or services from the projects meets programme requirements in line with the programme blueprint and projects dossier, and is to the appropriate quality, on time and within budget
- Facilitating the development of the blueprint with input and approval of the BCMs
- Managing the blueprint and ensuring that the capabilities delivered are aligned with it
- Managing the performance of the programme team
- Maximizing the efficient allocation of resources and skills within the projects dossier
- Managing internal and external suppliers to the programme
- Managing communications with stakeholders
- Initiating extra activities and other management interventions wherever gaps in the programme are identified or issues arise
- Reporting progress of the programme at regular intervals to the SRO.

### 4.8.2 Key attributes of the programme manager

The key attributes are:

- Ability to work positively with the full range of individuals and groups involved in the programme

- Ability to develop and maintain effective working relationships with other members of the programme management team, senior managers, the project teams and third-party service providers
- Necessary seniority to be able to take on the responsibilities required of the role
- Strong leadership and management skills
- Understanding of the wider objectives of the programme
- Credibility within the programme environment and ability to influence others
- Good knowledge of techniques for planning, monitoring and controlling programmes, including risk management
- Good knowledge of project management approaches such as PRINCE2
- Good knowledge of budgeting and resource allocation procedures
- Ability to find innovative ways of solving or pre-empting problems.

## 4.9 BUSINESS CHANGE MANAGER

There is a fundamental difference between the delivery of a new capability and actually realizing measurable benefits as a result of that capability. This difference is reflected in the complementary roles of programme manager and BCM. The programme manager is responsible for delivering the capability, while the BCM is responsible for realizing the resultant benefits by embedding that capability into business operations, and facilitating business changes to exploit that capability. The individuals appointed to each role must be able to work in close partnership to ensure that the right capabilities are delivered and that they are put to best use.

If a programme is implementing change across different parts of an organization, each should nominate a BCM. An integral part of the BCM role is an intimate knowledge of, and credibility in, the operational business.

Where there are multiple BCMs on a programme, they may all be members of the programme board; however, if there are too many, the board may become unwieldy. One option for dealing with this is to have separate BCM steering groups which deal with specific issues and have representation at programme board level. Some organizations use the term 'business change authority' (BCA) as a title for the BCM representatives; other organizations have used the term 'business change sponsor'.

It is likely that each BCM will be supported by a team to provide capacity and to ensure business understanding, commitment, engagement and adoption. These business change teams will need to ensure operational responsibility is allocated for the delivery of changes and identified benefits. This structure (possibly a matrix) must bridge between the formal organization of the programme and projects, and that of the organization's operations. Hence the business change management activities will have impacts both within the programme and project organization, and within the business operations.

Where substantial change in business operations is required, the individual appointed to the role of BCM will be responsible for creating the new business structures, operations and working practices. The BCM should have appropriate authority within the business areas to deliver the change and realize the benefits.

Exactly how many people will be required to ensure business benefits understanding, attribution, commitment and realization will depend on the number of business areas targeted for benefits realization, the scale and complexity of the changes proposed, and the level of visibility of the benefits hierarchy and benefits delivery that the programme requires.

The appointment of BCMs should be coordinated by the SRO in liaison with the sponsoring group representatives. The programme board is formed during Identifying a Programme, and it is important that an individual (or individuals) with a BCM perspective is involved in developing the programme brief and the programme preparation plan during Identifying a Programme.

The BCMs are key to providing the bridge between the programme and the business operations, since the individual(s) will be an integral part of the business operations. To realize benefits, the programme must be closely aligned with mainstream business activities. It is only when capability is integrated into business operations (business as usual) that the benefits will be fully realized.

Figure 4.4 illustrates a straightforward programme structure with multiple BCMs reporting directly to an SRO.

### Example

An Australian company that specializes in large-scale mergers uses MSP to manage the integration.

When setting up the programme to manage the change, it identifies key senior managers from one of the organizations who will take on responsibility for integrating each of the core functions: this would normally include financial processes, marketing and sales, procurement, human resources etc.

The individual who takes on this responsibility is nominally the MSP business change manager and is expected to prepare the two organizations for integration, manage the integration and then manage the benefits afterwards.

To achieve this, the BCM has to define the new working model, establish how the current systems will fit into this, the people, process and technology issues, and then drive the change through.

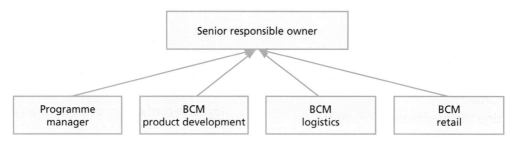

*Figure 4.4 Multiple BCMs reporting to the SRO*

### 4.9.1 Responsibilities of the business change manager

The role of BCM is primarily benefits-focused. The BCM is responsible, on behalf of the business operations and the SRO, for:

- Defining the benefits
- Defining the future operating state of the business area they represent
- Assessing progress towards Realizing the Benefits
- Achieving measured improvements
- Monitoring performance.

This need to define and realize benefits in terms of measured improvements in business performance means that the BCM must be 'business-side', in order to provide a bridge between the programme and business operations.

The BCM responsibilities comprise the following, which may be integrated into individual terms of reference and objectives:

- Maintaining the focus on realizing beneficial change
- Contributing to the development of the benefits management strategy
- Ensuring that the development and business responsibility for benefit profiles and the benefits realization plan are clearly attributed
- Identifying, defining and tracking the benefits and outcomes required of the programme
- Designing the future operating model ('to-be' state) and ensuring that it is contained and maintained within the programme blueprint
- Identifying organization changes that happen outside the boundary of the programme, which may affect the contents of the blueprint
- Preparing their sections of the organization for change
- Identifying opportunities and realizing benefits that arise during the programme, which might not have been originally profiled, and ensuring that the achievements are recognized
- Ensuring effective communications with all areas of the business that they represent
- Identifying and monitoring the performance metrics used to track the operational 'health' of the organization
- Implementing the mechanisms by which benefits can be realized and measured

- Monitoring business stability and ongoing capacity to cope with the level of change; this will include acceptable levels of performance variation (deterioration) whilst the change is embedded
- Reporting to the SRO on the readiness to change, achievement of outcomes and realization of benefits
- Advising the programme manager whether the work of the programme and each project covers the necessary aspects required to deliver the products/outputs and services/outcomes that will achieve the blueprint and lead to benefits
- Ensuring that there is no double-counting of benefits for which they are responsible
- Preparing the affected business areas for the transition to new ways of working; potentially, implementing new business processes
- Ensuring that business stability is maintained during the transition and that the changes are effectively integrated into the business
- Initiating business assurance reviews to ensure that capabilities are being embedded and established
- Optimizing the timing of the release of project deliverables into business operations
- Notifying delivery of expected benefits.

As the programme progresses, the BCM is responsible for monitoring actual outcomes against predicted results.

### 4.9.2 Key attributes of the business change manager

The BCM is a senior role who reports directly to the SRO in the programme and will have been nominated by a member of the sponsoring group. Any individual appointed as a BCM should:

- Be drawn from the relevant business area in order to demonstrate detailed knowledge of the business environment and have direct business experience
- Have ongoing operational responsibilities within their business areas. Their participation in the programme may be an integral part of their normal responsibilities in order to enable changes resulting from the programme to be firmly embedded in the organization
- Have the confidence of senior managers from the areas to be changed

- Understand the management structures, politics and culture of the organization(s) involved in the programme
- Have management skills to coordinate personnel from different disciplines and with differing viewpoints
- Have change management skills and enough experience to be able to bring order to complex situations and maintain focus on the programme's objectives
- Have negotiating skills, interpersonal fluency, comfort with ambiguity, dynamic prioritization
- Have access to specific skills including process analysis, benefits identification, modelling and analysis, and business continuity management.

The ideal BCM has a deep understanding of the organization's operational business, can identify, quantify and define benefits, and is skilled in change management tools and techniques.

Such people may not be easy to find. In the face of this dilemma some organizations have brought in external change management experts to fill these roles. However, this can lead to a lack of responsibility within the business, limiting take-up of capability and thus realization of benefit. The business operations must take responsibility for the programme to avoid being in a position where they are on the receiving end of change rather than initiating it.

A more effective approach is to place credible business individuals into the BCM roles and then put in place training and coaching to develop the benefits and change management skills that these individuals require.

In a UK government agency, there was a growing recognition of the adverse impact of current projects and programmes on the business. Concerns about the need to balance appetite and capacity for change had been raised, as had the overall lack of adoption (and benefits realization) across the organization.

A change management function and structure was put into place. This established a business change authority role at a directorate/business unit level. Three senior managers were appointed to fulfil the remit of the role, with 20% of their time dedicated to enabling change in their respective parts of the directorate. They were supported by a BCM who took on the coordination activities and managed a team of local change managers to work at the project level (sitting on the project boards), ensuring transition and maintaining business stability whilst enabling the change. Between 20% and 100% of their time was dedicated to this. Each of the change managers had a proven operational track record and had already gained the respect of the business management.

The team were mentored by an experienced change and benefits consultant, who provided advice and support for the team and raised internal competence.

This approach proved successful in ensuring that benefits were identified and delivered by the organization.

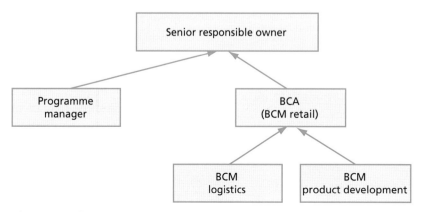

*Figure 4.5 Business change authority representing multiple BCMs*

Figure 4.5 illustrates how three BCMs may decide to coordinate their input through one person, the BCM for retail. In this situation, the BCM for retail will take the role of the business change authority (BCA) who speaks for retail, logistics and product development at the programme board.

## 4.10 BUSINESS CHANGE TEAM

The BCMs cannot deliver change alone. A business change team can be formed to help each of the BCMs take their stakeholders in their operational areas through the change cycle. Such a team considers the interests of those parts of the organization to be changed and will ensure that those parts are thoroughly prepared for the transition. The team's focus is on helping the operational unit through transition as smoothly as possible. It is a support function for when operational people need the most help.

Ideally the BCMs should be consistent throughout the life of the programme; however, the size and composition of the business change teams will evolve. For example, perhaps early in the tranche, only minimum support is required so the team can be kept small, whereas during transition, when the demands are higher, the team may expand. In some circumstances it is possible that some individuals may be members of more than one business change team for different BCMs, perhaps as change rolls out across different departments within an organization.

Reporting to the relevant BCM, such a team requires change management skills, operational knowledge and experience, as well as the influence and authority of appropriate senior managers.

Each tranche might make changes to different parts of the organization. For these reasons, the business change team needs to be reviewed at the beginning of each tranche.

Figure 4.6 illustrates how a complex organization might work, with a BCM for the corporate functions and the BCMs for logistics and product development being represented by the BCA.

## 4.11 PROGRAMME OFFICE

Programmes are major undertakings, often affecting large numbers of people and organizations and generating a substantial volume of information. The nerve centre and information hub of a programme is the programme office. All information, communication, monitoring and control activities for the programme are coordinated through the programme office.

The larger the organization and/or scale of change, the more likely it is that the programme office will be supporting multiple programmes. In organizations where the programmes are part of a portfolio, programme office activities may be provided by a corporate portfolio office, hub programme office, programme management office (PMO) or centre of excellence.

It is important to distinguish between the two distinct roles of the programme office. One is to provide support and guidance to the projects and initiatives. The other is to be the home for governance and control, including standards, approvals, financial monitoring, assurance, provision of health checks etc., and as such must be independent of the initiatives.

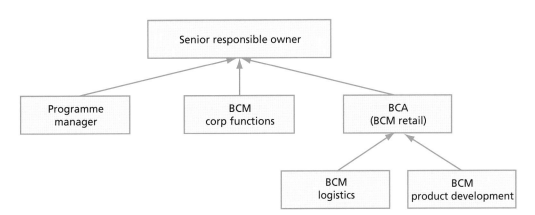

*Figure 4.6 Complex structure with BCA and BCM reporting to the SRO*

Appendix C expands on the roles of the programme office, and should be considered along with the guidance in the P3O publication, *Portfolio, Programme and Project Offices* (OGC, 2008).

## 4.12  PROGRAMME ASSURANCE

Assurance is the assessment of specific aspects to generate confidence that the programme is being managed effectively and that it is on track to realize the expected benefits and achieve the desired outcomes. Assurance, like audit, should be carried out independently of the programme management team; this may be by either an internal team and/or an external review team. Assurance may be focused on any number of aspects; please see Chapter 12 for examples of where assurance may be applied.

All programme management roles include a responsibility for making sure that assurance is carried out for the role's particular areas of interest, regardless of whether the programme will be subject to more formal audit scrutiny. For example, the SRO will require assurance that the programme's business case is being managed appropriately and that it remains aligned with strategic objectives. More formal independent assurance/peer reviews may be carried out by individuals or groups from elsewhere in the organization. There should be a clear brief for each assurance review. Assurance reviews may be carried out at any time during the programme and should be repeated in areas where problems have been identified and recommendations made for improvements.

It is important that there are integrated approaches to assurance and that all the dimensions of the programme are considered in planning. The integration therefore needs to be designed, planned and properly funded from the outset. Poor assurance integration will lead to overlapping reviews and an unnecessary load on the programme; or it could be too light, which would leave gaps and problems may not be spotted. In other words there should be an integrated approach to assurance which has been fully funded and is laid out in the assurance section of the quality and assurance strategy.

For further information on programme assurance, see Chapter 12.

## 4.13  ADDITIONAL GOVERNANCE ROLES

The following additional programme roles should be considered, though they may be part time or temporary during the different parts of the programme's life.

- **Risk manager** Provides expertise and management support for risk and issue management.
- **Programme accountant** Supports and ensures compliance to corporate accounting procedures, and also provides useful support in business case development.
- **Design authority** Provides expert advice or has responsibility for some corporate function, service, standard or strategy that will be affected, or a major programme outcome or change that needs to be controlled. This could be an IT or property infrastructure design, or a major service contract; it could also be a business process model or the programme blueprint or corporate 'target operating model'. The design authority provides expertise and guidance on a specific area to ensure that there is appropriate alignment and control when changes are being planned and implemented.
- **Benefits realization manager** Provides assurance and overview of the benefit profiles and realization plan. A key element of this role is to ensure that there are no scope conflicts between benefit profiles from different areas. This should sit at the corporate level or in the portfolio office, to give visibility across the whole portfolio of change, to ensure achievability and check that there is no duplication across the portfolio.
- **Procurement expertise** Should be involved early to ensure compliance with corporate strategies and alliances and provide advice. Most programmes will involve some aspect of procurement.

These are only a few examples; there are numerous other subject matter experts who could be used to help deliver a programme. An individual could be appointed with responsibility for any of the governance strategies/plans – for example, a communications manager or resource manager

There could also be specialist input on corporate functions, such as environment, estates, construction, or health and safety.

## 4.14 IMPLEMENTING AND MANAGING THE PROGRAMME ORGANIZATION

There is no single programme organization model that will fit every type of programme. Each programme should be directed and managed with the appropriate level of management resources to facilitate clear direction setting and effective management of ongoing progress, but without incurring excessive management overheads.

The programme organization will have to meet needs that include:

- The level of integration and overlap required with project organizations
- The need to split the responsibilities of the core programme roles across more than one individual to cope with large-scale programmes
- The requirement for building cross-organization structures
- Continual development of competency and individual performance.

The programme organization is defined in the organization structure in Appendix A. It is critical that the programme organization is compatible with the organization culture, and that careful consideration is given to how it interfaces and merges with other corporate groups and initiatives so that boundaries are clear.

### 4.14.1 Integrating programme and project structures

Designing the appropriate levels of engagement between the projects and the programme is a key part of establishing an effective programme organization. Project-level organization structures need to have clear leadership, direction-setting, decision-making and management, whether they are operating within a programme or independently. There are different forms of project organizations and different ways of integrating project organizations into a programme organization. Figure 4.7 shows some examples, thus:

- **Scenario A** Some projects will benefit from a dedicated project board to provide the required level of management direction and decision-making. The project board should have a clear set of responsibilities, agreed at the programme level, for directing the project and defining how the project should interface with the

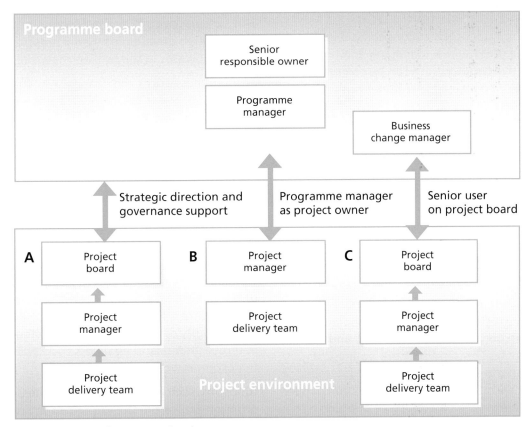

*Figure 4.7  Integrating project organizations*

programme. The chair of the project board will be the project executive. This scenario may be well suited to larger projects within the programme.

- **Scenario B** Projects that are central to the programme may work well with the programme manager fulfilling the project executive role and maintaining a very tight, direct link between the project and the programme.
- **Scenario C** The BCM may provide valuable user-side input and assurance to projects within the programme. In this scenario, the BCM may fulfil the senior user or project executive role on the project board.

It is important to consider how the BCM responsibilities are cascaded down to the project board and project teams. There is a link with the PRINCE2 senior user role, which could have an extended brief to include transitional stability and benefits achievement. Alternatively, a member of the business change team could be included within the project board structure, with a specific focus on transition, stability and benefits realization; this role could have a number of other possible titles, including 'business assurance', 'business champion' or 'voice of the business'.

### 4.14.2 Cross-organizational programmes

When two or more organizations come together to work on a programme, managing and directing their respective contributions can be complex. One example of cross-organizational working might be where one organization is providing the majority of the funding and purchasing capital assets such as a new building, while the other provides the staffing, infrastructure and systems for a new service facility. Both organizations require a return on their respective investments and so need to collaborate effectively to make the partnership deliver the required outcome. Each participating organization should have a clearly defined role that is agreed and understood by all the participating organizations.

One approach to designing an appropriate programme structure is to establish a separate entity for the purposes of coordinating and leading the programme. This separates the business of making the partnership work from the internal priorities of each participating organization. Figure 4.8 shows an example of a structure bringing together three organizations. The structure may

be a specifically created legal entity, or it may be based on formal terms of reference or contractual agreements.

In this example, the SROs from the three organizations become the sponsoring group for the programme, with a programme board comprising a BCM from each organization, the programme manager and the senior SRO. The decision on who would become the senior SRO is likely to be based on which organization is carrying the most risk.

The terms of reference and/or contractual arrangements will need to address issues such as board representation and responsibilities, appointment to and resignation from the board, etc. The challenges facing cross-organizational programmes are generally the same as for all major programmes. However, increased complexity can mean that different types of issue, with greater impact, can arise. Chapter 2 gives greater detail of aspects of programme management that present challenges and will need to be managed.

## 4.15 PROGRAMME ORGANIZATION WITHIN THE TRANSFORMATIONAL FLOW

This section covers how the programme organization governance theme is applied in each of the processes in the transformational flow.

Programmes evolve and change over their life, having both linear and cyclical characteristics. This is a progression from a state of ambiguity during Identifying a Programme, to gaining substance and shape during Defining a Programme, moving into delivery mode during Managing the Tranches and on to Closing a Programme.

There is an argument that the evolution of a programme and its different tranches implies a possibility of different leaders and managers for the different phases. If such a decision is taken, it will be necessary to balance the appropriateness of the leadership and management styles in the different tranches with the risk of a lack of continuity of leadership, management and in-depth understanding across the whole life of the programme.

During evolution, the programme will draw on different skills from the organization and may benefit from different styles of leadership and

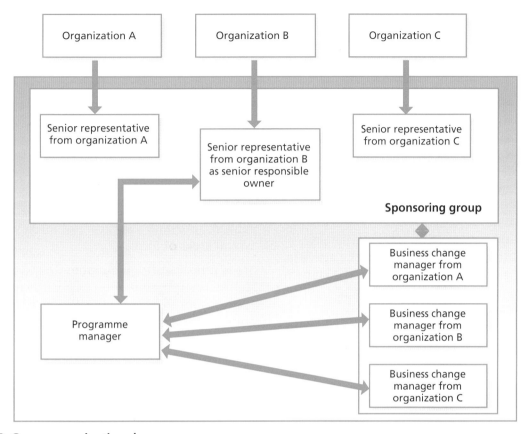

*Figure 4.8 Cross-organizational programmes*

management complemented by different skills, competence and knowledge, reflected in the make-up of the programme board and focus of individual responsibilities. How the styles may be varied across the tranches of the programme is illustrated below.

### 4.15.1 Identifying a Programme

The research/analysis-intensive nature of this phase means the team is often composed of subject matter experts. Such an environment can best be led by facilitating, providing guidance and offering suggestions, as there will still be considerable ambiguity at this stage. An 'instructing' management style would be both inhibitive and counter to the inherently exploratory nature of this phase. The leadership style must be suitably receptive and open.

More guidance is available in sections 14.2, 14.4 and 14.8.

### 4.15.2 Defining a Programme

Here the principle of design is paramount, and this must be supported by coordination across the different design groups and themes. Here the

management style must drive the coordination, whilst ensuring the primacy of the right and best elements emerging from across the design agenda. The leader must support the peer group working on the definition. There will be unique skills needed during Defining a Programme that will not be needed during delivery.

At this stage the organization structure document should be produced. More guidance is available in sections 15.3, 15.12, 15.17 and 15.18.

### 4.15.3 Managing the Tranches

These areas of a programme concentrate on outcome and delivery, so the activities and tasks to achieve this must be driven with a suitably focused style of leadership and management. What is expected or contracted to be delivered must be delivered. This more instructive style must ensure task completion with minimal disruption.

At the start of this stage the organization structure document is implemented; at the end it is reviewed and updated. More guidance is available in sections 16.2, 16.9 and 16.13.

### 4.15.4 Delivering the Capability

This is the process where we see many of the project management skills being deployed. The focus should be on delivery, with much project level activity, controls and governance being evident. The SRO should not be too involved with these activities, and the BCM should be satisfied that the quality of the work will enable them to deliver their benefits.

More guidance is available in sections 17.2 and 17.6.

### 4.15.5 Realizing the Benefits

The focus in this process is on communications, and the business change teams should be active in preparing the organizations for change. Skills such as business analysis and planning are important, as well as providing various levels of support in terms of training and backfill to support the organization going through the change.

More guidance is available in section 18.3.3.

### 4.15.6 Closing a Programme

Both ensuring benefits and closure of the programme require a management focus on ensuring that works are completed, adoptions are made, procedures are followed and changes are put in place. The management style required here has to focus on getting the job done, combined with the ability to analyse results and deal with the people issues arising from acceptance of the changes.

In this stage the organization structure document is reviewed and updated. More guidance is available in sections 19.2 and 19.8.

## 4.16 THE KEY ROLES

Table 4.1 provides a summary of the key roles and typical areas of focus.

There is no specific guidance for the two main control boards (sponsoring group and programme board) because they are forums where decisions are made and direction set with input from the four key roles. Therefore, guidance has been restricted to individuals rather than broadened to groups.

This in no way weakens or undermines the roles of the sponsoring group or the programme board, which are essential for any programme and have their responsibilities as set out in sections 4.5 and 4.7.

**Table 4.1 Programme organization and the key roles**

| Role | Area of focus |
| --- | --- |
| Senior responsible owner (SRO) | Ensuring that the programme has the necessary skills, resources and experience required to deliver the change |
| | Putting clear lines of authority in place |
| | Ensuring that sponsoring group members have a clear understanding of their roles |
| | Appointment of the programme manager |
| | Approval of the BCM appointment by the sponsoring group members |
| Programme manager | Design and appointment of the programme team |
| | Appointment of the programme office |
| | Facilitating the appointment of project management teams |
| | Ensuring that all roles have clearly defined responsibilities |
| | Ensuring that the organization design is managed through the programme lifecycle |
| | Induction of new members into the programme team |
| | Line management of the programme team |
| | Efficiency and competency of resources being deployed |
| Business change manager(s) (BCM) | Design and appointment of the business change team |
| | Induction and management of members into the business change team |
| | Development and performance of the individuals in the business change team |
| Programme office | Maintenance of organization information |
| | Advice and guidance on roles and responsibilities within the programme team |
| | Support in recruitment and appointments |

Vision 5

# 5 Vision

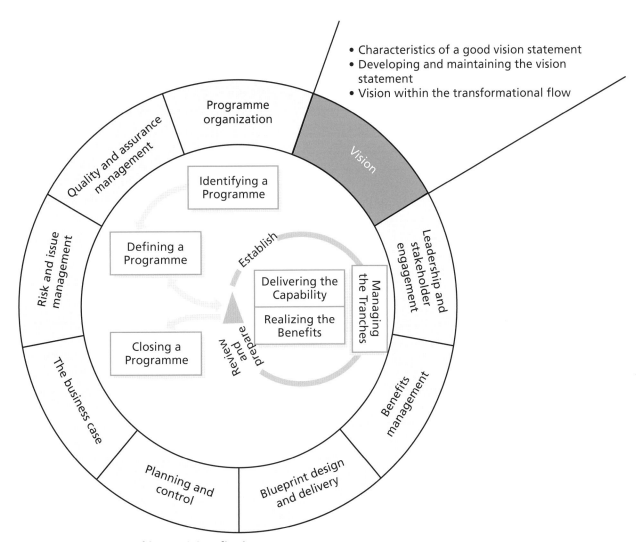

- Characteristics of a good vision statement
- Developing and maintaining the vision statement
- Vision within the transformational flow

*Figure 5.1 Overview of how vision fits into MSP*

## 5.1 INTRODUCTION

A vision is a picture of a better future. In MSP it is the basis for the outcomes and delivered benefits of the programme. As such it is a vital focus and enabler for the buy-in, motivation and activity alignment of the large community of stakeholders involved in any programme (see section 2.2.3, which discusses the principle of envisioning and communicating a better future). Figure 5.1 provides an overview of how the vision governance theme fits into MSP.

The vision statement encapsulates the vision and is used to communicate a high-level impression of the desired future 'to-be' state, in contrast to the blueprint, which is a much more detailed description of both the current organization and the changed organization. The two documents should be aligned and fully consistent with one another.

The vision statement is the outward-facing description of the future state following programme delivery (supported by the detail of the to-be elements of the blueprint). The vision statement will describe the new services, improvements and innovative ways of working with stakeholders, or any combination, and it should be used to engage and gain commitment from as many stakeholders as possible.

**Tip**

An MSP-based framework developed by a group of UK public authorities described the vision statement as a 'postcard from the future'. This helped programme teams to think about what the world would be like when the programme completes, capture the impact it would have on the organizations involved and describe the journey.

When any organization goes through transformational change, different stakeholders will not necessarily understand the big picture without such a vision statement, and it may need supporting interpretation to help explain the context.

## 5.2 CHARACTERISTICS OF A GOOD VISION STATEMENT

A good vision statement:

- Is written as a future state. It is not to be confused with an objective, strategy, intention or mission, all of which could begin with the word 'To'. Instead, it is a snapshot of the organization in the future.
- Can be easily understood by a wide variety of stakeholders; it is easy to communicate. This means it does not use jargon understood by only one group. It is clear in the vision statement how this better future is different from the present.
- Is written with the broadest groupings of stakeholders as the target audience.
- Describes a compelling future that engages the heart as well as the head. This does not mean it is emotional, but nor is it dry and factual.
- Sets out the current reality as part of the justification for the change – i.e. why the organization cannot stay where it is.
- Matches the degree of transformation change with the boldness of the vision conveyed. Vision statements should motivate everyone and need to do justice to the challenge of transformational change.

- Avoids target dates unless the vision is truly time-dependent. For example, the vision of a new international sports complex may be legitimately dependent on Delivering the Capability in time for hosting a major international event. However, in many other programmes the vision is not so time-dependent; the vision statement still remains valid even if timescales slip.
- Describes a desirable future, in terms of the interests of key stakeholders. Key benefits are implicit.
- Describes a vision that is verifiable but without too many detailed performance targets. A vision statement that contains an inspirational future that is not verifiable can breed scepticism among stakeholders. It should be clear when the organization has arrived at the future state. However, a primary purpose is consistent communication of the better future to a wide variety of stakeholders. Too many statistics and numeric targets will be a turn-off for some stakeholders and make the vision statement less memorable to many others. Such detail is more appropriate in the blueprint and its target performance levels.
- Is sufficiently flexible to remain relevant over the life of the programme. It does not contain too many constraints.
- Provides sufficient context and direction to enable the development of the blueprint.
- Is short and memorable but relevant. Some of the best vision statements are no more than a paragraph. The vision is communicated repeatedly at all kinds of events, and ideally stakeholders can recall it from memory almost word for word.

For further details on the vision statement, see Appendix A.

## 5.3 DEVELOPING AND MAINTAINING THE VISION STATEMENT

It takes time and the involvement of a number of people to draft a clear, compelling and inclusive vision statement. In transformational flow, work on the vision statement should begin soon after the programme mandate has been agreed and the senior responsible owner (SRO) has been appointed (see Chapter 14). The SRO would assemble a representative group of interested senior management and affected stakeholders and begin building outline vision statement options based on the information in the programme mandate (see the principle on leading change, discussed in section 2.2.2, and in particular the importance of assembling the right people first). Once agreed, the first cut of the vision is included in the programme brief under the heading of 'outline vision statement'; if the programme moves into Defining a Programme, the vision statement is communicated and refined, after which it is formalized in a standalone document.

**Tip**

There is a tendency for programmes to have weak vision statements, as they are often finalized quite early when it is not entirely clear what is required of the programme. The statement's development should be seen as iterative because a weak vision statement will not enable you to develop a blueprint. It is sometimes easier to do a high-level blueprint as part of developing the vision statement, which requires questions such as:

- What services will be added, changed or stopped?
- What processes will be different?
- What shape will our new organization be?
- Why are we changing?
- What will be the impact on our tools and technology?
- What values will need to change?

Using the answers from these questions you will be able to develop a more tangible vision statement that stakeholders will be able to identify with.

The outline vision statement from the programme brief is reviewed during the early activities within Defining a Programme to ensure strategic alignment and to test its viability. It is updated to create the programme's vision statement. The vision statement underpins the programme design and development (see discussion in section 2.2.1 of the principle of remaining aligned with corporate strategy).

The vision statement should be regarded as a constant and stable foundation for the programme. Improvements to its wording or, for example, embracing newly emerged business

drivers, may be allowed. However, if the vision statement does require major changes, there is a risk of:

- Confusing stakeholders, possibly even undermining the credibility of the programme
- Indicating that the current programme is no longer strategically aligned and that a possibly different programme is now required.

## 5.4 VISION WITHIN THE TRANSFORMATIONAL FLOW

This section covers how the vision governance theme is applied in each of the processes in the transformational flow.

The vision for the programme is the main thread that runs through the whole programme. By expressing the desired end-state in clear and concise language, it acts as a reference point against which the programme's direction of travel can always be assessed. It is the guiding light for the programme.

### 5.4.1 Identifying a Programme

At the outset of the programme there will be one or more strategic threats or opportunities, and the reaction of the organization's leadership to these will set the vision for the programme. These drivers may be described in the programme mandate and then be developed more formally to create the outline vision statement captured within the programme brief.

At this stage the programme mandate is reviewed and updated as required. More guidance is available in sections 14.2, 14.3 and 14.5.

### 5.4.2 Defining a Programme

Once into Defining a Programme, the outline vision statement is refined into the full vision statement. As a result of engagement with stakeholders it is developed further, and at this stage there is a clearer view of the impact and what it will mean to everyone. The vision statement should not be finalized until work on the blueprint and benefits has been undertaken, as this may show that the programme is able to achieve more or less than was originally thought and so some validation of the objectives for the programme can be undertaken.

More guidance is available in section 15.5.

### 5.4.3 Managing the Tranches

During the delivery of the programme, the vision statement acts as a beacon for the programme. When tough decisions are being taken or changes to direction are being made, the validity of those decisions should be assessed against the vision to ensure that the ultimate destination that was set will still be achieved. The vision should underpin much of the communications to make certain that stakeholders are engaged and, hopefully, understand the change that the programme is delivering.

### 5.4.4 Delivering the Capability

Project initiations can be set against the context of the vision statement. If each project clearly understands how it is contributing to an element of the vision, then its context will be much clearer and the project team will feel a greater involvement in the overall programme and its direction.

### 5.4.5 Realizing the Benefits

It is likely that the benefits of the change will be at the core of the vision statement. During this process the benefits will be pursued actively. There will, no doubt, be reluctance to change or even resistance: the contents of the vision statement should be used to underpin communications and help to mobilize the departments affected to deliver the new or changed services or ways of working.

### 5.4.6 Closing a Programme

The ultimate test of the vision during closure will be whether it has been achieved. It may be that the programme is closing and has achieved its objectives, but the vision is still alive and will outlive the programme. Ideally, progress towards achieving the vision should be evident, although some of the benefits may remain to be realized.

## 5.5 THE KEY ROLES

Table 5.1 summarizes the key roles and typical areas of focus.

There is no specific guidance for the two main control boards (sponsoring group and programme board) because they are forums where decisions are made and direction set with input from the four key roles. Therefore guidance has been restricted to individuals rather than broadened to groups.

This in no way weakens or undermines the roles of the sponsoring group or the programme board, which are essential for any essential programme and have their responsibilities set out in Chapter 4.

**Table 5.1 Vision and the key roles**

| Role | Area of focus |
|---|---|
| Senior responsible owner (SRO) | Engaging the sponsoring group in the development of the vision statement |
| | Producing the vision statement document |
| | Gaining the endorsement of the sponsoring group and senior support and commitment for the vision |
| | Ensuring that the organization is capable of achieving the transformation described |
| | Maintaining focus on the vision statement |
| | Authorizing any changes or formal interpretations to the vision statement |
| Programme manager | Developing programme documentation aligned to the vision statement |
| | Ensuring that the vision statement underpins the programme communications plan |
| | Coordinating the development of the blueprint based on the vision statement |
| | Designing the delivery of capability to align with the vision statement commitments |
| | Processing any changes or updates to the vision statement |
| Business change manager(s) (BCM) | Supporting the SRO in the development of the content relating to the business areas to be changed, and contributing to the content of the vision statement |
| | Interpreting the vision statement in the context of their business operations |
| | Assessing the impact of the vision statement on business operations |
| | Communicating the vision statement to their particular areas of the business |
| | Delivering the operational changes needed to achieve the desired end state |
| Programme office | Configuration management of the vision statement document |

# Leadership and stakeholder engagement

6

# 6 Leadership and stakeholder engagement

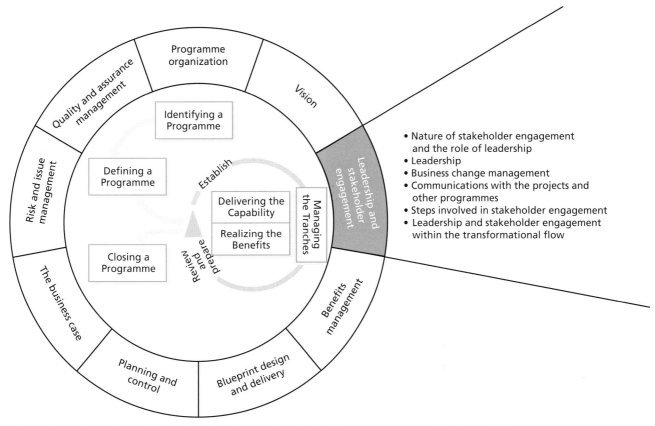

*Figure 6.1 Overview of how leadership and stakeholder engagement fits into MSP*

## 6.1 INTRODUCTION

A stakeholder is any individual, group or organization that can affect, be affected by, or perceive itself to be affected by, a programme. One key aspect of the 'leading change' programme management principle (see section 2.2.2) is that it actively engages stakeholders in the following ways:

- Leaders use the programme vision statement to influence and persuade stakeholders to commit to the beneficial future.
- Business change managers (BCMs) engage their operational stakeholders, leading them through the uncertainty of transition to the new ways of working.
- A focus on benefits (see section 2.2.4) recognizes that a 'benefit' is only such when it is perceived to be advantageous by one or more stakeholders. In a community of different

interests and attitudes, the leader must engage stakeholders so that benefits are identified, clearly communicated and understood, owned and realized, and the threats to realizing those benefits are reduced (see Figure 7.5).

- Some stakeholders will be identified as resources within the delivery of the new capability – some with unique or scarce skills and competencies.

How a programme engages its stakeholders is crucial to its success. Figure 6.1 provides an overview of how the leadership and stakeholder engagement governance theme fits into MSP.

There are many illustrations of programmes that have failed because of inadequate stakeholder engagement. This underlines the importance of this governance theme.

For example, a multi-agency programme that was restructuring a significant part of a public service was, in most respects, well led and well managed. However, the leaders of the programme failed to engage a key group of stakeholders in one organization; consequently, these stakeholders failed to own the realization of a stream of benefits for that part of the organization. The result was that the programme significantly underperformed, realizing fewer benefits than if these stakeholders had been committed to the programme and its vision.

## 6.2 NATURE OF STAKEHOLDER ENGAGEMENT AND THE ROLE OF LEADERSHIP

Managers sometimes forget the obvious: stakeholders are individuals or groups with feelings, perceptions, desires and influence. In any transformational change, there will be those who:

- Support or oppose it
- End up gaining or losing when benefits are realized (see Figure 7.5)
- See only a threat, perhaps convinced that they will lose despite all evidence to the contrary
- Are inherently indifferent to the change. They may become helpful or unhelpful, depending on how they themselves are managed and influenced
- May become either supporters or blockers of these benefits depending on how and to what level they are engaged.

Programme managers need to think of stakeholder engagement not just as a system of tasks and managing things, but also as a way of achieving influence and positive outcomes through effective management of relationships.

Strong leaders understand that people need to be engaged as more than resources to be used or obstacles to be removed. This will include considering matters of internal politics, and individual emotions and motivations.

Good leaders take seriously the attitudes and agendas of individuals. They need to understand the challenges that transformational change brings for people. Such leaders are likely to be more successful in influencing people around them, and in turning stakeholders from blockers into advocates.

One mechanism that some programme leaders employ to influence key stakeholders is to conduct early 'visioning' workshops to help draft the programme vision statement (see Chapter 5). Such a workshop is an opportunity:

- To engage the right stakeholders early (the 'leading change' principle), even including clients and suppliers
- For leadership to explore and define what might be called the 'do-nothing vision'.

The 'do-nothing vision' allows the leaders to create and foster the belief in the need for change: 'We can't stay where we are because this is what will come about ….' This is also sometimes known as the 'burning platform' or 'burning bridge', on the premise that you can't stay on either and you have to jump from the platform or cross over the bridge. Skilful leaders, effectively using communications, stories, visions and metaphors, manage perceptions of the current reality, the beneficial future and the tension between the two in order to build and maintain the organizational impetus and commitment to change. The do-nothing vision is often a useful way to show potential blockers the possible negative impact of their actions, and bring them round to support the change.

## 6.3 LEADERSHIP

Understanding the essential nature of leadership is helped by contrasting it with that of management, as shown in Table 6.1.

This distinction does not mean that managers cannot be leaders or that leaders cannot be managers. People occupying roles in the programme's management team need to display both sets of competencies and outlooks. Nor does it mean that leadership is exclusive to the senior

**Table 6.1 Leadership and management**

| Leadership is … | Management is … |
| --- | --- |
| Particularly required in a context of change. It clarifies the 'as-is', the vision of the future, and thrives in the tension between the two | Always required, particularly in business-as-usual contexts, and focuses more on evolutionary or continual improvement |
| Inclined to clarify the 'what' and the 'why' | Focused on the 'how' and the 'when' |
| More concerned with direction, effectiveness and purpose | Concerned with speed, efficiency and quality |
| Most effective when influencing people by communicating in face-to-face situations | Most effective when controlling tasks against specifications or plans |
| Focused on meaning, purpose and realized value | Focused on tasks, delivery and process |

responsible owner (SRO) and the sponsoring group. A best-practice programme evidences dispersed leadership: at some time or other, all roles in the management team must display leadership qualities. However, the SRO, the sponsoring group and programme board roles generally need to display leadership on a more continual basis.

**Example**

Research carried out at the Cranfield School of Management using a sample of 15 strategic programmes across seven industry sectors revealed multiple attributes of programme management work, each conceived by individual programme managers at one of four different levels, or 'mindsets'.

The research showed that the levels were cumulative: managers with a higher-level mindset could also conceive their work in terms of the lower levels, enabling them to move between levels as appropriate to a given situation. Managers with a lower-level mindset could only see that lower level.

Table 6.2 lists the 17 key behavioural attributes of programme management work identified in the Cranfield research, with a summary description of the conception for each attribute found at either end of the scale (levels 1 and 4). It is clear that the conceptual agility of managers with a level 4 conception was linked to higher leadership traits than for those at lower levels. However, an individual's level of conception did not always correlate with their level of seniority within programme governance. For example, a programme manager might be alert to wider stakeholder issues, but their SRO might not, thus inhibiting the effectiveness of that programme manager. Overall the principle of 'leading change' (section 2.2.2), in particular the ability to live with uncertainty, was found to be a key characteristic of managers able to operate at the higher levels.

## 6.4 BUSINESS CHANGE MANAGEMENT

Business change management considers how change happens in its broadest sense – within individuals, within teams and within the organization – and how people can be led through such change.

A programme is always commissioned in a wider context of change. At this macro level of viewing change, a programme may be seen as a part of a larger strategic change initiative or part of a corporate portfolio of change.

At a micro level, each individual is affected by the programme and experiences their own cycle of change as they transition from the old way of doing things to the new.

Change is everywhere and iterative: it is often best represented as a circular process rather than linear. There are several well-established change management models, each one with merit. Figure 6.2 shows one such model, with parts of the transformational flow mapped onto each step.

Business change management and ensuring organizational commitment to change should be a dominant programme concern and focus of action for the management team. In response to this, a BCM must be effective in leading an operational team through a transition cycle that embeds new working practices.

## Table 6.2 Conceptions of programme management

| Attributes | Cumulative conceptions of programme management | |
|---|---|---|
| | Level 1 | Level 4 |
| **Relationship between self and work** | | |
| Granularity of focus | Plans in detail | Selects detail with external and future focus |
| Emotional attachment | Emotionally detached, factual | Committed to outcomes |
| Disposition for action | Procedural trouble-shooter | Intuitively reconfigures and makes the rules |
| Approach to role plurality | Focused, single role | Adopts multiple viewpoints |
| **Relationship between self and others** | | |
| Relationship with team | Supportive and responsive | Confidence-inspiring leader, able to influence behaviour |
| Approach to conflict and divergence | By seeking procedures | Facilitates towards creative solutions |
| Education and support | Assists with problem solving | Coaches to enable influence |
| Use of questions | Own clarification | To challenge, encourage creative thinking and reframe purpose |
| Expectations of others | Contracted effort | Exploits and extends individuals' talents |
| **Relationship with programme environment** | | |
| Adaptive intent | Does what worked in the past | Adapts self and environment to suit purpose |
| Awareness of organizational capabilities | Assumes departments can deliver | Awareness of the shortcomings; prepared to go outside |
| Approach to risk | Procedural. Manage out internal risks | Ready for the consequences of failure |
| Approach to face-to-face communications | Reports facts in consistent style | Sells vision with cultural sensitivity |
| Approach to governance | Reports in hierarchy | Embeds programme structure within business |
| Attitude to boundary | Follows change control | Shapes to meet emerging and changing needs |
| Attitude to time | Schedule driven; reschedule when necessary | Conscious of issues of timeliness and maturity |
| Attitude to funding | Budget driven | Aware of budget uncertainties: creates budget from achievement |

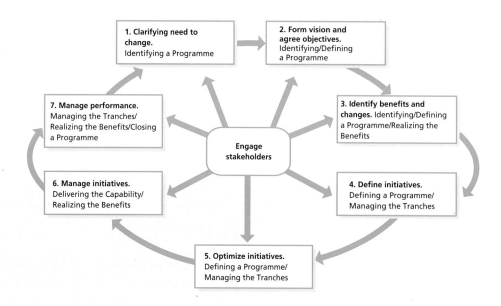

*Figure 6.2  Example of a change process model*

## 6.5 COMMUNICATIONS WITH THE PROJECTS AND OTHER PROGRAMMES

Whilst projects within the programme will need to communicate with their local stakeholders, the programme will need to control this to ensure that the communications are consistent, clear, timely and accurate.

A good place to start is with some general stance or policy within the stakeholder engagement strategy (see Figure 6.3, step 3). Some typical examples of solutions are:

■ A general guideline, briefed to the projects through the programme office and the programme manager, that planned, routine communications are first reviewed by the programme office

- Certain identified stakeholders are always referred to the SRO or to the programme manager, or to the person in the programme specifically responsible for maintaining the relationships with these stakeholders
- Certain stakeholders may have nominated 'custodians' through which all communications are channelled
- Certain topic areas identified as 'sensitive' must always be referred up to the programme for communication, e.g. industrial relations
- Regular communications briefings are given to constituent projects so that they stay on message (e.g. via the provision of presentation packs)
- Wherever possible, project communications are aligned with the overarching programme communications plan.

Whatever the approaches taken, care should be taken to allow the projects to manage their local communications whenever this is reasonable. Too much control of communications by the programme can easily disempower the projects as well as generating new sources of discontent from stakeholders within the projects themselves.

Keeping communications consistent across other programmes is a necessity in a corporate portfolio environment, and also in multi-agency programmes driven by external factors (e.g. educational, health,

economic, environmental, transport and other services driven by legislative reform). Failure to achieve coherence risks confusion and a lack of stakeholder confidence and buy-in.

## 6.6 STEPS INVOLVED IN STAKEHOLDER ENGAGEMENT

Programmes that stress the management of stakeholders can lapse into relying on planned communications that are little more than a task list with a bias toward outbound information. This does not sufficiently engage stakeholders, who generally do not appreciate being managed. In such an approach, the management is more of perceptions, objections, messages and communications rather than of the stakeholders themselves. As stakeholders are people (even if they are being engaged as part of a wider group or organization), attempting to manage them from a purely mechanistic mindset is unlikely to work.

The steps in the cycle of activities do have to be managed within the programme, because if they are not managed effectively the quality of the engagement with stakeholders and the essential two-way communication will suffer.

Figure 6.3 illustrates the stakeholder engagement cycle that underpins the MSP stakeholder engagement strategy. Each step in this cycle is described in the following six subsections.

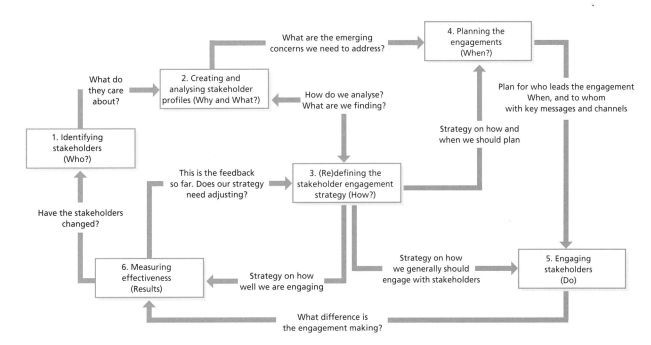

*Figure 6.3 Stakeholder engagement cycle*

### 6.6.1 Identifying stakeholders ('Who?')

Stakeholder engagement begins with identifying all the stakeholders involved in or affected by the programme and its outcomes. As the programme's vision statement and blueprint are developed, these documents provide the basis for identifying further stakeholders and what outcomes they want.

During the life of the programme, stakeholders will change. Some stakeholders will participate in the programme in advisory or assurance roles; some will be important in assessing the realization of the programme's benefits; others will have an audit or assurance perspective.

Programmes are likely to have large numbers of individual stakeholders. It can therefore be useful to organize the programme's stakeholders by category such as: users/beneficiaries; governance (management boards, steering groups, audit); influencers (e.g. trade unions, the media); and providers (suppliers, business partners). These high-level categories can be broken down further, or alternative groupings can be identified in order to organize communication by shared interests. In this way, key messages can be targeted at and consultations undertaken with the relevant people. Groupings should be practically identifiable rather than abstract; for example, 'employees based in the Dublin office' is a readily identifiable group, whereas 'members of the public who support human rights' is not. This exercise may identify the same individuals in different categories and groupings, but it is often a useful way of differentiating between stakeholders with multiple interests.

### 6.6.2 Creating and analysing stakeholder profiles ('Why?' and 'What?')

Identifying stakeholders is only the first step. Analysis means gaining an understanding of the:

- Influences, interests and attitudes of the stakeholders towards the programme's outcomes
- Importance and power of each stakeholder.

Gathering this information together into a single source can reveal important insights about a programme's stakeholders. Stakeholder information is consolidated into a document called stakeholder profiles; this one document contains all information about stakeholders and the stakeholder map. Within the document, there will be a profile of each of the stakeholder groups. See Appendix A for descriptions of stakeholder map and stakeholder profiles.

Tip

Some organizations create a stakeholder register to summarize the key information from the stakeholder profiles. It can be used to show the current status of the different groups and is much easier to review at a programme board.

#### 6.6.2.1 Stakeholder map

The programme's stakeholder map, which forms part of the stakeholder profiles, shows the stakeholders, their interests, and the areas of the programme that affect them. For example, some stakeholders will be concerned with how the programme will affect their working environment while others will be concerned about how the programme will change the way customers are handled. The stakeholder map in Table 6.3 compares the various stakeholders against their interests in a programme dealing with urban regeneration following the construction of an international sports complex.

Because of the evolving and potentially volatile nature of a programme, the stakeholder profiles (including the stakeholder map) should be regularly revisited and checked to see whether other stakeholders have now appeared, new interests have emerged or earlier assessments of stakeholders should now be changed. As with all information in MSP, the objective is not to create the map but to use it to inform decisions, so revising it throughout the programme is key to ensuring its maximum contribution.

The stakeholder profiles will need to be updated whenever new stakeholders are identified or the interests of existing stakeholders change.

#### 6.6.2.2 Further analysis

Stakeholders' influence and interests, whether rational and justifiable or emotional and unfounded, must all be taken into account. They will affect the business change process and hence the programme. Fears may be unfounded or perceptions mistaken, but must be addressed.

**Table 6.3 Example of a stakeholder map for a sports complex programme**

| Interest areas / Stakeholders | Sports facilities | Transport infrastructure | Public transport service | City image/prestige | Local economy | Housing | Hotel accommodation | Local environment | City taxes |
|---|---|---|---|---|---|---|---|---|---|
| Planning department | | ✓ | | | ✓ | ✓ | | ✓ | |
| City mayor | ✓ | ✓ | ✓ | ✓ | ✓ | ✓ | | ✓ | ✓ |
| City government | ✓ | ✓ | ✓ | ✓ | ✓ | ✓ | ✓ | ✓ | ✓ |
| Transport department | | ✓ | ✓ | | ✓ | | | | |
| Sports minister | ✓ | ✓ | ✓ | ✓ | | | ✓ | ✓ | |
| National government | | ✓ | ✓ | | ✓ | ✓ | | | ✓ |
| Local residents | ✓ | ✓ | ✓ | | ✓ | ✓ | | ✓ | ✓ |
| National sports council | ✓ | | | | | | ✓ | ✓ | |
| Tourists | ✓ | ✓ | ✓ | ✓ | | | ✓ | ✓ | |
| Athletes | ✓ | | | ✓ | | | ✓ | | |
| Rail company | | ✓ | ✓ | | ✓ | | | | |
| Local businesses | | | ✓ | ✓ | ✓ | ✓ | | ✓ | ✓ |

It is useful to analyse the significance and potential influence of each stakeholder against their areas of interest. This analysis will also help to:

- Prioritize stakeholder engagement
- Focus programme resources to contribute the most towards successful outcomes
- Ensure communication channels are well exploited
- Align message content, media, frequency of engagement and level of detail to meet the relevant needs of the stakeholders.

The communications channels may need to be worked to engage stakeholders who cannot be engaged directly by the programme. In such cases, working through partners, industry groups, volunteer organizations etc. may be required.

One of several techniques for analysing stakeholders is to consider each stakeholder in terms of their influence on the programme and their potential interest in the programme outcomes and plot these on a matrix.

The level of their importance to the programme and its impact on them will determine the level and type of stakeholder engagement the programme should undertake. For example, in the programme to exploit an international sports complex illustrated in Figure 6.4, the sports minister will have high interest in the programme, and also high influence upon it and so is a key player and should be treated accordingly: high interest × high influence = high impact. By contrast, the local residents, despite having a similarly high interest in the legacy of the sports

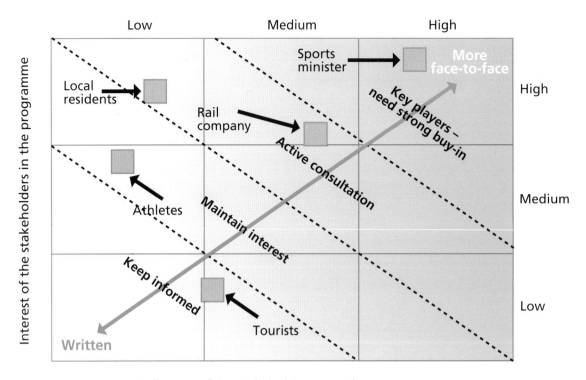

**Figure 6.4 Influence/interest matrix of a sports-complex programme**

complex, don't have so much direct influence on the programme or its outcomes; hence the primary mode of engagement is active consultation.

As stakeholders may move to different positions on the matrix as the programme progresses and capabilities are delivered, it is important to rework the stakeholder analysis regularly. For example in Figure 6.4, the importance of engaging the tourists towards the latter stages will become more crucial to the success of the main event being staged in the complex and they should therefore be moved towards 'maintain interest' (or higher) in the matrix.

Another kind of analysis examines stakeholder attitude. The attitude of a stakeholder towards the programme might be negative. The aim of the targeted elements of the programme communications plan (step 4) might well be to influence that stakeholder to a neutral position or better.

Collectively, all the identification and analysis information – in the form of a stakeholder map, an influence/interest matrix or any kind of similar analysis – is gathered together into the stakeholder profiles document.

### 6.6.3 (Re)defining the stakeholder engagement strategy ('How?')

The key question a stakeholder engagement strategy answers is: 'How will the programme effectively engage with the stakeholders?' The programme management team must specify:

- How stakeholders will be identified, categorized and grouped
- How the analysis of a stakeholder's influence and interest in the programme will be measured and assessed
- How the importance and impact of a stakeholder to a programme will be assessed
- Approaches for engaging with stakeholders, including specific mechanisms which could be applied, and roles and responsibilities for the engagement process
- How stakeholder analysis information will be processed, stored and reviewed
- How the interfaces between the programme and its projects' stakeholders will be managed
- What channels will be used and in what circumstances
- How feedback and dialogue will be managed
- How the success of the stakeholder engagement will be measured.

This will ensure that the engagements always support consistent and cohesive communications. See Appendix A for details on the content of the stakeholder engagement strategy.

If programme management teams are not physically co-located, this increases the risk of uncoordinated and inconsistent engagement with particular stakeholders. Some stakeholders are likely to exploit any apparent inconsistencies to support their local agendas. Geographically dispersed teams will find that they acquire greater control and influence through employing a rigorous stakeholder engagement strategy.

Implementing the stakeholder engagement strategy means considering a range of factors including:

- The scale of cultural, organizational or societal change
- Managing expectations over an extended period
- Adequate resource and energy to ensure:
  - Business ownership of the overall programme
  - Stakeholder buy-in and involvement
  - Public relations (PR), marketing and communications expertise to support the programme
  - Clarity and consistency of messages and benefits
- Maintaining documents such as the programme communications plan and stakeholder profiles as valid tools for engaging stakeholders.

For further information about the contents, see Appendix A.

The programme management team should actively adjust and redefine the stakeholder engagement strategy. The programme office will often be called upon to conduct such reviews or to give a view on who is best equipped to do so. Independent PR and communications specialists can make an important contribution at such reviews.

### 6.6.4 Planning the engagements ('When?')

Communications are best planned after defining how the programme will engage the different stakeholders as reflected in the stakeholder engagement strategy.

Engagement is more active and embracing than communication. It covers including stakeholders in decision-making and implementation, as well as consulting with and informing them. And communication is central to all of these and any change process.

The greater the change, the greater the need for clear communication about the reasons and rationale behind it, the benefits expected, the plans for its implementation and its proposed effects.

The objectives of the communications process are to:

- Keep awareness and commitment high
- Ensure that expectations do not drift out of line with what will be delivered
- Explain what changes will be made and when
- Describe the desired future end state (see section 2.2.3).

Successful communications will be judged on the ability to meet these objectives.

Tip

Successful communications are based on four core elements:

- **Stakeholder identification and analysis** Send the right message to the right audience
- **Message clarity and consistency** Ensure relevance and recognition, and engender trust
- **Effective system of message delivery** Get the right messages to the right stakeholders in a timely and effective way
- **Feedback collection system** Assess the effectiveness of the communications process.

Messages must be consistent. Leaders undermine their own credibility and risk hesitancy among stakeholders if they give out inconsistent messages.

Messages should be appropriate in number, focused, simple, brief and derived from the programme's objectives. It is useful to establish key phrases ('touchstone statements', 'sound bites' or 'word bites' are alternative terms) as the foundation for more complex communications and then to repeat these throughout the programme.

This also ensures that the programme and its organization are seen to be speaking with one voice.

Many organizations have access to public relations and communications specialists. People with such skills should be used wherever possible to help shape the programme communications.

### 6.6.4.1 Programme communications plan

The programme communications plan describes what will be communicated, how it will be communicated, by when, and by whom, during the programme. It should be defined and implemented as early as possible and then maintained throughout the programme.

Using information from the stakeholder profiles, the programme communications plan should be designed to:

- Raise awareness amongst all stakeholders of the benefits and impact of the planned outcomes.
- Gain commitment from stakeholders in the target business area(s) to the changes being introduced – thus ensuring the long-term success of the improvements.
- Keep all stakeholders in the target business area(s) informed of progress before, during and after implementation or delivery of programme outcomes.
- Promote key messages from the programme.
- Demonstrate a commitment to meeting the requirements of those sponsoring the programme (the sponsoring group).
- Make communications truly two-way (i.e. a dialogue, not a broadcast) by actively encouraging stakeholders to provide feedback and ensuring that they are informed about the use of their feedback to influence the programme. All types of feedback should be expected, and responses to it carefully considered. Feedback may sometimes be negative, impractical or harshly critical.
- Ensure that all those responsible for projects have an understanding of the scope, nature and outcomes of the programme.
- Promote outcomes to maximize the benefits obtained from the new business operations.

It is often advantageous to communicate early successes (sometimes referred to as 'quick wins') to those directly concerned with the business operation and to other key audiences, especially where rapid progress in realizing benefits needs to be seen. The aim is to secure commitment and build momentum.

The programme communications plan should answer the following questions:

- What are the objectives of each communication?
- What are the key messages?
- Who are the stakeholders the communications are trying to reach?
- What information will be communicated and by whom?
- What reaction might the stakeholders have to the information communicated?
- What sensitivities do we need to be aware of?
- When will information be disseminated and what are the relevant timings?
- How much information will be provided and to what level of detail?
- What mechanisms will be used to disseminate information?
- How will feedback be encouraged; what will be done as a result of feedback?
- How will feedback be recorded, reviewed and resolved?

The answers to these questions may be different for each stakeholder. The stakeholder map, developed during analysis, can also be extended to list the specific communications activities for each stakeholder group.

### 6.6.4.2 Communication channels

Communication channels should be established to ensure stakeholders' expectations of the programme are managed and maintained throughout the programme's life.

The channels used for communications may be a mixture of participative approaches, for example seminars or workshops, and non-participative media, for example announcements or newsletters. The effectiveness of each channel should be monitored as the programme progresses. Changes should be made to cater for the evolving requirements of the stakeholders, as their knowledge increases and demand for information grows. Some possible channel options are summarized in Table 6.4.

**Table 6.4 Communication channels**

| Channel | Purpose and benefits |
| --- | --- |
| Seminars, workshops, videoconferences and live webcasts | Powerful tools for engagement with specific groups of stakeholders. A key benefit is that they provide the programme management team with an opportunity for direct contact with stakeholders and for obtaining first-hand feedback on issues directly affecting them. |
| Café conversations | These are unstructured meetings where a broad issue is aired with those stakeholders who are concerned enough to attend. Such meetings are useful means of gaining information as well as engaging stakeholders early in the process, helping to give them a sense of involvement in the change that is still emerging. |
| Press/media packs and briefings | The press and media are vehicles for getting messages about the programme to an external audience and for providing the programme team with confirmation that their work is significant and important. |
| Bulletins, briefings, announcements, press releases, blogs (electronic- or paper-based), internet and intranet | There are two types: (1) general information about the programme for all audiences and (2) specific information relevant to one or more stakeholder groups. General information should provide an update on the programme, addressing issues of concern to all stakeholders, such as overall progress or any changes to the programme objectives. The more specific information should provide the particular stakeholder(s) with information relating to their own issues. Such may be distributed via intranet home pages, websites or email. However, it is important to make sure that stakeholders have access to email or the home pages, are aware of their existence and want to visit them. In addition to electronic media, it is often useful and more convenient to distribute in paper form, such as newsletters. Frequently asked questions (FAQs), together with appropriate responses, are often included. |
| Site exhibitions | Static or rolling displays are useful in providing a continuing presence and awareness within the organization about the programme. |
| Video, CD, DVD, webinars, podcasts and vodcasts | CDs are useful for presenting large amounts of information about the programme by enabling individuals to search for information relevant to their particular interests. Video films and DVDs, when targeted appropriately, are a cost-effective means of communication to large, widely dispersed audiences and can be used to provide updates on progress and for selling the key programme messages in a visually appealing and effective manner. Video, DVDs and podcasts circulated over a restricted network have the added advantage of conveying tacit aspects of the personalities and passions of leaders in the programme, in a way that purely written media rarely achieve. |

## 6.6.5 Engaging stakeholders ('Do')

The processes of identifying and analysing stakeholders may well start to engage them to some degree. For example, identification could involve stakeholders in early workshops; often an effective method of analysis is to ask the stakeholder and listen: 'First seek to understand, then to be understood.'

In terms of the concepts presented in Table 6.4, able programme managers will always recognize the need for more subtle and informal means of communication. The programme management team will often need to influence, lobby, cajole, manipulate, co-opt, flatter and apply pressure to stakeholders in order to maintain momentum and keep the programme on track.

## 6.6.6 Measuring effectiveness ('Results')

It is easy for the programme management team to believe its own myths, such as:

- 'Everybody who needs to know, knows'
- 'People are generally positive towards the change, and if they are not, they soon will be when they see the benefits being realized.'

Simple methods of checking perceptions include sampling stakeholder communities. One simple question early in the programme might be 'What is the programme's vision?'

Communications specialists agree that people do not retain information until they have heard it several times. Feedback will reveal under-communication or miscommunication.

Good programme managers will not wait for the end-of-tranche reviews or an external audit to find out how effective the programme's stakeholder engagement is. They make it their business to gain this evidence in person.

An independent review of stakeholder perceptions can provide a valid sense-check on programme assumptions about stakeholder perceptions and commitment, and could be included as part of a programme health check.

## 6.7 LEADERSHIP AND STAKEHOLDER ENGAGEMENT WITHIN THE TRANSFORMATIONAL FLOW

This section covers how the leadership and stakeholder engagement governance theme is applied in each of the processes in the transformational flow

Leadership sets the direction for the programme and brings the whole team with it as it moves towards the vision. Stakeholder engagement runs through all processes in the transformational flow, since the programme will only succeed if it has the active support of committed stakeholders.

### 6.7.1 Identifying a Programme

Stakeholder engagement is prevalent in all aspects of everyday programme delivery. From the outset, the techniques are being used; the formation of the sponsoring group is the result of stakeholder analysis, as is the formation of the programme board and the appointment of the SRO. During the early days of the programme, there is likely to be a relatively small group of strategic stakeholders who are involved in the initiation activities; consideration should be given to who the high-impact stakeholders are and the challenges that will be faced. The programme brief would most likely identify stakeholder support as a risk – either opportunity or threat, for example.

More guidance is available in section 14.2, which discusses sponsoring the programme, and section 14.8, which covers approval to proceed.

### 6.7.2 Defining a Programme

During Defining a Programme, the stakeholder engagement is likely to spread from this core group, expanding the extent of engagement as more is known about the programme and its

likely impact. The programme preparation plan will have set out the governance arrangements, and the formal documentation (stakeholder map and profiles) should start to appear early in the definition process. Once the vision, blueprint and benefits begin to stabilize, the engagement should become more intense to create greater understanding, engender support and identify and plan for resistance.

During this stage, the programme communications plan, the stakeholder engagement strategy and the stakeholder profiles all need to be created. More guidance is available in sections 15.4, 15.13, 15.17 and 15.18.

### 6.7.3 Managing the Tranches

When the programme moves into full delivery, communications should be regular and focused. There will be an opportunity at the launch of the tranche to increase awareness with various management communication events that will raise the profile of the programme. Following on from this should be communications that reinforce and widen the scope of messages to ensure that the programme maintains control of the agenda. Stakeholder priorities and support may change as delivery progresses, and the stakeholder analysis stored in the stakeholder profiles must be actively maintained so that it remains accurate. At the start of each tranche the stakeholder engagement strategy and the programme communications plan should be implemented: these should be reviewed and updated when a tranche finishes.

More guidance is available in sections 16.2 and 16.5.

### 6.7.4 Delivering the Capability

As the projects are being launched, it is an opportunity to engage stakeholders in the process as part of teams or various advisory groups. The projects themselves may also be a source of valuable knowledge about the stakeholders and be able to provide good news stories that can be used to support broader communications. It is also very important that the programme maintains control over project level communications. The project perspective and priorities may be different from those of the programme, and this situation will have to be managed.

Projects provide an opportunity to review and update the stakeholder profiles, as individual projects are likely to identify additional project level stakeholders that had not been involved at a programme level. The programme communications plan applies as much at the project level as it does across the programme. More guidance on engaging stakeholders is available in section 17.3.

### 6.7.5 Realizing the Benefits

Just about the only tool available to a programme to prepare the organization for change is stakeholder engagement and communications. This process starts as soon as the programme becomes public knowledge and resistance and support emerges. By understanding the perspectives of different groups and communicating effectively, the programme can complete pre-transition and support the preparation for change. It may well be that work within this process will be endeavouring to promote the positive effects of the programme as the change is happening, and resistance may be at its highest. Something that senior managers view as a benefit may have detrimental effects on other individuals, so it is important that this is managed.

At this stage, active use of the programme communications plan continues, and the stakeholder profiles need to be reviewed and updated. More guidance is available in sections 18.2.4, 18.3.2 and 18.3.4.

### 6.7.6 Closing a Programme

Effective communication at the closure of the programme can make the difference between it being remembered as a success or failure. The programme, however successful, will not please everyone. It is therefore essential to take a sensitive approach to the needs of various stakeholder groups. Ensure that communications are carefully targeted and that they are positive about the achievements.

In common with most programme documents, when closing a programme a final review and update should be made of the programme communications plan, the stakeholder engagement strategy and the stakeholder profiles. More guidance on notification, feedback and disbanding is available in sections 19.4, 19.7 and 19.8.

## 6.8 THE KEY ROLES

Table 6.5 is a summary of the key roles and typical areas of focus.

There is no specific guidance for the two main control boards (sponsoring group and programme board) because they are forums where decisions are made and direction set with input from the four key roles. Therefore guidance has been restricted to individuals rather than broadened to groups.

This in no way weakens or undermines the roles of the sponsoring group or the programme board, which are essential for any essential programme and have their responsibilities set out in Chapter 4.

**Table 6.5 Leadership and stakeholder engagement and the key roles**

| Role | Area of focus |
| --- | --- |
| Senior responsible owner (SRO) | Engaging key stakeholders early and at appropriate milestones throughout the programme |
| | Leading the engagement with high-impact stakeholders and anticipating stakeholder issues that may arise |
| | Briefing the sponsoring group and gathering strategic guidance on changing business drivers |
| | Showing visible leadership at key communications events and ensuring the visible and demonstrable commitment of the sponsoring group |
| | Ensuring the creation, implementation and maintenance of the overall stakeholder engagement strategy |
| Programme manager | Developing and implementing the stakeholder engagement strategy |
| | Day-to-day implementation of the whole stakeholder engagement process |
| | Developing and maintaining the stakeholder profiles |
| | Controlling and aligning project communications activities |
| | Ensuring effective communications with the project teams |
| | Developing, implementing and updating the programme communications plan |
| Business change manager(s) (BCM) | Engaging and leading those operating new working practices through the transition, generating confidence and buy-in from those involved. Active stakeholder engagement is a major part of discharging this role |
| | Supporting the SRO and taking specific responsibility for stakeholder engagement in their part of the organization |
| | Support to the programme manager in the development of the stakeholder engagement strategy and programme communications plan |
| | Alerting the programme manager to the net winners and losers (if any) in their area of change |
| | Providing information and business intelligence for the stakeholder profiles |
| | Briefing and liaising with the business change team |
| | Communicating with affected stakeholders to identify new benefits and improved ways of realizing benefits |
| | Delivering key communications messages to their business operations |
| Programme office | Maintaining information relating to the stakeholders |
| | Maintaining an audit trail of communication activity |
| | Collating feedback and ensuring that it is logged and processed |
| | Facilitating activities specified in the programme communications plan |

# Benefits management

7

# 7 Benefits management

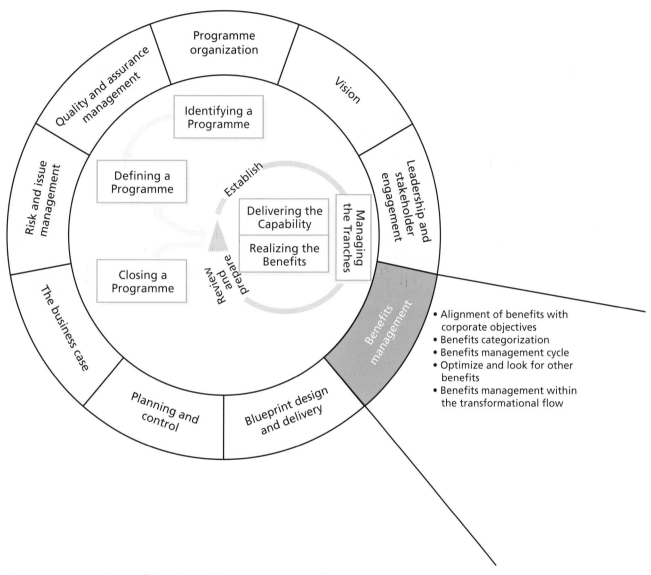

*Figure 7.1 Overview of how benefits management fits into MSP*

## 7.1 INTRODUCTION

Benefits management is at the very heart of programme management: programmes are primarily driven by the need to deliver benefits. This is achieved by projects creating outputs, which build capabilities, which transition into outcomes that serve the purpose of realizing benefits for the organization. However, it is likely that the programme will have some negative impacts as well as improvements. Where a negative effect of the change can be forecast, then this is termed as a dis-benefit. Benefits and dis-benefits can be summarized as follows:

■ A **benefit** is the measurable improvement resulting from an outcome perceived as an advantage by one or more stakeholders, which contributes towards one or more organizational objective(s).

■ A **dis-benefit** is the measurable decline resulting from an outcome perceived as negative by one or more stakeholders, which detracts from one of more organizational objective(s).

Organizational objectives in this instance may be corporate objectives that are aligned with and delivered by the programme.

Benefits and dis-benefits are anticipated when a change is conceived and, while there may be uncertainty relating to its extent, the benefit or dis-benefit itself is not a risk because it is planned to be realized. There may be some risk about the extent of its ultimate value or impact.

These definitions recognize that there will invariably be winners and losers; however, the role of the programme is to deliver the organization's benefits, while recognizing the sensitivities of the stakeholders. Programmes are driven by benefits; without them the programme would not exist. The work to analyse and develop benefits is a key input into the business case. It provides the information in terms of performance improvement (benefits) that justifies the investment in delivering the change. This chapter outlines how benefits should be identified, evaluated and managed to ensure that the programme successfully achieves the vision. Figure 7.1 provides an overview of how the benefits management governance theme fits into MSP.

Realization of benefits is most likely to take place within the business' operational environment. The programme will deliver new capabilities such as business processes, new assets, systems, functions, services or sets of working practices. The programme will then support the business operations in implementing these and managing the effects on performance during the transition and achieving the outcomes. Realization of the full set of benefits may not happen until long after the final project in the programme has been completed. Figure 7.2 depicts how all these elements interact.

Programmes normally serve to deliver corporate objectives. Figure 7.2 illustrates how.

■ The corporate objectives drive the development of the programme vision
■ The vision is expanded into a blueprint for the future organization
■ The blueprint defines what the projects need to create

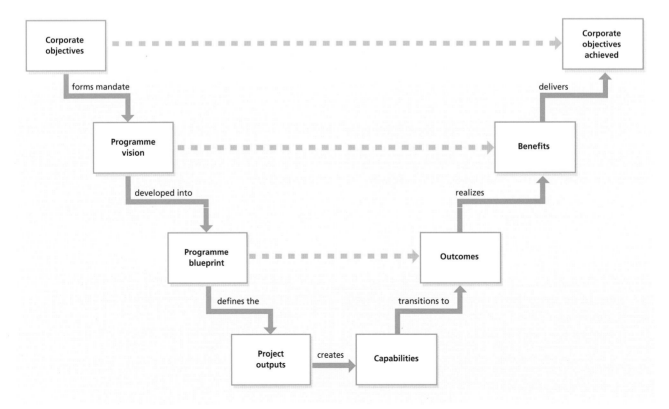

*Figure 7.2 Strategic context of benefits management within a programme*

- The projects deliver outputs which create capabilities
- The capabilities are transitioned into outcomes
- The outcomes enable the realization of benefits
- The benefits are then achieved and contribute to the achievement of the corporate objectives.

Undertaking benefits management allows delivery against the programme management principle of 'focusing on the benefits and threats to them' (see section 2.2.4). For this reason, benefits management is integral to the other governance themes and is a key driver in the transformational flow.

Given its importance to the programme, it is not surprising that benefits management drives many aspects of programme management (see Figure 7.3) including:

- Aligning and validating the integrity of the blueprint against the projects, activities and associated organizational changes needed to deliver the new capabilities and benefits
- Defining the aggregate of achieved benefits, expected benefits, costs to date and expected cost against the business case; providing a crucial test of the ongoing viability of the programme

- Prioritizing benefits to allow the programme to create maximum value under given constraints and make the right trade-off decisions if required
- Planning the programme (benefits realization is a major foundation for this aspect)
- Engaging with stakeholders to understand impact and helping win support
- Defining what is a fit-for-purpose capability, establishing what the critical quality-checking mechanisms throughout the programme would be and checking that they are aligned with the requirements in the blueprint
- Informing end-of-tranche reviews to enable decisions on changes to the programme going forward and underlying governance to be made
- Ensuring that the costs associated with Delivering the Capability are balanced with the value of the benefits in the business case.
- Monitoring the risks and issues that may impact benefits realization.

Benefits management stretches from conception of a programme to beyond its closure and ensures that the programme:

- Does the right things – is aligned with strategy
- Focuses on the right set of benefits
- Is aware of any positive and negative impact it might generate

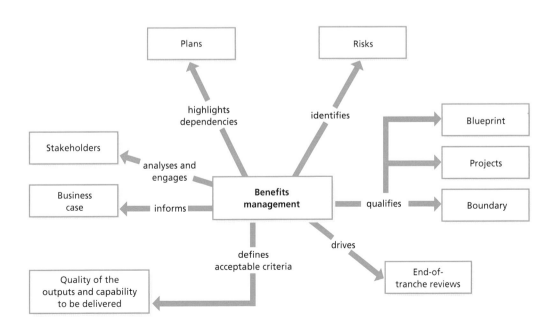

*Figure 7.3 Benefits management interfaces*

- Identifies, plans, validates, measures and reviews benefits
- Is tightly aligned to the transformational flow processes.

There are many techniques that programmes can use to help get the best value from investment in change. In the context of a programme, there are techniques that can be applied at project level to help deliver optimized outputs and at programme level to inform the programme objectives and maximize value across the projects. More guidance can be found in the Best Management Practice guide *Management of Value*.

## 7.2 ALIGNMENT OF BENEFITS WITH CORPORATE OBJECTIVES

Organizations cannot stand still. Their environment continually changes and they must evolve to survive and grow. They define objectives to describe how they want to evolve; and they deploy projects and programmes to make these changes happen. All the current and future change activities form the corporate portfolio. The portfolio reflects an organization's appetite across a range of dimensions, e.g. risk, rate of change, budget and commitment to provide to current customers, markets and stakeholders. Strategy provides the context and balance for planning, running and completing a change portfolio. Individual programmes must link their intended benefits clearly to corporate objectives.

Programmes deliver transformational change rather than incremental changes, e.g. improving another similar product or service offering. (See the 'envisioning and communicating a better future' principle, covered in section 2.2.3.)

Figure 7.4 shows a simple view of the cause and effect of the programme delivering change. The organizational changes – sometimes enabled by project outputs, sometimes initiated in other ways – result in desired outcomes, which realize planned benefits. In turn, benefits should contribute, directly or indirectly, towards one or more of the corporate objectives. See also Table 7.1.

Changes may cause side-effects and unintended consequences, which can lead to dis-benefits but also opportunities for realizing additional benefits.

**Figure 7.4 Path to benefits realization and corporate objectives**

It is important to note that benefits management may well continue beyond the end of the programme because:

- Benefits may take longer to materialize than it is reasonable to maintain the programme structures
- Other benefits may have to be realized, but will need to be owned and managed to pre-agreed target levels that are yet to be achieved
- Benefits can manifest themselves at any time and may not require the programme structure to be in place to realize them
- Beyond the end of the programme, the BCM would continue to have responsibility for realization even though the formal structures may well have been disbanded
- Unexpected benefits should be captured and reported to ensure the full value of the programme is recognized.

## 7.3 BENEFITS CATEGORIZATION

Categorizing benefits can help organizations to better model their priorities and planning (see section 7.4.2) and ensure that there is a balanced portfolio of benefits. By categorizing benefits effectively, organizations are able to:

**Table 7.1 Differences between outputs, capabilities, outcomes and benefits**

|  | Output | Capability | Outcome | Benefit |
|---|---|---|---|---|
| Description | The deliverable, or output developed by a project from a planned activity | The completed set of project outputs required to deliver an outcome; exists prior to transition | A new operational state achieved after transition of the capability into live operations | The measurable improvement resulting from an outcome perceived as an advantage by one or more stakeholders and which contributes towards one or more organizational objective(s) |
| Rationale | Answers at least in part the fundamental question 'What do we need to create to enable the change?' | Answers the question 'What will we need to have in place to enable the new operating state?' | Answers the question 'What is the desired operational state of the organization using these new things?' | Answers the question 'Why is this justified?' (i.e. it explains what a programme delivers) |
| Example | An individual component of an e-commerce system, application, hardware, new business processes training etc. | An e-commerce system tested and ready to go into operation and with trained staff | Transformed client service organization, faster processing, fulfilling and charging for web-based orders | Increased sales revenues of x% |

- Balance the mix of benefits that are being sought and the associated risk profiles
- Enable effective reporting and tracking by category
- Identify potential overlaps of benefit counting
- Understand the impact of changes on different parts of the organization
- Track the relationship between objectives and benefits
- Help to manage changes to priorities within the programmes – if there is a strategic change in the value types being sought, the programme will be more agile in its ability to see the impact across the programme
- Help to create a common set of terminology for referring to benefits and bring greater transparency
- Enable a portfolio-level view of benefits across programmes and projects through consistency.

There are many different ways to categorize benefits. The following benefit categories are well established, but they are not exhaustive.

- Value
- Financial impact
- Corporate objective
- Stakeholder impact
- Timeline
- Level of risk.

Any categories can be used and they can be applied in sequence or combined: for example, a timeline can be used to categorize benefits into short-term and longer-term, then value can be applied to further detail them as economic, effective or efficient; financial impact can define whether they are cashable or non-cashable.

The programme needs to decide early on how it will categorize its benefits. It is almost certain that an individual benefit will be categorized against more than one (if not all) categories as they show different perspectives on the benefit. The categories to which a benefit belongs are best documented in the benefit profiles (see section 7.4.1.3). In carrying out this analysis, care should be taken not to double-count benefits.

### 7.3.1 Value

The three Es can be a starting point when defining and organizing benefits and could lead to further sub-categorization:

- **Economic benefit** A financial improvement, releasing cash, increased income or the better use of funds (for example, credit rating)
- **Effectiveness benefit** Doing things better or to a higher standard (for example, fewer failures)

- **Efficiency benefit** Doing more for the same or the same with less (for example, processing more enquiries but with the same number of people).

These value types cover the vast majority of potential benefits and are very useful for identifying potential programme benefits. Grouping each benefit under one of these headings will enable analysis and the relationship between different benefits and changes.

A corporate objective could impact on all three types. For example, an objective of cost reduction could provide a positive impact (benefit) on economic and efficiency, but this might be to the detriment of the quality of services provided, so creating a negative (dis-benefit) on effectiveness.

### Example

A UK local authority in the southwest implemented a strict regime for the approval of initiatives based on benefits.

All new initiatives were required to illustrate which of the strategic objectives they contributed to. Each initiative had to explain its economic, effectiveness and efficiency impact on the organization. Additionally, where the effect was financial, this would be declared as cashable or non-cashable.

This provided a balanced view of the impact and illustrated where, for example, an economic gain may have a negative impact on effectiveness. The organization's executive could then make decisions with a more holistic understanding of the likely impact of the investment.

### 7.3.2 Financial impact

Based on the financial impact that benefits generate for their organization, they can be categorized as:

- **Cashable** For example, benefits such as lower supply chain costs, staff savings or lower running costs that are realized in the form of reduced unit costs which can release cash
- **Non-cashable** For example, staff time savings which can be re-invested in improved services but cannot be released as cash.

Predicted cashable benefits should be validated with the finance department, which will have to account for the money saved later. Often there are good reasons why benefits remain non-cashable: e.g. releasing staff might not be a valid short-term option. To make non-cashable benefits real, it is most important to agree them with the relevant business areas, including deciding on a realistic conversion ratio: e.g. what percentage of the potential staff time savings can be realistically converted to other value-adding activities. If this is not done, then all that has been delivered is spare time.

### 7.3.3 Corporate objective

Benefits can also be categorized by the type of corporate objective they support. Each organization will have different objectives and priorities that they wish to achieve; Table 7.2 contains examples of the common objectives that may relate to benefits. Each of these objectives may have an impact on one or more of the three value types: economic, efficiency or effectiveness.

### 7.3.4 Stakeholder impact

Programme outcomes and benefits have different effects on different stakeholders. These effects may be perceived as positive or negative. The same outcome can generate positive benefits for one group of stakeholders, while causing negative effects, called dis-benefits, to other groups. The complex nature of programmes seldom creates simple divisions in stakeholder groups, e.g. as in those who are supporting or opposing the programme. The programme hence needs to investigate very thoroughly the benefits it generates and the effect they have on stakeholders.

Stakeholders who perceive a programme as impacting them negatively will try to resist it. This resistance may become a major risk for the programme. The programme should therefore explore organizational change options that allow it to minimize dis-benefits. If the programme does not succeed in this, there remains the risk that dis-benefits may grow to unacceptable levels and eventually undermine the business case for the programme.

The matrix in Figure 7.5 provides an example of a stakeholder impact assessment of creating a new sports complex in a town. There are a number of

**Table 7.2 Examples of corporate objectives**

| Corporate objective | Benefit description |
|---|---|
| Increased flexibility | Delivers outcomes that allow an organization to respond to strategic demands without incurring additional expenditure |
| Internal performance improvement | Changes that are internal to the organization, such as improved decision-making or more efficient management processes |
| Enhanced personnel or HR management | A better-motivated workforce may lead to a number of other benefits such as flexibility or increased productivity |
| Policy or legal compliance | This enables an organization to fulfil policy objectives or to satisfy legal requirements where the organization has no choice but to comply |
| Process improvements | These are 'more with same' or 'same with less' that allow an organization to do the same job with less resource, leading to reduction in costs, or to do more with the same resource |
| Enhanced quality of service | Improvements to services, such as quicker response to queries and providing information in a way the customer would prefer, give rise to fewer customer complaints and less costly service failures |
| Reduced costs | Improvements in control and reduction of operating costs |
| Improved revenue generation | Changes that enable increased revenue, or the same revenue level in a shorter timeframe, or both |
| Reduced environmental impact | Changes that reduce carbon footprint or mitigate the environmental impact of the organization |
| Risk reduction | Changes that enable an organization to be better prepared for the future – for example, hedging currency risks. They may also relate to public safety or the safety of vulnerable groups. |
| Strategic fit | Benefits that contribute to strategic fit, or enable the strategic direction through long-term investments or market positioning |

possible benefits, but not all stakeholder groups will see benefits in the same way, and the matrix is a good way of illustrating winners and losers from a change.

Where an organization's benefit is an individual's dis-benefit (e.g. increased efficiency may require staff to work longer hours or increase their personal productivity), the programme must be sensitive to this in its communications.

Early stakeholder engagement and analysis will help to identify such dis-benefits as well as possible new benefits. See Chapter 6 for more information about stakeholder engagement.

### 7.3.5 Timeline

Different benefits will materialize at various points during and after the programme's life. Timing the realization of benefits is of obvious importance: not only will the advantage a benefit generates for certain stakeholders vary depending on when it is delivered, but it might also be necessary to produce short-term 'quick wins' to keep stakeholders supportive of the initiative.

In complex programmes, early generation of benefits may be required to fund later tranches: identifying and managing the risk associated with this level of dependency is essential.

### 7.3.6 Level of risk

It is essential to understand the level of risk associated with the achievement of the benefit, as this contributes to understanding the overall level of risk for the programme. The best way to use this classification is to associate a numeric value with the level of risk and use this to factor the amount of the benefit that is achievable.

For example, numeric levels could be applied to individual benefits as follows:

- Low risk = 90% of the value is achievable
- Medium risk = 60% of the value is achievable
- High risk = 30% of the value is achievable.

For example, if a benefit has been identified that is worth £100,000, but there are a number of risks associated with it and its likelihood of being achieved is medium, you might only account for £60,000 in the benefits forecast, as this is the most likely benefit realization. If effort is put into removing the risks, then the £100,000 would still

| Key benefits and dis-benefits by stakeholder | Improved city image | Improved training facilities | Increased visitor attractiveness | Enhanced community facilities | More jobs | Faster central city access | Change traditional local landscape | Pressure on local housing prices | Legacy maintenance costs |
|---|---|---|---|---|---|---|---|---|---|
| National government | | | | | | | | | |
| City mayor | | + | + | | | | | + | − |
| Athletes | | + | + | | + | | | | − |
| Tourists | | | + | + | + | | | | |
| Residents | | | | | | | + | + | |
| Employers | | + | | + | + | + | | + | |

Positive impact

Negative impact

*Figure 7.5 Benefits distribution matrix of stakeholders (example)*

be achievable. This helps to reflect the uncertainty associated with benefits and create more accurate forecasts.

Managing the threats to benefits is one of the fundamental MSP principles: 'focusing on the benefits and threats to benefits realization'.

## 7.4 BENEFITS MANAGEMENT CYCLE

This section describes a generic four-step cycle for managing benefits on any programme (see Figure 7.6).

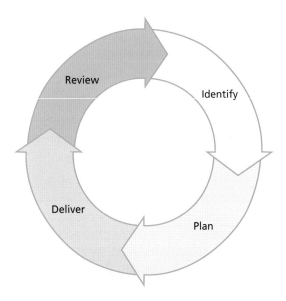

*Figure 7.6 Benefits management cycle*

The benefits management cycle is continuous and iterative throughout the programme. The cycle is supported by continuing activities to optimize and identify further benefits (see section 7.5). The following sections describe the steps of the cycle that continue throughout the programme.

### 7.4.1 Identify benefits

The benefits management cycle starts as early as possible by identifying likely benefits and mapping them, preferably by working from the corporate objectives back to the enabling project outputs (see Figure 7.2). This should start during Identifying a Programme when developing the programme brief.

The optimal way to identify benefits is to engage key stakeholders who can provide different perspectives on where benefits might be realized. These perspectives and insights should help to generate an initial list.

> **Tip**
>
> Benefits should be described in ways that are meaningful to the business and operational users. This will avoid any misunderstanding between the programme and business as usual.

Benefits may then be categorized in a number of different ways, as described in section 7.3.

Once the benefits are categorized, the programme can analyse the overall mix and possibly adjust the scope of the programme to ensure that it will deliver the required balance of benefits.

Where a benefit has been identified but there is a high risk that it may not be achieved, it may be tracked as a risk opportunity if there is insufficient justification to develop a benefit profile. The same applies to a benefit identified as a result from a major change in programme direction. The key thing is that the opportunity is recorded and tracked. This approach should be defined in the benefits management strategy and, if necessary, the risk management strategy, to ensure that such benefits are not lost or missed.

### 7.4.1.1 Benefits modelling and maps

Programme outputs, capabilities, outcomes and benefits are interrelated (as shown in Table 7.1), and corporate objectives are not achieved by accident. It is important for programmes to carefully model the flow between these elements and monitor and manage their interdependencies thoroughly.

A benefits map shows the relationship between outputs, capabilities, outcomes, benefits and the objectives. A benefits map is important because benefits do not typically happen in isolation, and there are cause-and-effect relationships between the elements. Failure to deliver a specific output or capability may appear to have a minor effect from the project perspective but have a massive impact on benefits realization. The map illustrates a total 'picture' of the changes, shows the inputs for each benefit and how they fit into this total picture. The benefits map should include any dependencies that are outside the boundary or control of the programme, as they may affect the realization of benefits.

The example of a benefits map in Figure 7.7 shows:

- The corporate objective (on the right)
- Short- and longer-term benefits leading to the corporate objective
- The outcomes achieved after transitioning the new capability into live operation
- The new process underpinned by the new IT systems.

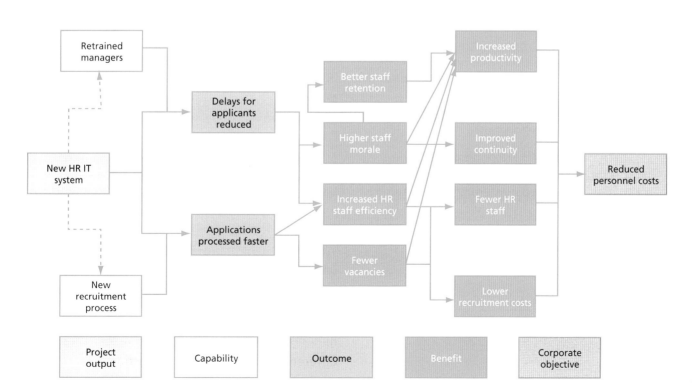

*Figure 7.7 Benefits map: new HR system example*

The benefits map can be created working from right to left, from corporate objectives to longer-term and short-term benefits. It should then define the project outputs and organizational changes required. Where the outputs are a given, for example in an emergent programme (see Chapter 1), the benefits map may need to be developed from both ends and joined in the middle.

Benefit maps are excellent ways of providing a high-level view of what the programme must achieve, and should be considered for inclusion in the programme brief.

The benefits map contributes to the benefits realization plan, showing the realization sequence through a chain of benefits. Timescales can be developed from the benefits map to inform the creation of the schedule within the benefits realization plan.

### 7.4.1.2 Benefits management strategy

The benefits management strategy defines the programme framework for realizing benefits. It is a key component of the programme's governance. It sets out the rules of engagement on how to identify, design, monitor and review the benefits management cycle.

The strategy should set out what represents a benefit to the organization, specific measures of benefits achievement that are acceptable within the programme, standard ways in which they should be calculated and how to ensure that there is no double-counting of benefits.

The benefits for a public sector defence organization are often vastly different from those of a commercial venture; consequently a coherent benefits management strategy would define how each will measure the value from an investment.

In an environment that has established portfolio management for its programmes and projects, a generic benefits management strategy template may be provided to the programme, setting out how benefits will be managed (or at least setting out a framework of policies or guiding principles for programmes).

In this situation the programme management team should develop the benefits management strategy to ensure its compliance with the corporate portfolio needs.

The strategy must also prescribe the context within which the projects will operate, how they will reference and contribute to programme benefits, the controls that will be put in place and how assurance will work. The projects are critical in providing the capability that the operations will need in order to realize benefits. If the capability is inappropriate or inadequate, the potential benefits will be undermined. PRINCE2, for example, defines the need for a project benefits review plan; in a programme environment this would be defined by the programme.

Where the responsibilities for programme benefits are widely spread across the organization(s) and the 'how to' of realization is complex, a clear and robust benefits management strategy is essential: without such a strategy people may be measuring the same benefit with different measures and reporting at different frequencies.

For details on the content of a benefits management strategy, see Appendix A.

### 7.4.1.3 Benefit profiles

A benefit profile describes a single benefit or dis-benefit, with its attributes and interdependencies, and supports the building of a detailed benefits realization plan.

Typically, a benefit profile is created for each benefit, with a description and an operational owner, as soon as the benefit is identified. Population of many of the other fields is generally achieved through stakeholder engagement. As a minimum, a benefit profile should be written for each key benefit in the programme business case.

The minimum contents of a benefit profile should be those used for the benefits validation tests described in section 7.4.2.2.

Concentrating efforts on a few core benefits will reduce the overhead of creating, maintaining and pursuing numerous benefits. The three types (economic, effective and efficiency) provide the three main starting points for benefits.

The business change managers (BCMs) will normally be responsible for the benefit profiles. However, they may work closely with a wide range of individuals across a number of functions to develop the profile and attribute specific responsibilities to managers across the broader organizational management structure. This should be explained in the benefit profile and defined in the benefits management strategy.

Accountability for the overall set of benefits remains with the senior responsible owner (SRO) but the BCM would be expected to take responsibility for identifying, developing, validating and managing the delivery of the benefit, as profiled, within the programme environment.

For further details on benefit profile, see Appendix A.

### Tip

Some organizations use **benefits registers** to summarize information that exists in benefit profiles, which then exist as separate additional information where the full detail is maintained.

The register can provide an overview of the programme's benefits in a similar way to the risk register providing a view of the risks to the programme.

The benefits register becomes the summary document that should be regularly reviewed by the programme board.

## 7.4.2 Plan benefits realization

Once the benefits have been identified, the programme will need to understand how they fit together, attribute responsibilities, validate that they are credible and plan for delivery.

Some benefits will take much longer to materialize than others. It is important to consider shorter-term benefits as well as the longer-term ones to

ensure that there is sufficient ongoing focus and commitment to the programme. Initial benefits demonstrate to stakeholders that the programme is making a tangible difference, and that these early benefits are the stepping stones for achieving subsequent benefits. Benefits that are not going to be realized for many years will generate less commitment and enthusiasm. Using the benefits map, benefit profiles and a benefits realization plan (see section 7.4.2.3), the interrelations and dependencies between different types of benefits can be shown as well as their realization managed.

### 7.4.2.1 Benefits attribution

Accountability and responsibility for benefits, collectively and individually, is a key requirement for successful programme benefits management. Each benefit should be defined by appropriate competent individuals, who are then responsible for its successful delivery. It is important that benefit responsibility remains with those business units affected. Dis-benefits responsibilities should also be clearly allocated.

One way to make this more meaningful is to link benefits realization to personal performance targets.

The aim is to bring transparency to the way in which the actions to realize the benefits will be delivered and by whom.

### 7.4.2.2 Benefits validation

Benefits are described in detail in benefit profiles (see Appendix A). The definition of a benefit should pass four critical validation tests:

- **Description** What precisely is the benefit?
- **Observable outcomes** What are the verifiable differences that will be noticeable between pre- and post-programme implementation?
- **Attribution** Where will this benefit arise? Can this programme claim its realization? Is the accountability and responsibility for delivering the change clear and agreed?
- **Measurement** How and when will the achievement of the benefit be measured?

An identified benefit that does not pass these four basic tests is by definition not a benefit. Many programmes struggle to deliver benefits or are perceived as underperforming, because what they wanted to achieve, and where and how they would measure it, was not defined thoroughly enough at the start. Defining and describing benefits in detail should not be treated as an afterthought but be at the core of any programme.

Programmes with benefits that are struggling to pass these validation tests may find that they are trying to profile an outcome rather than a benefit.

### Tip

Benefits are best titled with a change term at the beginning (such as 'increased', faster', 'lower', 'cheaper', 'bigger') and should be accompanied by a measurement (such as percent, monetary value etc). Avoid generic terms like 'better' or 'improved' without further details, as these terms are not specific enough for further analysis.

### 7.4.2.3 Benefits realization plan

The benefits realization plan is a complete view of all the benefits, their dependencies and the expected realization timescales and is derived from the benefits map (see Appendix A). It is used to track realization of benefits across the programme and set review controls.

The benefits realization plan will be developed alongside the programme plan (see Chapter 8 for information on the blueprint, Chapter 9 for details of planning and Chapter 10 for an explanation of the business case) to ensure alignment and viability across:

- Delivery of capability
- Management of transition
- Realization of benefits
- Expected costs
- Related risks.

Also, to ensure the right focus on benefits, it is acceptable to combine the benefits realization plan and the programme plan in one document.

The development of the benefits realization plan should be closely integrated with the programme's strategy for stakeholder engagement. The benefits realization plan should also identify benefit reviews to formally assess the realization of benefits.

For details of the content of a benefits realization plan, see Appendix A.

### 7.4.3 Deliver benefits realization

This is discussed in more detail in Chapter 18. Benefits realization has three stages:

- Pre-transition
- Transition
- Post-transition.

Delivery of benefits realization is principally linked to the stages above, when the capabilities delivered by the projects are transitioned into outcomes, and the legacy working practices are removed to establish the new operating model.

One of the key areas of focus during the delivery step is the measurement of benefits: without this the realization of benefits cannot be managed. Benefits should always be quantifiable and measurable.

There is often a tendency to be over-optimistic when defining and setting target measures for the expected benefits from a programme. Over-optimistic expectations can create buy-in and commitment from stakeholders, but the support will quickly evaporate at the benefits reviews (see section 7.4.4) when the reality is understood. However, less optimism in setting expectations may stop the programme from even getting started – so a balance is required. One way to achieve this balance is to define the metrics that will be used to track progress towards meeting the corporate objectives and realizing the programme's benefits. These key performance indicators (KPIs) help to avoid creating unrealistic and non-measurable expectations.

A common cause of problems when trying to measure improvements is not having a baseline of the performance from the time before the programme started. This should be captured in the blueprint 'as-is' state and used as the baseline against which performance changes are measured.

When using KPIs note that:

- Some KPIs may not be suitable for benefits measurement
- Some KPIs may need to be adjusted as a result of operational changes (the programme may need to define new KPIs and provide processes and tools to support them)
- Current KPIs may need to be supplemented by other measures to assess the benefits realized

- Performance criteria from relevant or affected contracts, service level agreements, compliance targets etc. should be reviewed to ensure change congruence (e.g. any penalties that might be incurred because of deterioration in performance)
- Some measures may be subject to fluctuations from normal process variation or seasonal trends. It is important that this is understood and reflected in plans.

Measures – and the targets set against these measures – can have a very distorting effect upon operations if they are not considered in the overall context of achieving the programme's objectives.

During delivery, the BCM should be carefully monitoring business performance metrics to ensure that changes are in line with predictions. The BCM should also monitor for early warnings of significant issues that might arise which could have significant impacts and that may require transition to be stopped or contingency measures to be deployed.

### Example

A public health service was targeted by its government to reduce waiting times in accident reception units. The target was measured in terms of the time that elapsed between a patient registering at arrival and being examined by a medic. In order to meet the tough targets set, accident units adopted a system of triage: initial assessment and prioritization by a nurse. The target did nothing to improve the speed at which the injured were actually treated. On the contrary, scarce clinical resources were diverted to perform the triage so that the target was met.

## 7.4.4 Benefits reviews

Benefits reviews may be time- or event-driven and should, as a minimum, take place at the end of each tranche to ensure that benefits realization is still on track and, if not, immediate changes should be made to the benefits realization plan. The outcome of a benefits review might also require the programme to review the projects dossier to ensure that alterations in benefits realization are considered.

Benefits from the capability delivered in one tranche will often not appear until later tranches. Benefits reviews should cover future benefits as well as benefits that should have been realized to date. Thus:

- For realized benefits, input from stakeholders (including the BCMs responsible for the changed operations) will provide realistic information and evidence of what has been achieved to date.
- With expected benefits it is important to ensure they remain valid and valuable with regard to:
  - Perception of stakeholders across the programme
  - Any changes to the business environment – internal and external.

Benefits reviews can also be undertaken at any formal gated review process that takes place within the organization. The objectives of a benefits review are to:

- Assess and update the individual benefit profiles and the benefits realization plan to ensure that the planned benefits remain achievable and have not changed in scope or value
- Check that the overall set of benefits included within the benefits map and benefits register remains aligned to the programme's objectives and to reprioritize or realign them as necessary
- Inform stakeholders and senior management of progress in benefits realization and help to identify any further potential for benefits
- Assess the performance of the changed business operations against their original (baseline) performance levels
- Assess the level of benefits achieved against the benefits realization plan
- Review the effectiveness of the way in which benefits management is being handled, so that lessons can be learned and improved processes can be developed and implemented – for example, refining the definition of benefits or improving the understanding of the organization's ability to deliver.

Such reviews will require the benefits realization plan, along with its benefits map and relevant individual benefit profiles, to be adjusted or re-worked. If there are fundamental concerns about the effectiveness of benefits management, the benefits management strategy itself should be revisited.

After the programme closes, support is often required to help business operations take full advantage of the new services delivered. This is achieved by ensuring that the BCMs are fully engaged with the programme from the outset and have responsibility for delivering the benefits and performance improvement. Additionally, once the programme has been closed, the responsibility for setting up and managing the benefits reviews moves to the BCM.

## 7.5 OPTIMIZE AND LOOK FOR OTHER BENEFITS

The lessons learned and opportunities to improve performance in any of the steps in the benefits management cycle should be under continual improvement. The programme environment never stands still: new benefits could emerge that were overlooked in earlier analysis. Changing strategy and new organizational drivers mean that the programme must be responsive to these and look for opportunities to identify benefits, just as risks are continually reviewed and identified.

During transition and realization, the BCM will be in constant dialogue with different stakeholders. A common phenomenon is that when such stakeholders buy into the programme and its benefits, they are informed and creative enough to identify new benefits and to optimize the realization of existing ones. At this point, the cycle starts again, as new opportunities may have been identified that will feed into the identification step, and modelling and profiling will be undertaken.

## 7.6 BENEFITS MANAGEMENT WITHIN THE TRANSFORMATIONAL FLOW

This section covers how the benefits management governance theme is applied in each of the processes in the transformational flow.

During its life, a programme will have to transform a number of project outputs into benefits. It will encounter deviations in output performance and need to address the impact that this could have on benefits realization. It must react to changes in its environment, adapt its benefits accordingly and constantly explore opportunities for further benefits. Ultimately, the programme will close, but benefits management will continue. The programme will have to manage transition, close down and entrust ongoing benefits management to the new business-as-usual operations.

### 7.6.1 Identifying a Programme

The programme mandate contains an overview of key corporate objectives and expected benefits that a programme must deliver. As part of developing the programme brief, the programme confirms its understanding of these objectives and provides an initial assessment of whether and how it will be able to deliver the benefits. Initial 'as-is' information is captured for the blueprint and provides the baseline from which performance improvements can be sought.

The programme type will affect the focus on benefits. A compliance programme may be justified through the avoidance of negative effects or non-compliances, potentially avoiding adverse legal implications. A vision-led programme is likely to have a greater focus on benefits.

More guidance is available in sections 14.3, 14.5 and 14.8.

### 7.6.2 Defining a Programme

During Defining a Programme, the benefits management strategy will be created; this may initially be part of the governance arrangements in the programme preparation plan. While the benefits management strategy defines the practices and governance arrangements for benefits management, the main focus of the programme from a benefits perspective is the detailed definition, allocation of ownership and planning of the benefits themselves.

Benefit profiles are established, which describe the benefits in more detail. Relationships between outputs, outcomes and benefits are developed and depicted in the benefits map. The sequence and timing of benefits realization is defined in the benefits realization plan. Together with the projects dossier, which describes which projects generate the outputs, and the blueprint that defines future capability, the documentation created for benefits in this phase should contain a complete picture of the programme's viability.

More guidance is available in sections 15.7, 15.8, 15.9, 15.13, 15.17 and 15.18.

### 7.6.3 Managing the Tranches

Managing the Tranches maintains the strategic oversight of the delivery of capability and the preparedness for change. Problems or indicators of instability should be managed through the programme board.

The activities during Managing the Tranches ensure that the benefits context is considered while:

- Conducting regular benefits reviews
- Monitoring for any strategic changes
- Assessing the eventual impact of changes
- Aligning the programme to strategic change
- Checking the project activities against the blueprint and benefits realization plan.

More guidance is available in sections 16.2, 16.12 and 16.14.

### 7.6.4 Delivering the Capability

While projects continue to deliver their commissioned outputs, the programme ensures that they remain aligned to the benefits realization plan. The BCM provides support and expertise and assesses any project alterations for their benefits impact.

Engagement with stakeholders remains a high priority to fine-tune requirements, review design solutions and conduct user acceptance testing. Stakeholders will only be able to realize agreed benefits when the appropriate outputs are delivered.

More guidance is available in sections 17.4 and 17.5.

### 7.6.5 Realizing the Benefits

Realizing the benefits is the fundamental focus of benefits management. This stage is particularly concerned with implementing the benefits realization plan and the benefit profiles.

In addition, programmes should:

- Always be alert to the possibility of new benefits
- Look to accrue greater benefits, on top of those already realized
- Be adjusted if benefits do not appear to be reaching their target levels.

Chapter 18 provides greater detail and guidance.

### 7.6.6 Closing a Programme

Closure of the programme is a crucial milestone for benefits management. Once the programme closes, no further new capabilities will be provided by it, while benefits can and should continue to be realized.

As part of the closure process the benefit profiles, benefits map, benefits management strategy and benefits realization plan are all reviewed and updated. They will form a reference point for any post-programme benefits activities.

Finally, the programme must ensure that ongoing support is in place. Many benefits will continue to be realized, and new applications for the created outputs might emerge, providing opportunities for further benefits, unanticipated to date. An individual must be found within operations who will take responsibility to continue embedding change. This could be the BCM from the programme.

More guidance is available in sections 19.2 and 19.5.

## 7.7 THE KEY ROLES

Table 7.3 summarizes the key roles and typical areas of focus.

There is no specific guidance for the two main control boards (sponsoring group and programme board) because they are forums where decisions are made and direction set with input from the four key roles. Therefore, guidance has been restricted to individuals rather than broadened to groups.

This in no way weakens or undermines the roles of the sponsoring group or the programme board, which are essential for any programme and have their responsibilities set out in Chapter 4.

**Table 7.3 Benefits management and the key roles**

| Role | Area of focus |
| --- | --- |
| Senior responsible owner (SRO) | Reports to the sponsoring group on the delivery of the programme benefits as described in the benefit profiles |
| | Ensures that the programme and the business areas affected maintain a focus on benefits delivery |
| | Ensures that the benefits management strategy is created, adjusted, improved and enforced |
| | Maintains a focus on business performance sustainability during transition |
| | Chairs benefit reviews involving relevant stakeholders, business managers and possibly internal audits |
| | Liaises with the sponsoring group on the validation of all benefits claimed by the programme |
| | Authorizes benefits achievements |
| Programme manager | Develops the benefits management strategy on behalf of the SRO with the BCMs and relevant stakeholders from the affected business areas |
| | Develops the benefits realization plan in consultation with the BCMs, relevant stakeholders and members of the project teams |
| | Ensures that the delivery of capability is aligned to maximize the realization of benefits |
| | Initiates benefit reviews as part of benefits realization plan or in response to any other triggers |
| Business change manager(s) (BCM) | Identifies and quantifies the benefits with the support of relevant stakeholders, the programme manager and members of the project teams |
| | Delivers particular benefits as profiled: this extends to ensuring that commitments and actions that have been attributed to operational areas are delivered |
| | Provides information to support the creation and delivery of the benefits realization plan |
| | Develops and maintains the benefit profiles |
| | Ensures there is no double-counting of benefits |
| | Maintains engagement with key individuals responsible for benefits delivery within the operations |
| | Sets business performance deviation levels and early-warning indicators to support realizing benefits |
| | Initiates benefit reviews after the programme has closed |
| Programme office | Monitors the progress of benefits realization against plan |
| | Gathers information for the benefits reviews |
| | Produces performance reports as defined by the programme manager |
| | Maintains benefits information under change control and maintains audit trails of changes |

# Blueprint design and delivery

# 8 Blueprint design and delivery

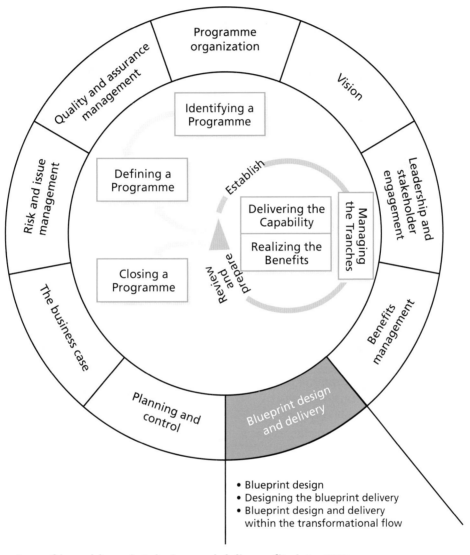

*Figure 8.1 Overview of how blueprint design and delivery fits into MSP*

## 8.1 INTRODUCTION

The programme's vision statement provides early and valuable information as a description of the desired outcomes in customer-focused terms. As it is a description at a summary level, it needs to be expanded and developed into a blueprint. It is the blueprint that provides a usable basis for modelling benefits and designing the projects dossier.

The blueprint is not concerned with how to get to the future state. The 'how' is dealt with when designing the projects dossier (i.e. examining different solutions and routes to get to the defined future state) and the optimum set of solutions and routes is selected.

The new capability occurs when the outputs from projects are ready for operational use – once transition is completed and the outcomes have been achieved. Many programmes choose not to deliver all the new capability at the same time because such a major concentrated change is often too big a risk.

Figure 8.1 provides an overview of how the blueprint design and delivery governance theme fits into MSP.

The programme plan is designed to show when and how the new capability will be delivered in step changes. These step changes are achieved through a series of tranches. A well-designed, tranche-based programme plan will be the result of careful consideration of the following:

- Feasibility studies or similar to discover the best way forward where there is uncertainty early in the programme
- Quick wins – benefits realized early are valuable and boost confidence
- Incremental expansion of capabilities delivered in earlier tranches.

The blueprint, projects dossier, programme plan, benefits realization plan and the business case will be developed iteratively and will require close integration to ensure that the benefits to be realized are driving the desired transformation. It is often necessary to consider more than one design of the future organization, and to examine different possible approaches for delivering the capability. Each of these various approaches will have a different mix of time, cost, risk and benefits. It is the responsibility of the senior responsible owner (SRO) and programme team to discover the optimum mix that produces the most acceptable business case.

## 8.2 BLUEPRINT DESIGN

The blueprint is a model of the future organization, its working practices and processes, the information it requires and the technology that supports its operations. The future organization is designed to deliver the outcomes and benefits described in the vision statement. When delivered, the future organization has to be capable of achieving the desired outcomes and realizing the expected benefits. The blueprint is used throughout the programme to maintain the focus on delivery of the new capability.

Blueprints have their origins in other management disciplines such as business architecture planning and enterprise architecture planning. Some organizations have an overall blueprint for the entire business. In these contexts, each programme (or standalone project) is briefed to deliver a discrete part of that corporate blueprint.

'Target operating model' is a term often used to describe the organization's future state; this term can be used as an alternative to blueprint if appropriate.

Tip

- Involve staff who are not just subject experts but are able to envision the future – remember, every programme should aim to produce a good design for the future organization
- Make substantial use of knowledge from other appropriate change initiatives, from inside the organization and from other organizations
- Use external facilitation to enable radical thinking and challenge existing expectations.

The programme manager is responsible for organizing activities to ensure that the blueprint is appropriately authored and signed off. Where the programme manager and BCMs have suitable skills and experience, they can be the authors of the blueprint, but it is important to emphasize that the knowledge of what the business does now and how it will function in the future comes from the business change managers (BCMs), who should be the main contributors.

Where they do not have the skills, it is the responsibility of the programme manager, assisted by the BCMs, to engage appropriately skilled and knowledgeable people as the authors. (See also section 2.2.2 on the importance of assembling the right people first.)

While the precise format of a blueprint will depend on the characteristics of each programme, and may contain words and diagrams, a consistent overall structure is recommended.

The **POTI model** sets a high-level scope of what must be included and integrated in an effective blueprint:

| | |
|---|---|
| P | Processes, business models of operations and functions including operational costs and performance levels |
| O | Organizational structure, staffing levels, roles, skills requirements, organizational culture, supply chain and style |
| T | Technology, buildings, IT systems and tools, equipment, machinery and accommodation |
| I | Information and data required for the future business operations and performance measurement |

### 8.2.1 Future state

Whereas the primary purpose of the vision statement is communication of the intended future, the primary purpose of the blueprint is specification and ensuring coherence of the entire future state and the solution set that will underpin it. Programmes do not deliver the desired capability all at once. There can be several defined points in the future, at which tranches deliver elements of the change. The blueprint shows the intermediate future states as they are planned to be at the end of each tranche. Intermediate blueprints are part of the overall blueprint document and should be defined for each step change in capability delivered at the end of each tranche.

Intermediate blueprints help to shorten the planning horizons so that the detailed design work is done at the appropriate time. This would predicate and support the step-based changes in capability and benefits realization (see section 8.3.3 for more on step changes).

The blueprint describes the elements of the future organization. It is the combination of these elements that enables outcomes. These elements have a close relationship with outputs, but a more complex relationship with outcomes. The example in Figure 8.2 explains this point further.

Once the outcomes are achieved, the benefits can be realized; this relationship is further explained in Chapter 7.

### 8.2.2 Current state and gap analysis

Each programme has to plan and manage the journey from where the organization is today to the future as outlined in the vision statement. An understanding of the current state and the gap (the difference between current and future

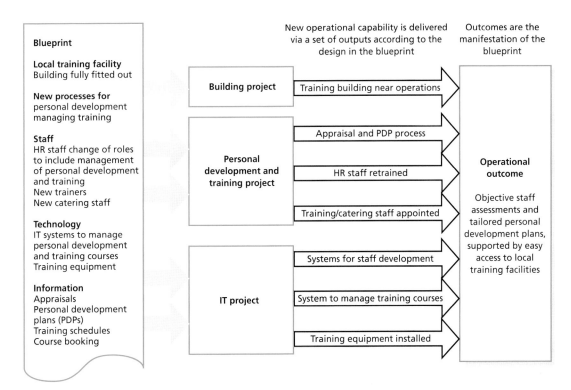

*Figure 8.2 Relationship between blueprint, outputs and outcomes*

states) is essential to be able to effectively explore alternative approaches to delivering the new capability.

The initial analysis of the gap is a comparison between the current organization (described in the current 'as-is' state section of the blueprint) and the design for the future organization (described in the future 'to-be' state section of the blueprint).

Elements of the blueprint, such as processes, technology etc., are compared as they are now with how they need to be. These are high-level descriptions; more detailed analysis will be carried out by the projects.

In Figure 8.3, the final blueprint shows a new front-office operational capability. As this does not exist today, the gap to close is establishing this new capability. For more on how this is done, see the discussion of options analysis and the projects dossier in section 8.3.1 and Chapter 9.

**Tip**

Good documentation of the current state is often missing. Use this opportunity to encourage programme staff to create good documentation and not to inflict the same problem on future change initiatives.

Lack of information about the current state represents a risk that the programme will need to manage. Without baseline information about how the organization functions at this time, it will not be possible to develop baseline measures for benefits.

For programmes that will adopt current projects, and for emergent programmes where projects are already under way, the programme should analyse each project's definition and current status to:

- Understand the requirements and specifications of the project
- Identify its outputs
- Identify its dependencies with other projects
- Find out how far into delivery it is.

The programme blueprint should be designed to reflect the merging of the project designs and to ensure that the validated cohesive future operations are delivered. It is refined throughout the programme to maintain, as a minimum, alignment with the organization's strategy at key learning points, such as at the end of a tranche.

## 8.3 DESIGNING THE BLUEPRINT DELIVERY

Figure 8.4 shows the nature of collaboration with other themes. The design of the blueprint and its delivery is carried out iteratively with benefits management (see Chapter 7) until an acceptable business case starts to emerge.

Output from this work then informs other work done in Defining a Programme, and refinements which take place during Managing the Tranches, to ensure effective management of the programme.

The blueprint provides the basis of the initial requirements that will be set for each project.

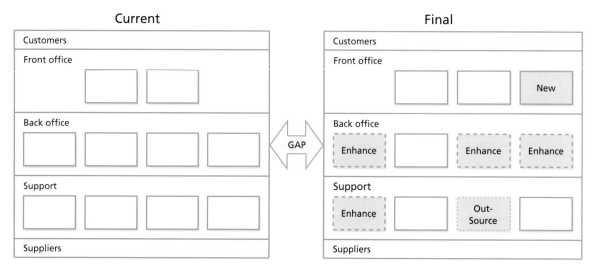

*Figure 8.3  Showing the initial analysis of the gap*

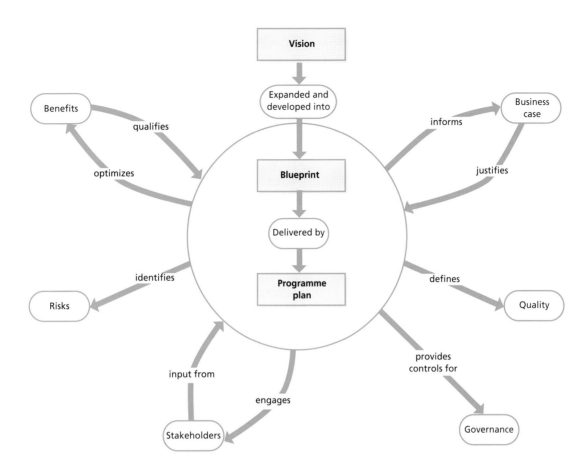

**Figure 8.4 Blueprint design and delivery in collaboration with other themes**

### 8.3.1 Options analysis

The project outputs will provide the means to enable the organization to change, thus delivering the future organization as described in the blueprint. In many cases there will be more than one way to create or acquire the outputs. Each approach will have different costs, timescales and risk. Each approach will also enable different degrees of improvement. Before the design of the projects dossier is finalized, a range of different solutions (and therefore approaches) should be considered. These need to be modelled to link outputs as enablers to outcomes which then lead to benefits. These models should be assessed to see which option produces the most acceptable business case. The ideal option/model has low cost and low risk, is quick to deliver and produces high benefits. Unfortunately, this option is rarely available and the programme will need to optimize its approach by balancing these three dimensions.

### 8.3.2 Optimizing the approach

Optimizing the approach is about finding the best mix of future-state solutions to deliver the new capability and the timing of that delivery via tranches. This is done by cross-working and iteration between the benefits management activities discussed in Chapter 7 and the activities in this theme.

It is important to test the chosen set of solutions from a number of key perspectives in order to make sure it is viable; for example:

- Will the organization be able to acquire adequate funding?
- Will there be sufficient capability available to manage the work when required?
- Will programme and project staff have appropriate skills and experience?
- Have the risks been identified and assessed?
- When will the benefits materialize and what are the associated levels of risk?
- Is an acceptable business case emerging?

If this test shows an acceptable business case is not emerging, it will be necessary to adjust the blueprint and/or the approach. At this point there are generally only three options available:

- Be less ambitious and design a blueprint in which the gap between the current state and future state is smaller
- Find a different approach and solutions which can deliver the blueprint addressing the constraints (i.e. more quickly, for less cost, with fewer threats) or with greater benefits
- Close the programme.

See also sections 2.2.4 and 2.2.5.

### 8.3.3 Step changes through tranches

Only when an acceptable business case seems possible should consideration be given to arranging the solutions into projects. Other factors now need to be considered:

- Combine several small pieces of work into one project
- Create logical groupings of projects to enable effective management. These groupings should take into account:
  - Discipline, skills, knowledge, technology, facilities etc.
  - Existing team-working arrangements
  - Geography and culture
  - Current projects.

See discussion of the principle of developing a coherent capability in section 2.2.6.

How and whether to adopt existing projects should be considered. Analysing and taking designs from their individual plans and definitions into a blueprint can help to provide a first definition of the boundaries of the emerging programme. Treatment of the rest of the preparation for an emergent programme should ideally follow the same process as a new programme. However, as work is already in progress on current projects, there may be overriding practical constraints. The following criteria may be helpful:

- **Proximity to delivery** Projects close to completion (particularly where there is a high degree of confidence of successful improvement as a result of their outputs) could be allowed to continue

- **Strategic fit** Projects which do not closely align with the current organization policy and strategy may be candidates for premature closure, especially if they are not close to completion
- **Re-use and adaptation** Projects that are mid-lifecycle but not a good strategic fit may have completed work to date that can still be of value if adapted to the vision of the emerging programme. Research results, designs and prototypes are some examples of assets that might be of value.

In MSP the programme plan is designed to deliver the new capability in tranches. These step changes in capability should be carefully planned to support the realization of the appropriate, desired benefit(s). A tranche:

- Is made up of one or more projects or activities
- Delivers a step change in capability for the organization, as described in the intermediate blueprint
- Includes transition activities to achieve the outcomes defined for the tranche.
- Provides a control point at which the programme can be re-directed or stopped.

Where a tranche has its own business case, it is worth noting that benefits may be delivered after the tranche has been completed, and this should be factored in to the benefits realization plan and the tranche business case.

Programme tranches provide control and decision points for objectively assessing the programme's direction and viability.

In practice, an organization may run a programme with overlapping or parallel tranches. When deciding whether or not to have overlapping tranches, there are four considerations to evaluate:

- **Ongoing commitment to the programme** When coming to the end of a tranche where the organization remains committed to the vision, and progress to date means that delivery confidence is high, then the start of the next tranche may be brought forward – thus the subsequent tranche will overlap the end of the current tranche.
- **The nature of the programme** Ideally, there should not be dependencies on projects' outputs between tranches.
- **The risk appetite of the organization** Clearly, there is an increased risk associated with overlapping tranches, and the willingness to accept this increased risk will depend on the individual organization's culture and attitude to risk.
- **Structure of the programme** Given the increased risk, the programme should be structured around planned reviews at key decision points; these may be time- or event-driven.

Overlapping tranches are more likely to occur in large and complex programmes. However, it should be recognized that having tranches running concurrently increases risk because:

- The outputs from the projects for a tranche which is due to close later may not be required if the programme terminates at the end of an earlier tranche, thus wasting money
- The governance arrangements for the later tranche will need to be in place for the projects, thus increasing cost, complexity and administration
- At the end of tranche, a programme may change direction rather than stop, and investment in the projects already under way for later tranches may be wasted as the projects need to be redefined or stopped

- A programme with multiple concurrent tranches will be more difficult to stop or re-direct because there will not be a single stop/go point where the changes can be made; consequently the programme could run out of control.

One important purpose of a tranche is to use what has been learned so far to inform the direction of the remainder of the programme, increasing the likelihood of success. This is much more difficult with overlapping tranches, which are unable to take advantage of this information when they start and therefore may be less successful. Where overlapping tranches are designed into programme delivery, the levels of assurance should increase proportionately to reflect the increased risk.

As ends of tranches provide the programme with an opportunity to review future direction and viability, and go/no-go decisions, overlapping tranches add risk and should be avoided if possible. It is necessary to tightly control projects which overlap tranche ends and ensure that there are appropriate governance arrangements for the project in the event of the programme closing. If there are multiple projects running through a tranche end, it is much more complex to stop or divert the programme. The project lifecycle stages should be aligned as closely to the end of tranche as possible.

The programme also needs to maintain momentum so it is likely there will be some project activity preparing for future tranches, but it should be managed carefully. Some examples of the types of project work that might start in one tranche whilst delivering in another could include:

- Feasibility studies
- Market research
- Product testing
- Early stages of a major procurement
- Prototyping of a complex solution
- Situations in which project outputs are needed whether the programme continues or not.

Pragmatism is the key, and avoiding major expenditure or committing to contracts before approval to move to the next tranche is recommended. Where possible, the project delivery lifecycle should be designed to link a management stage end with the programme tranche end, in order to maximize control.

Judgement is required to establish the appropriate balance between maintaining control of the programme (to enable it to be stopped at the end of the tranche) and not losing too much momentum as the programme moves from one tranche to another. Monitoring the business environment during tranche delivery should provide plenty of indication of the organization's ongoing need for the programme.

The tranche ends when the Realizing the Benefits transition stage is completed, the outcomes are achieved and adequate assurance reviews have been completed to inform the rest of the programme. Further benefits will be realized in the post-transition phase.

Each tranche delivers part of the final future state described in the blueprint, and it may have an associated intermediate blueprint. This part of the

blueprint should provide a clear understanding of what the tranche has to deliver (see also section 8.2.1). The complete blueprint document therefore contains several sections: the 'as-is' state; sections for the intermediate future state for each tranche; and the final 'to-be' state for the end of the last tranche. Benefits realization planning (see Chapter 7) should help to identify points during the programme where sufficient projects will have delivered/completed for benefit reviews and progress assessments to take place.

Figure 8.5 shows how blueprint sections are used to describe the current state, intermediate future states at the end of each tranche, and the final future state at the end of the last tranche. In this example, tranche 1 is designed to deliver part of the new front-office operational capability and one of the back-office enhancements, and to outsource a support capability. Tranche 2 is designed to

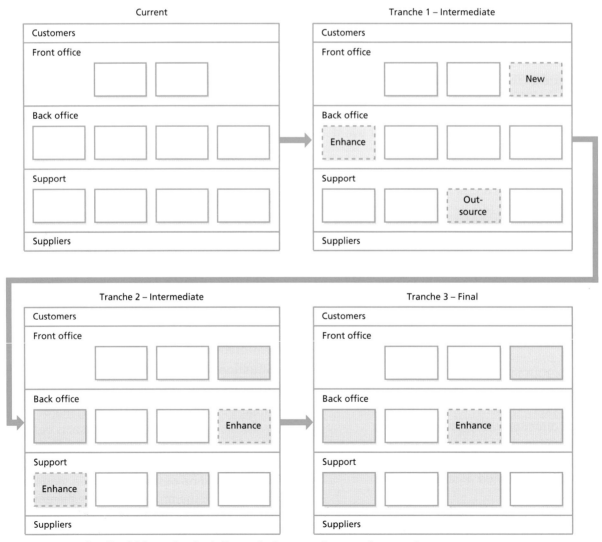

*Figure 8.5 How the final blueprint is delivered via step changes in tranches*

deliver the remainder of the new operational capability, the other back-office enhancement and the support enhancement. The final tranche, tranche 3, is designed to deliver the third back-office enhancement.

## Tip

One area sometimes overlooked in blueprint design work is service arrangements. As the organization will operate differently in the future, it might have a different infrastructure, IT systems, manufacturing plant etc. As well as designing these new systems, it will be necessary to design new service management arrangements to support them.

A good starting point for developing the blueprint is to identify what services will be needed, what will be stopped and what will be altered. From the answer to these questions the POTI model can be developed.

Figure 8.6 shows a sample programme schedule indicating the grouping of projects into tranches and the review points.

Once the overall design of the delivery is accepted, the timing of delivery can be considered (see Figure 8.6). The nature of the change required will determine the thinking at this point. Some programmes need to explore different delivery options, as early in the programme there isn't sufficient data or knowledge to decide which is the best route. The result of this exploration in an early tranche determines the arrangement of the later tranches. Early tranches may be designed as pilots or proofs of concept. The most important outputs from such tranches are the lessons learned that enable the programmes to be refined and steered to success. Some programmes might be driven by a strategic initiative (or similar). Just because an initiative is part of strategy, this does not guarantee that it will succeed. A good programme

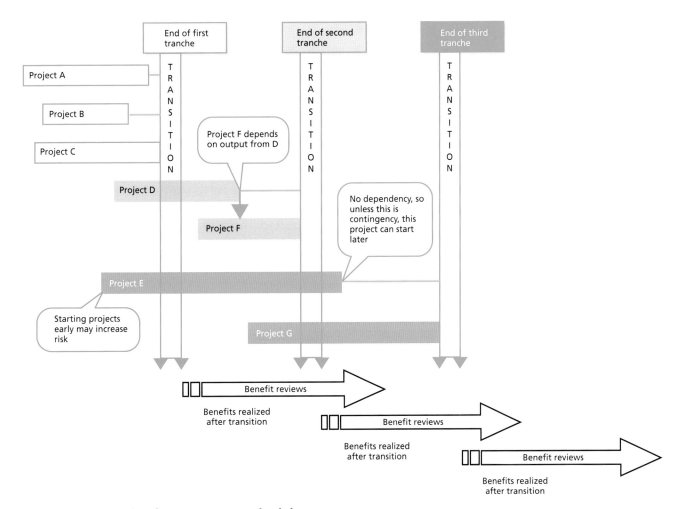

*Figure 8.6  Example of a programme schedule*

will attempt to prove (or disprove) the hypotheses embedded in the strategy as cheaply and quickly as possible.

### Example

A company that sells mobile phones changed its strategy from shop-based to internet sales. Fortunately, they decided to test this hypothesis.

A small-scale pilot showed the cost of sales greatly reduced, but the lack of face-to-face contact with customers was a major dis-benefit as the company lost the close understanding of customer requirements. This had been its great strength over the competition. The company also found that too many phones were being returned, increasing operating costs.

The lessons learned from this test enabled the firm to refine its approach. The internet became more a means to entice customers into its stores. The cost of this learning was insignificant compared with the original plans to switch to the internet in one major change, which probably would have put the company out of business.

Delivery can be incremental. Early tranches might deliver core changes, with later tranches building on that core. This provides quick wins, and as each change is smaller, it reduces the risk. (See also the transformational flow chapters in Part 3.)

## 8.4 BLUEPRINT DESIGN AND DELIVERY WITHIN THE TRANSFORMATIONAL FLOW

At each tranche end, and when a major change to the programme is proposed, the definition, scope, delivery status and expected benefits of the programme need to be revisited:

- Before transition, to check against the blueprint to ensure that the capability described is ready to be delivered and that the business is prepared and sufficiently stable to cope with transition
- After transition, to test whether the new capability has delivered the desired outcomes, enabling the improvements and benefits required

- To use the lessons learned to adjust the future state, the delivery approach and plans for at least the next tranche, to maximize those aspects that worked well and to minimize (or eliminate) those that didn't generate adequate benefits.

This section covers how the blueprint design and delivery governance theme is applied in each of the processes in the transformational flow.

### 8.4.1 Identifying a Programme

The work on the blueprint starts to emerge in the programme mandate when the 'as-is' state is documented, in effect developing the understanding of how things work at the moment. In the programme brief the outline vision statement is developed, which will include the major outcomes that need to be achieved and the required benefits. These will be important inputs to the blueprint.

### 8.4.2 Defining a Programme

This is when the major design work is done. Once the vision statement has been refined, the work on designing the 'to-be' state (and the intermediate steps to reach it) is undertaken. This work is done in parallel with developing the benefits and the projects. Without a blueprint, developing the benefits will be impossible as there will not be a start and end state to analyse, and identifying the projects required to deliver the 'to-be' state will be at best guesswork. It is important to remember that the baseline performance information in the blueprint, which illustrates the 'as-is' state, is also an important input to the benefits performance baselining.

More guidance is available in sections 15.6, 15.9 and 15.14.

### 8.4.3 Managing the Tranches

During the delivery of a tranche, the blueprint is a critical document for maintaining direction and control. Any changes to the programme should be analysed in terms of what the impact will be on the future state being created by the projects, and reflected in the blueprint. Strategic drivers may change, project delivery may become problematic or the business may struggle to cope with the level of change; all of these may lead to changes to the blueprint. The specific focus needs to be on ensuring that the intermediate blueprint for this tranche can be achieved and will enable the outcomes and underpin the realization of benefits. As part of the end-of-tranche review, the blueprint should be reviewed to ensure that the future intermediate blueprint and the final future state are still valid and viable.

More guidance is available in sections 16.7, 16.9 and 16.13.

### 8.4.4 Delivering the Capability

The blueprint provides the basis for developing the requirements for the projects. The mandates for the projects are defined in the projects dossier; however, the content of the blueprint should provide a key input to the development of the more detailed design of the project briefs. The blueprint will provide the majority of the requirements for the project, and the acceptance of the project outputs should be measured against their ability to satisfy the capabilities defined in the blueprint. This means that the blueprint provides the key quality criteria for the projects as well.

More guidance is available in section 17.5.

### 8.4.5 Realizing the Benefits

The blueprint 'as-is' state will define the baseline performance of the organization prior to change. This comprises important inputs to the baseline measurement for the benefit profiles. Changes to these performance baselines inform both the benefits and the progress towards the future state. Benefit reviews investigate whether the benefits have been achieved and assess whether the capability defined in the blueprint delivered what was needed to support the changes.

More guidance is available in sections 18.2.2. and 18.3.3 (enacting the transition represents the step from one blueprint stage across to the next one).

### 8.4.6 Closing a Programme

The success of the programme will be measured on whether it delivered a coherent capability, as defined in the blueprint and the associated benefits. The final review of the programme should check how it was controlled and whether it has been successful or not. It should focus not only on whether the blueprint was delivered, but also whether the programme managed any changes of direction effectively through the blueprint. The final state may look very different from what

was envisaged in the early blueprint, but the final version of the blueprint should reflect what now exists.

More guidance is available in sections 19.3 and 19.5.

## 8.5 THE KEY ROLES

Table 8.1 provides a summary of the key roles and typical areas of focus.

There is no specific guidance for the two main control boards (sponsoring group and programme board) because they are forums where decisions are made and direction set with input from the four key roles. Therefore, guidance has been restricted to individuals rather than broadened to groups.

This in no way weakens or undermines the roles of the sponsoring group or the programme board, which are essential for any essential programme and have their responsibilities set out in Chapter 4.

**Table 8.1 Blueprint design and delivery and the key roles**

| Role | Area of focus |
|---|---|
| Senior responsible owner (SRO) | Providing strategic direction for the work of the design of the blueprint and analysis of delivery options |
| | Ensuring sponsoring group authorization and commitment to the 'to-be' state, demonstrated through active cooperation; for example, making appropriate resource available to assist with the design of the blueprint and analysis of delivery options |
| | Ensuring that the blueprint document remains aligned with the strategic direction of the organization and will promote a coherent capability |
| | Providing the interface to the sponsoring group and other key stakeholders, maintaining their buy-in; for example, as the design of the future organization becomes clearer |
| | Providing advice and direction to the programme manager and BCM(s) as required, including risks or issues identified during blueprint design and delivery |
| | Ensuring that the programme board assesses and understands the implications of the blueprint and its delivery |
| Programme manager | Ensuring that the blueprint document is authored and assembled in collaboration with the BCM(s) |
| | Working closely with the business change manager(s) to ensure that the blueprint, programme plan, benefits realization plan and benefit profiles are consistent and able to deliver the business case |
| | Ensuring the programme has access to competent resources to create the blueprint |
| | Ensuring that appropriate options appraisals to select the optimal 'to-be' state take place |
| | Ensuring that the management of changes is undertaken with an impact assessment on the blueprint |
| | Communicating the details of the blueprint to the relevant projects and other programmes |
| | Ensuring that the planned step changes in operational capability are clearly understood by the project teams |
| | Ensuring that uncertainties and ambiguities relating to the content of the blueprint are captured as risks |
| | Contributing to managing stakeholder expectations |
| Business change manager(s) (BCM) | Leading the development of the content and taking responsibility for the delivery of the design into business operations |
| | Consulting with and gaining support from senior business managers for the 'to-be' state |
| | Ensuring that the planned step changes in operational capability are clearly understood by the operational areas |
| | Providing and coordinating essential input to the blueprint with the assistance of experienced operational staff and specialists, and (where appropriate) authoring (at least part of) the blueprint |
| | Ensuring that 'as-is' and 'to-be' information from the blueprint is used to construct the benefit profiles |
| | Aligning the creation of the capability within the blueprint with benefits realization through approval of project outputs |
| | Ensuring that operational changes during the life of the programme are being reflected in the evolving 'as-is' state in the blueprint |
| Programme office | Providing or locating information and resources that can assist with the design of the blueprint |
| | Facilitating impact assessments of changes on the blueprint |
| | Maintaining configuration control of the blueprint |

# Planning and control

9

# 9 Planning and control

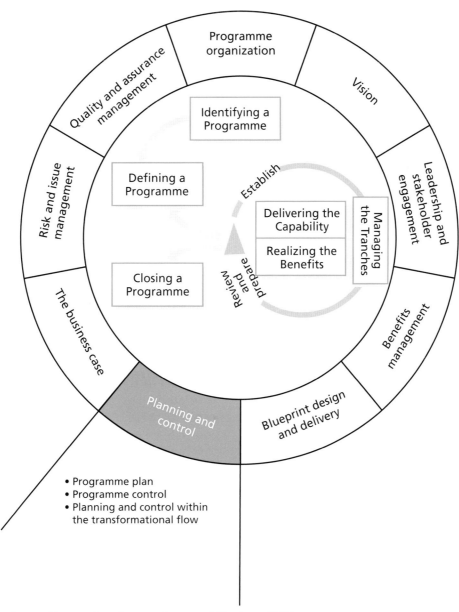

*Figure 9.1 Overview of how planning and control fits into MSP*

## 9.1 INTRODUCTION

Figure 9.1 provides an overview of how the planning and control governance theme fits into MSP. Planning and control are key to the success of any transformation programme and should be seen as distinctly separate concepts and activities.

### 9.1.1 Programme planning

The preparation of the programme plan involves:

- Processing large amounts of information
- Extensive consultation
- Building the plan.

During its early iterations the programme plan will include many unknowns and a high level of ambiguity.

## 9.1.2 Programme control

Programme control provides supporting activities and processes that run throughout the lifecycle of the programme to:

- Refine and improve delivery
- Minimize the impact of ambiguity
- Bring certainty wherever possible
- Justify the continuance of the programme.

The management and control of the programme should be based on experiences from the previous tranches.

## 9.2 PROGRAMME PLAN

The programme plan is not a master plan that is created and then left on the shelf. It is a key control document for the programme, which forms a complete picture of how the programme is going to work. When constituent project plans are developed later, they will be aligned with, but not embedded in, the programme plan in all their detail. This enables the programme manager, on behalf of the senior responsible owner (SRO), to implement a planned and controlled environment that can be monitored and maintained throughout the life of the programme. For further details of the contents of a programme plan, see section A.4 in Appendix A.

Developing the programme plan (see Figure 9.2) requires an understanding of the:

- Level of detail in the programme plan needed to:
  - Provide adequate information about progress to enable decision-making
  - Identify pressure points and other issues that may affect progress
- Tools to be used to monitor and maintain the programme plan, including how:
  - Information from the programme plan will be presented to stakeholders
  - Information from the programme plan will be distributed, to whom, and when (see Chapter 6)
  - Project-level information will be integrated at the programme level.

Whilst benefit profiles and the benefits realization plan are often initially developed separately from the programme plan, collaboration between these activities is critical. The total set of benefit profiles, together with the benefits realization plan, need to be integrated with the programme plan to ensure that the dependencies on project delivery and transition are properly considered. A close link also needs to be established with risk management activities.

A number of the governance strategies have associated plans, and it is perfectly acceptable to integrate these plans into the programme plan for simplicity where appropriate.

Developing and maintaining the programme plan requires the ongoing coordination of all the project plans. The focus for programme planning

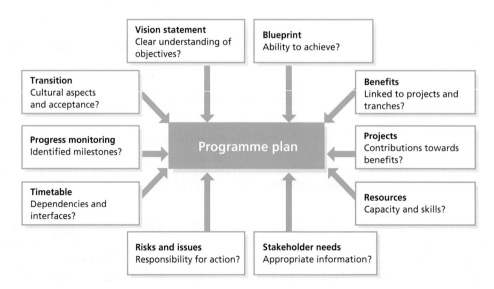

*Figure 9.2 Contributions to the programme plan*

is on the interdependencies between the projects and any dependencies on external factors outside the control of the programme. This makes programme planning and monitoring a complex task.

The programme's journey is longer and more complex than those of its constituent projects. Some programmes require considerable exploration in the early tranches to discover a successful way forward. Early programme designs will have very little detail for the later tranches, and estimates for the duration and cost of these may be based on huge assumptions. Whilst projects may also refine their plans into more detail as they progress, their degree of uncertainty (and their reliance on learning as they complete each phase/stage) is typically much less than in a programme. Decision makers in programmes will often rely far more on judgement as opposed to the more structured methods employed in projects.

### 9.2.1 Resources

Any input required by a project or programme is known as a 'resource'. The term covers people, assets, materials, funding and services. Shared resources (those resources that will be used by two or more projects) should be planned and managed by the programme. Developing the programme plan will identify those resources that need to be shared between projects. Minimizing resource-sharing between projects will help prevent bottlenecks occurring. Against that, maximizing resource-sharing will help promote knowledge-sharing, organizational learning, efficiency and fluent working.

It is important to remember that resources (especially people) have finite availability, skills and experience. The combination of these factors reflects their ability to contribute to the changes required. This will determine the maximum pace at which work can progress. Programmes must ensure that planning at all levels does not disregard the limits of competence, otherwise unrealistic plans may be developed. Of all the resources that a programme will consume, it is often availability of competent resources that presents the major challenge.

Although people are often expected to work together in teams in a programme or its projects, they may have no previous working relationships

with one another. Team building should be employed to help to get such groups up to speed quickly and working effectively together.

Many people (amongst other resources), in addition to being on more than one programme or project at the same time, have operational obligations. The acquisition of such resources needs careful consideration: in particular, how conflicts will be resolved when a resource is required in more than one place at the same time. Preparing in advance for such problems will make it easier to prioritize when necessary. If such issues are not quickly resolved with tact and diplomacy, there will often be confusion and tension.

It is common for organizations to overestimate their own capacity and ability when embarking on a transformation programme. An independent assurance or a P3M3 maturity assessment should be considered in order to baseline the existing maturity. This will help the organization to assess its internal resource capability for delivering a programme.

The resource management strategy describes how resources will be identified, acquired and managed. It will provide direction on how to address resource problems.

### 9.2.2 Resource management strategy and plan

A major part of programme planning is to consider what resources the programme will require, and how they will be acquired, used, shared and managed effectively. How this will be approached is defined in the resource management strategy. Programme resources will include:

- The programme's financial needs as expressed in budgets, expenditure profiles and accounting procedures
- Specialist skills, where and when they will be made available; for example, procurement or market expertise will be needed early in the programme lifecycle
- Staff and other personnel involved in the programme. This includes those who will be affected by its outcome(s), even if their involvement may be minimal (as they will need to be available at the right time to change to the new way of working)
- Assets that the programme will use, e.g. buildings and equipment

- Systems, services and technology that the programme will use as part of delivery.

The resource management strategy and plan includes the requirements for procurement and contract management within the programme. Procurement and contract management activities must be aligned with corporate policies and standards, and may require tailoring to suit the particular needs of the programme.

The resource management strategy should be developed alongside the programme plan to ensure that the resources required match the planned activities and timescales.

The resource management strategy is implemented through the resource management plan, which reflects the timeline for the requirement of the resources, when and who will be implementing them.

For further details of the resource management strategy and plan, see Appendix A.

### 9.2.2.1 Resource-sharing

Shared resources represent a set of dependencies between the programme and its projects and therefore need to be managed effectively and used efficiently. Scarcity of shared resources often creates more critical constraints on the progress of the programme than even the logical dependencies between project outputs.

Typical examples of resource-sharing are:

- **Staff** Where people are involved with more than one project within the programme
- **Infrastructure or facilities** For example, where office space may need to be shared
- **Information** For example, where a group of projects may be updating a shared repository
- **External service providers** Where several projects make use of the same service provider.

### 9.2.3 Risk management

Implementing the programme plan will inevitably have risks associated with it. Individual projects may face critical risks that, should they materialize, could affect the entire programme. All assumptions must be managed as risks. The identification of these, together with suitable responses, should form part of the programme's risk management activities. Such activities and contingency for risk should be included in the programme plan, based

on the risk management strategy. For further details on risk management, see Chapter 11 and Appendix A.

### 9.2.4 Projects dossier

The projects dossier contains a summary description of all the projects that together, through their combined outputs, will deliver the required intermediate and final 'to-be' states as described in the blueprint. These outputs allow the organization to acquire the capabilities described in the vision statement. The blueprint should inform the requirements and specifications that are required to be delivered by the project to achieve the outputs.

The projects dossier includes information on existing projects to be absorbed into the programme, and new projects to be commissioned by the programme (see Chapter 17).

> **Tip**
>
> Some programmes use the term 'project register' as an alternative to projects dossier as the generic term for the document that contains the necessary details about the projects.

The projects dossier should include the following information about each project:

- A description of the project and its objectives
- Requirements and their relationship to the blueprint
- Specific outputs that are required
- Time constraints that the project should work to
- Its dependencies with other projects
- Its anticipated budget (if available) based on the business case
- The contribution it will make to the programme's benefits.

These will form the basis of the project briefs that will be developed by the programme to give each project a thorough and rapid start. For further details on the content of the projects dossier, see Appendix A.

One of the objectives for designing the projects dossier is to place clear and direct accountability on the projects, while avoiding a spaghetti-like tangle of interdependencies. This can be achieved by ensuring that the delineation of the project boundaries maximizes the internal consistency of the projects and minimizes the number of interfaces and dependencies between the projects.

### Tip

The term 'workstream' is often used to describe the logical grouping of projects and activities together to enable effective management. This is particularly relevant where there are many projects within a programme or where their management control would be enhanced by subgrouping them.

Workstreams may delineate projects against a variety of criteria, including (but not restricted to):

- **By discipline** Programmes are typically multidisciplinary, whereas projects are often seen as belonging to a single discipline. Projects can be defined and scoped such that each involves a single discipline – for example, IT, construction, policy, business process
- **By location** Multi-site or regional projects are inherently difficult to manage, largely because of the communication overheads between members of the project teams. Projects may be scoped by grouping activities that can be achieved on a single site
- **By outputs** (e.g. an IT system or a building) Projects may be defined such that each is responsible for a single set of outputs, or outputs that are closely related.

One of the key factors for defining a workstream is to concentrate dependencies, as much as possible, within the workstream.

Workstreams are not time-bound; they exist for as long as the delineation criteria are valid. Within MSP, workstreams may run through a number of tranches but must be scheduled in such a way that is optimal to enable programme control; in particular, if the programme is stopped or re-directed, then the workstream will need to be changed accordingly.

The management of workstreams may require a layer of management to exist between the project managers and the programme manager. Someone who has overall responsibility for a group of projects that have been assembled into a workstream could be called a workstream manager.

There may be other business activities outside the scope of the programme that could conflict with or contribute to the programme's objectives. These should be identified and any possible opportunities or threats defined so that appropriate action can be taken if required. As such they need to be escalated by the programme manager to the SRO, the sponsoring group or the management of the corporate portfolio (where this exists) and managed as a programme risk.

Projects must be managed by effective teams to achieve success. Potentially, all of the following are worth considering when forming good project teams.

- Design smaller projects if the change is big or complex
- Combine work in small packages into one project
- Consider skills, knowledge, technology and facilities that are likely to be available when the work needs to be carried out
- Maintain existing team-working arrangements
- Geography and culture – project teams that are spread across different regions or countries can be difficult to manage.

Critical inputs for this aspect of programme planning come from the blueprint and its delivery (see Chapter 8).

### 9.2.5 Deadlines and constraints

The drivers for the programme may include immovable deadlines over which the programme has little or no control. The staging of an Olympic Games is a good example. These time-related drivers will naturally constrain the overall timescales within which the programme must operate. It is important not to lose sight of realism when such constraints exist. A programme is obliged to concentrate on the delivery of the high-priority capabilities – those that maximize benefits. It should recommend exclusion of capabilities that cannot be delivered before the deadline.

### 9.2.6 Scheduling

A key step in the planning process includes constructing a schedule of project delivery that demonstrates realization of benefits aligned with the strategic objectives that set the context for the programme. In order to achieve this, the programme needs to:

- Integrate the increasing refinement of individual project plans (as each project proceeds through its stages) into the programme plan to inform and assess progress
- Respond to project exception situations (by external influences or internal variances) that cause a reassessment of the programme plan
- Recognize business peak load periods when operational resources may not be available or when transition would increase the risk to business performance
- Continually monitor and review progress against the programme plan, including looking forward so as to anticipate emerging risks to the programme plan.

Treating each project as a 'black box' (being concerned just with key inputs and outputs, not the detail) enables the programme manager to schedule projects according to their dependencies, and to assess the impact of any potential slippages. Key elements within individual projects should be revealed within a dependency network diagram (see Figure 9.3), especially where this clarifies major interdependencies between projects.

Often there is a combined dependency. Here, until all the outputs from a group of projects are ready for operational use, there is not a capability on which to base and complete an operational transition. In Figure 9.3, transition cannot start until all the outputs from the four projects are complete and ready for operational use.

The programme plan's schedule provides the overall sequence and timetable for the programme by incorporating the dependency network and the timescales for each of the projects.

### 9.2.7 Priorities

Priorities are a key factor influencing programme scheduling. The effect on staff and the rest of the programme of delaying or bringing forward a particular project can be significant. Prioritization should focus on critical programme activities, for example:

- Specific projects, such as procurements, whose outputs are prerequisites for future projects
- Resource requirements, such as specific skills that may be scarce

- Early benefits realization, such as reduced operational costs, that will help engender continued commitment and enthusiasm for the programme.

## 9.3 PROGRAMME CONTROL

Programme controls should be established at the earliest opportunity, with assurance arrangements being defined in the programme mandate and being further developed in the programme preparation plan.

As soon as the programme is under way and is being managed tranche by tranche, all the definition and planning work comes into play so that there is a fluent, orderly construction and delivery of the new capability, resulting in the new outcomes being achieved.

End-of-tranche reviews are the critical control points in the programme delivery cycle, where the ongoing viability of the programme is assessed. The end-of-tranche review is the point where a decision is made as to whether the programme should continue, based on the ongoing desirability and viability of the blueprint, benefits, availability of finance, and ability to meet the corporate objective.

Managing the programme does not mean micro-management of the projects within it. Communicating the right information between the programme and its projects is a major consideration when establishing programme controls. Projects should be empowered but need clear tolerances and limits, in order to ensure that they do not exceed their delegated authority. Allowing the project managers to manage their projects within the tolerances set by the programme is an essential part of good programme management.

Equally, there need to be similarly effective flows of information from business operations into the programme to enable the monitoring of benefits and business performance.

The aim of the programme is the realization of expected benefits, through the achievement of the desired outcomes. The aim of the projects is the delivery of the required outputs and capability. This difference may lead to tensions between the project and programme planning and control processes. One of the greatest challenges in

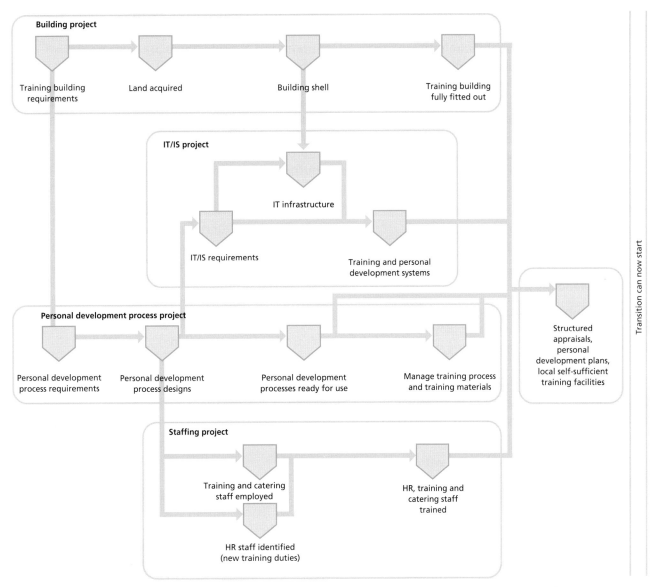

*Figure 9.3 Example of a dependency network showing how projects depend on other project outputs*

running a programme is therefore to reconcile project objectives and accountability with overall programme goals and programme-level consistency and control. Factors such as project management experience, programme risk and available margins should all be assessed when determining how tightly the programme should control its projects. All of these factors are then reflected in the monitoring and control strategy, which sets out the approach the programme will take to applying these internal controls (see Appendix A for details of the contents).

The communication flow between the programme, its projects and business operations should aim to re-use information contained in standards introduced as part of the programme governance.

Project documentation such as the project initiation documentation (PID), highlight reports, exception reports, and issue and risk registers will provide much of the information required by the programme. Part of the role of the programme office is to support this reporting (see also Appendix C).

### 9.3.1 Monitoring and control strategy

The monitoring and control strategy sets out how the programme will be controlled internally. This particularly focuses on:

■ How the programme will maintain governance and controls over its projects and change activities

■ Ensuring that projects are started up in a controlled way, and that they have appropriate stages defined that enable the programme to approve, stop or re-direct projects effectively to ensure that they remain aligned to the evolving programme

■ How project interdependencies will be managed

■ How the programme will ensure that it is running efficiently and is optimized to meet its objectives

■ The contents, structure and format of the programme plan.

Note, specific controls relating to how projects and the programme are interfaced will be contained in the various governance theme strategies, e.g. for risks or stakeholders.

The monitoring and control strategy content is set out in Appendix A and its deployment plan is embedded within the programme plan.

### 9.3.2 Dependency management

Programme control is about managing dependencies. There are basically three types of dependencies:

■ **Internal dependencies that are within the programme** These are dependencies that can be managed within the boundary of the programme, and may reflect how the projects depend on each other to deliver the blueprint and the benefits.

■ **Intra dependencies on other programmes or projects** These are the dependencies that are external to an individual programme but are still within the perimeter of the organization's programme and project management environment, most likely linked to the scope of another programme or within a corporate portfolio.

■ **External dependencies outside the programme environment** Those dependencies that extend beyond the boundaries of all the programmes into other parts of the organization or even other organizations. These are dependencies that are outside of the control of the programme management environment, potentially in business operations, other partners, external dynamics such as legislation and strategic decisions and approvals.

An effective dependency network can be created by looking at the projects only in terms of their inputs and outputs (the black box approach referred to in section 9.2.6). The network provides a crucial control tool for the programme manager. It helps to identify where a particular project has a dependency on an input, but no group or individual has responsibility for delivering it, and a project can see a dependency by others on its outputs. This helps to communicate priorities and the impact of delays across the programme to project teams.

Quite often, projects list assumptions in their documentation. In a programme environment, the validity of these assumptions may be dependent on the existence of other projects or activities. Some examples of dependencies that could be influenced by the assumptions in other projects include:

■ Decisions on direction

■ Policy or strategy papers to be signed off

■ Outputs from other projects

■ Skills and specialist knowledge

■ Funding

■ Involvement of partner or other organizations.

**Tip**

Workstreams can be used to concentrate dependencies within one group or team, for example IT. There may be a number of projects in an IT workstream, where the skills and knowledge across the various projects will be able to work together to manage dependencies and share experiences more easily than if they were operating separately.

Dependencies represent uncertainty, and as such are risks to the programme.

### 9.3.3 Starting projects

A programme should have good knowledge about the overall requirements for each project, even before the project has started. Projects in a programme should be started with a thorough brief to give them a running start. The project brief should:

■ State the project's objectives, scope, outputs, constraints and interfaces

- Provide direction and clarity about how the project will contribute to delivering some of the new capability
- Make specific reference to how the requirements relate to the blueprint
- Explain how this new capability relates to outcomes and benefits
- Define the authority delegated to the project, with clarity about how and when it needs to escalate to the programme
- State how and in what format the project will report progress to the programme
- Provide guidance on the standards to which the project should conform through its management activities.

### Tip

For a PRINCE2 project, a well-prepared brief from the programme may allow the project to effectively meet the requirements of the first process, 'Starting up a Project', enabling it to go straight into 'Initiating a Project'.

## 9.3.4 Integration of information

Circumstances may require one or more pre-existing projects to be adopted into the programme. In these cases the relevant project information should be integrated into the design of the blueprint and programme plan (see Chapter 8). The approach to information integration should be defined in the information management strategy, and the details for implementing the strategy in the information management plan.

The main areas to cover under the integration of programme and project information are:

- Strategic-level changes that alter the programme's blueprint, vision statement or business case and will have an impact on live projects, or those due to start soon
- Responsibilities and accountabilities from the programme management governance strategies that may have an impact at the project level
- Tolerance levels for project-level costs, timescales and quality
- Project milestones and review points.

### 9.3.4.1 Information management strategy

Information is at the core of any programme. Decisions must be made at the outset on how to make sure that information is reliable and robust. During the lifecycle, assessing the ongoing viability of the programme and its ability to achieve the outcomes will depend on rigorous management of the information about the progress of projects and the stability and performance of the business.

The information management strategy document defines the required activities. See Appendix A for more details.

### 9.3.4.2 Information management plan

The information management plan sets out the activities and timetable for putting the governance designed in the information management strategy into practice. This will include setting up the filing structures and applying appropriate controls.

See Appendix A for more details on the contents of the information management plan.

## 9.3.5 Progress monitoring

The programme management team will need to establish monitoring early in the implementation of the programme plan. This monitoring process should result in management intervention to address issues, preventing the programme drifting off target.

### Tip

Where PRINCE2 is being used, progress monitoring can be integrated with the process of the 'Directing a Project', with the programme manager and programme board being the escalation point for exception reports that take the project out of tolerance: in particular, where an exception threatens a programme dependency, where there should be minimal tolerance.

The end of each tranche is a key review point (or milestone) at which a formal assessment of progress and benefits realization must be made. The length of a tranche may warrant assurance reviews between tranche ends. For this, there might be something tangible available (for example a prototype) that can be used to assess the likelihood of achieving the benefits required.

In addition to tranche event-related reviews, the programme may also be subject to gated reviews at key points to assess its continuing viability against the business case.

All these assurance reviews may involve internal audit, peer-level assessors or external scrutiny, depending on the type of programme and its governance requirements. For further details on reviews, see Chapter 12 and Appendix D.

The completeness, timeliness and relevance of information are critical if monitoring is to be worthwhile. A programme that has anything more than trivial levels of incomplete, out-of-date or inaccurate information is a programme that is out of control. The design of data collection, information flows and timing of reporting must also be practical and do-able. The information management strategy describes how this coherent information will be delivered and managed within the programme, and the information management plan defines how and when it will be implemented.

### 9.3.6 Project control

Each project should have its management processes, but these will need to be consistent across projects with clearly assigned responsibilities and governance. Project governance should be formally integrated with programme governance to ensure that the projects remain aligned with the objectives of the programme. As already stated, a well-managed programme will start its projects with a clear brief. The programme manager should continue to guide the projects, focusing on matters such as project interdependencies, and the impact on projects from strategic or programme changes, risks and issues.

If a project is overlapping a tranche end, wherever possible a management stage should be built into the project delivery lifecycle to enable programme control. If the programme changes direction or is closed, the future for the project can be aligned appropriately, and it may continue in standalone mode or move under the governance of a different programme.

### 9.3.7 Planning and controlling transition

Whilst an estimate of the length of the transition period should be considered when developing the overall programme plan, more detailed transition planning is not practical until sufficient progress has been made in each individual tranche. Detailed transition planning requires both knowledge of the specific project outputs and the state of readiness of the operations which are due to change. Transition plans form part of the larger benefits realization plan.

Some organizations have seasonal demands. For example, retail outlets that depend heavily on seasonal trade do not normally want to make significant changes over that period. Transition planning needs to take account of such constraints.

Often there will be more than one concurrent programme and several projects, all of which are due to deliver change in a similar period. Careful planning is required to avoid change overload. This is an area where a corporate programme office and portfolio control can help the organization to avoid such pitfalls.

Change to an organization, its people, working practices, and information and technology needs to be planned and managed carefully. This must allow the cultural and infrastructural migration from the old environment to the new one. The planning and control aspects of transition management will go hand in hand as the tranche approaches completion and continues until the new business operations are self-supporting and fully embedded. Maintaining existing business operations is an important consideration during transition, since new operations will be introduced while the existing ones are still operating. See the discussion of leading change in section 2.2.2.

Successful benefits realization depends on the identification and effective management of all the business changes stemming from the delivery of the project outputs.

The scope of a project is usually (and rightly) too narrow to include all the necessary activities to embed a change and realize its full benefits.

The programme manager and business change managers (BCMs) work closely together to manage all aspects of transition. Figure 9.4 shows an example of the sequence towards realizing benefits through pre-transition, transition and post-transition. These three phases of transition are described more fully in Chapter 18. The following three sections give a summary of key points from that chapter, with reference to numbered points in Figure 9.4.

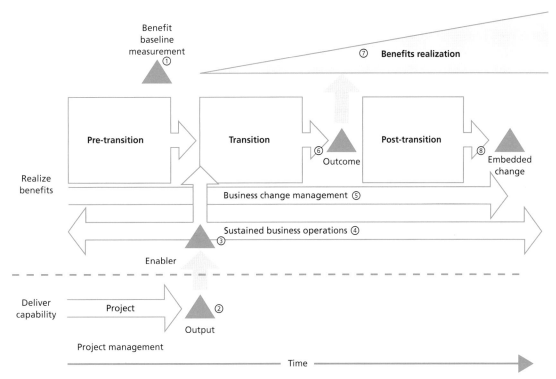

*Figure 9.4 Simple example showing outputs, transition management and benefits realization*

### 9.3.7.1 Pre-transition phase

This is the build-up to transition. In effect, it starts as soon as the programme becomes public knowledge. Stakeholders will be taking a view on the programme and its impact on them.

The work to develop the blueprint 'as-is' state will define the baseline performance levels (1), which will be measured for progress towards the anticipated future-state performance. The measures are key to monitoring the stability of the organization.

Stakeholder engagement and leadership will be critical in the build-up to the change, and the vision will need to be 'sold' extensively.

Prior to giving the go-ahead to deliver transition, a review and 'stop/go' decision needs to be made as to whether the business operations are adequately prepared to accept the capability and go through transition.

### 9.3.7.2 Transition phase

In this simple case, the transition is a single output from a single project in a single business unit. The project has delivered its output (2) which is received by the business unit as an enabler (3), to take into its operations (4). Particular business changes may be required (5) for this single enabler

to embed the enabler into the operations. In most programmes it is more complex, with many outputs relating to many outcomes.

This takes the business unit to a state where there is achievement of the planned operational outcome (6). Meanwhile, benefits realization may sometimes be already under way (7) and so should be tracked by the BCM responsible. Such tracking may yield valuable information, for example about realization of dis-benefits during transition. Care must be taken, though, that such tracking does not unduly disturb operations and the transition itself.

### 9.3.7.3 Post-transition phase

This is where activities to embed the change take place. The aim of post-transition is to achieve a prevailing outcome: a change that sticks (8).

Much of this change or transition management is defined in Realizing the Benefits as part of the transformational flow, led by the appropriate BCMs. However, in planning these types of change leadership actions, they may identify particular business changes that need to be included in the benefit profile and in the benefits map. This in turn means that the associated costs of such business changes need to be accounted for by the programme.

The post-transition activities are absolutely critical; it is often the case that failure to focus on this area is the reason that change fails to stick.

All this guards against one of the common reasons for programmes failing to realize their expected benefits: project outputs are planned and accounted for, but necessary business changes are not.

The post-transition stage may extend beyond the life of the programme itself, at which point the BCM will take on all responsibilities associated with Realizing the Benefits.

## 9.4 PLANNING AND CONTROL WITHIN THE TRANSFORMATIONAL FLOW

This section covers how the planning and control governance theme is applied in each of the processes in the transformational flow. Effective planning and control is essential to the programme. It synchronizes, coordinates and monitors all of the programme activities. It plays a key role in making sure that the boundaries between each of the flow processes are respected so that there is a clear and controlled end to each one and start-up for the following one.

### 9.4.1 Identifying a Programme

The programme preparation plan is produced and approved in Identifying a Programme. It describes the work to be carried out in Defining a Programme and how it will be controlled. It also provides basic governance arrangements for use in Defining a Programme until the full governance framework for the programme has been developed and approved.

For an emergent programme, information about and decisions on existing projects will be output from Identifying a Programme and will need to inform the work in Defining a Programme as the full set of plans are developed.

More guidance is available in sections 14.5, 14.6, 14.7 and 14.8.

### 9.4.2 Defining a Programme

Whilst this theme focuses on the programme plan, it cannot be developed in isolation from the development of other plans. In this process a full set of plans and governance arrangements are developed. These are used to direct and

control work in the programme and its projects. The outputs from Defining a Programme may be re-visited towards the end of each tranche. These plans and governance arrangements may be refined in the light of the lessons learned so far and any changes in external circumstances, such as corporate strategy.

More guidance is available in many parts of this guide, especially sections 15.2, 15.10, 15.11, 15.13, 15.14, 15.16, 15.17 and 15.18.

### 9.4.3 Managing the Tranches

The full set of programme control documents are used to direct work, ensuring that activities are started according to the schedules which are part of these plans. This covers all work in the programme except starting projects, which are managed in Delivering the Capability. The monitoring and control strategy defines how to monitor and control the programme. It is a key document in this process.

During Managing the Tranches, the focus is principally on the control mechanisms that help to maintain the direction and momentum of the programme.

As the end of each tranche approaches, these plans and governance arrangements are reviewed and refined for the next tranche (see section 9.4.2).

More guidance is available in sections 16.2, 16.3, 16.10, 16.11, 16.12, 16.13 and 16.14.

### 9.4.4 Delivering the Capability

Projects within the projects dossier are started according to the schedule in the programme plan. The programme's plans and the blueprint are used as a project starts to explain to the project teams how their outputs will need to integrate with those of other projects in order to produce a capability ready for transition.

In this way each project will be aware of dependencies with other projects and with other programme activities.

Reporting arrangements should be agreed with each project. Information from projects is used to update programme documents, such as the programme plan. The effectiveness of monitoring the programme will therefore be dependent on how well all of the projects plan, monitor and control their own activities.

More guidance is available in sections 17.2, 17.5, 17.6 and 17.7.

### 9.4.5 Realizing the Benefits

Collaboration between the projects and those carrying out other programme activities is critical. BCMs and other operational staff will need to be aware of project progress to help them prepare for transition. Projects will need input from operational staff at various points in their lifecycle, such as requirements capture.

Transition is a very critical point in programmes, as this is where the change to the organization actually takes place. Many programmes have faltered at this point, wasting the considerable effort and good work expended so far. Preparation and implementation of the transition plan is a critical piece of work.

The BCM has a key role to play in:

■ The alignment of projects
■ Ensuring the inputs, business requirements and time constraints
■ Providing expertise from operational staff in assessing designs, prototypes and similar items
■ Considering how well these proposals are likely to work in a full-scale operational environment.

If there is a business change team, then a member of the team may work alongside or as part of the project board representing the BCM in the day-to-day decision-making of the project.

More guidance is available in sections 18.2.3, 18.3.3 and 18.4.2.

### 9.4.6 Closing a Programme

Unless closing prematurely, the programme will need to have successfully delivered all the outputs from all the projects as listed in the projects dossier.

A review of the programme is important, and this should include all of the programme control documents – not just to determine if it was successful but to assess how well it was managed and controlled. If the programme was not adequately planned and if it was not properly monitored and controlled, it less likely to be successful. Another consequence of such inadequate management is that the data collected is likely to be poor. You might be aware that the programme did not succeed but it might not be clear by how much or why.

More guidance is available in sections 19.2, 19.3, 19.4, 19.6 and 19.8.

## 9.5 THE KEY ROLES

Table 9.1 provides a summary of the key roles and typical areas of focus.

There is no specific guidance for the two main control boards (sponsoring group and programme board) because they are forums where decisions are made and direction set with input from the four key roles. Therefore, guidance has been restricted to individuals rather than broadened to groups.

This in no way weakens or undermines the roles of the sponsoring group or the programme board, which are essential for any essential programme and have their responsibilities set out in Chapter 4.

**Table 9.1 Planning and control and the key roles**

| Role | Areas of focus |
| --- | --- |
| Senior responsible owner (SRO) | Consulting the sponsoring group and other key stakeholders, maintaining their buy-in, especially in preparing for and carrying out transition |
| | Leading the ongoing monitoring and review activities of the programme, mid-tranche and end-of-tranche, including commissioning formal reviews such as audits/health checks, if required |
| | Monitoring progress and direction of the programme at a strategic level and initiating management interventions where necessary |
| | Authorizing the resource management strategy |
| | Authorizing the monitoring and control strategy |
| | Ensuring that adequate assurance is designed into the control mechanisms |
| | Authorizing the projects dossier, programme plan, and the required monitoring and control activities |

*Table continues*

**Table 9.1 continued**

| Role | Areas of focus |
|---|---|
| Programme manager | Designing the projects dossier, resource management strategy, monitoring and control strategy and the required assurance activities |
| | Design of the programme plan |
| | Ensuring that the blueprint, programme plan, benefits realization plan and benefit profiles are consistent and able to deliver the business case and remain aligned |
| | Development of the resource management strategy and deployment of the plan |
| | Development of the monitoring and control strategy and its deployment |
| | Establishing and managing the appropriate governance arrangements for the programme and its projects |
| | Ensuring that key programme documentation is current |
| | Creation and issuing of project briefs |
| | Identifying and managing programme dependencies |
| | Progress-reporting to the SRO and the programme board on project, business case, programme plan and blueprint achievement |
| | Adjusting the projects dossier, blueprint and plans to optimize benefits realization |
| | Managing stakeholder expectations and participating in communications activities to inform stakeholders of progress and issues |
| Business change manager(s) (BCM) | Consulting with the programme manager on designing the projects dossier and scheduling the tranches and constituent projects to ensure that the transition will align with the required benefits realization |
| | Ensuring that changes are implemented in the business |
| | Ensuring that the business continues to operate effectively during the period of change |
| | Providing adequate and appropriate business and operational resources to the programme and its projects to ensure that outputs are designed, developed and assured to give them the best chance of enabling the scale of improvements required |
| | Making sure that operational functions are adequately prepared and ready to change when transition starts |
| | Ensuring that plans are in place to maintain business operations during the change process until transition and handover is complete; also providing input to the reviews |
| | Planning the transition within operational areas, accommodating requirements to maintain business operations |
| | Ensuring that the focus remains once transition is completed, to establish the new ways of working and ensure that old practices do not creep back |
| Programme office | Supporting the development of planning, control and information management arrangements |
| | Gathering information and presenting progress reports on projects |
| | Supporting the programme manager in the development of reports |
| | Providing the programme teams with information and resources that can assist with the design of documentation. Establishing and operating the programme's information and configuration management systems, procedures and standards |
| | Collecting monitoring and measurement data and keeping the information up to date |
| | Collecting and presenting information on business performance |
| | Ensuring that there are coherent and common project-level standards in place for all document management arrangements for the programme |

# The business case

10

# 10 The business case

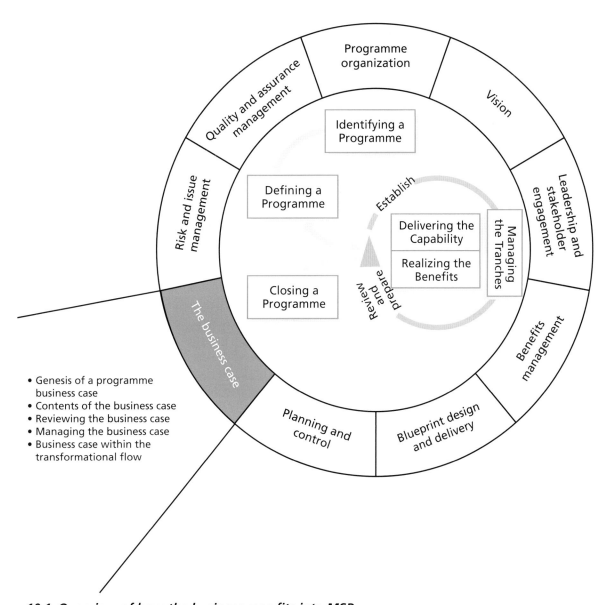

Figure 10.1 Overview of how the business case fits into MSP

## 10.1 INTRODUCTION

The senior responsible owner (SRO), the sponsoring group and the programme board must have confidence at every stage that the programme is still viable. In MSP the business case provides the vital test of the viability of the programme. It answers the question 'Is the investment in this programme still worth it?'

Since this viability question is ongoing, the business case cannot be static. It provides more than the basis for initial approval to kick off the programme. It is actively maintained throughout the programme, continually updated with new information on benefits, costs and risks.

The business case is an aggregation of specific information about the programme:

- Value of the benefits
- Risks to achieving the benefits

- Costs of delivering the blueprint
- Timescales for achievement.

The business case presents the optimum mix of information used to judge whether or not the programme is (and remains) desirable, viable and achievable. It identifies the added value of managing the change as a whole in a programme (see section 2.2.5) as well as the added costs of the programme over and above project costs. The business case effectively describes what the value is – including the added value – to the sponsoring organization from the outcomes of the programme. Managing the business case is about making sure that the balance of benefits, costs, timescales and risks is optimized throughout the programme.

Figure 10.1 provides an overview of how the business case governance theme fits into MSP.

## 10.2 GENESIS OF A PROGRAMME BUSINESS CASE

### 10.2.1 Programme mandate

A programme begins most effectively when it is launched in the context of a clear corporate strategy. Good strategy is robust enough to cope with continually changing business drivers, both internal and external (see Figure 10.2). Ideally, the strategy will suggest the optimum route for

programme delivery and the prioritization of new and existing work against it. The programme mandate provides the strategic trigger at the start of a programme. The programme mandate may be a consolidation of information from a number of documents, policies and directives. Collectively, this programme mandate informs and directs the activities of programme identification (in Identifying a Programme) and definition (in Defining a Programme). A programme mandate might contain a suggested business case, and should at least provide much of the raw material for outlining one. For further details on what the programme mandate should contain, see Appendix A.

### 10.2.2 Programme brief

If the programme mandate provides the trigger and context for a programme, it is the programme brief that develops the programme concept and provides the basis for an initial assessment of the viability and achievability of the proposed programme. As such, the programme brief does provide an outline business case, the formal basis for assessing whether such an investment is viable or achievable, before committing to the detailed programme definition work. If the programme mandate is flawed, the process of developing the programme brief should reveal this.

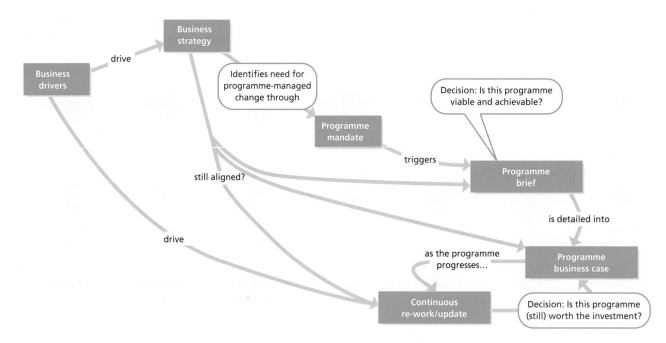

*Figure 10.2 Genesis of a programme business case*

Achieving success requires a realistic view of the organization's competence, capacity and culture to accommodate change. Just because a venture looked a good idea in a strategic planning session does not necessarily mean it can stand further scrutiny.

The programme brief contains the outline vision statement (the picture of the future beneficial state) and benefits, which should be validated against the organization's strategic objectives.

At this summary level of detail, the programme brief allows the SRO to consider several scenarios or options in a way that might not be practicable once the programme has narrowed down and some of these options are detailed in the programme definition. This early work has the freedom to consider sometimes quite radical alternatives to what might be expected – a freedom that is more restricted once Defining a Programme begins.

### 10.2.3 Link with benefits

Definition of the programme benefits evolves through the programme mandate and programme brief, and then significant analysis and development work is done during Defining a Programme to develop the understanding and potential of the benefits that the programme can realize. Part of this work is to gain an understanding the level of risk that will be associated with the investment.

The work on benefits is intrinsically linked to the development of the business case, as it is the input information that will provide the justification for the investment. The anticipated financial savings would be expected to exceed the cost of the projects to deliver the capability.

The analysis isn't always so simple, and some business cases may be based on achieving value or benefits that are not entirely balanced by the costs of delivery. This may be particularly the case with a compliance programme, for example, where the benefits may be the avoidance of negative consequences rather than actual positive effects.

### 10.2.4 Link with projects

There will be individual project business cases as well as the business case for the programme. A project business case is about balancing the costs,

timescales and risks relating to delivering the project outputs, and the context and contribution to the realization of directly enabled benefits.

The programme's business case is broader than a project business case. The programme business case embraces the wider horizons of strategic outcomes arising from the programme's projects. It is more than a summation of the project business cases (where they exist). It will also include the cost of business changes required in the programme and additional benefits realization costs, showing how these integrate with the project outputs to achieve the corporate strategic objectives.

The business cases for the programme and the projects are continually monitored, reviewed regularly, and updated as necessary to ensure that progress remains aligned to the strategic objectives (see Figure 10.2). In the most serious case, an escalation of a major issue from one of the projects could result in the programme's business case becoming unviable.

## 10.3   CONTENTS OF THE BUSINESS CASE

The programme's full business case sets out the overall costs, the planned benefits realization and the risk profile of the programme, in order to assess its viability and make appropriate management decisions about its continued viability.

The business case is developed by iteration through stages of formulation and analysis (see Figure 10.2), and is compiled from other information, including the:

- Blueprint
- Benefits realization plan
- Risk register
- Resource management strategy and resource management plan
- Programme plan.

The level of detail and completeness of the business case will reflect the degree of certainty associated with the programme at that point. Initially, the programme may tolerate high levels of uncertainty; estimates will be very approximate, with high levels of potential variance. The blueprint may be going through frequent iterations as well.

There may be options in the outline business case (programme brief) that are carried forward into Defining a Programme; these options consider alternative means of how the programme's final capability could be delivered and embedded. Each option will require detailed consideration to be able to compare the likely costs, benefits and risks.

In Defining a Programme, the business case should be developed in tandem with the early iterations of the blueprint, programme plan and benefits realization plan (the business case is an aggregation of information from these and other sources). These documents will be developed in parallel and will require close integration to ensure that the benefits to be delivered are driving the programme's transformation.

Developing the business case alongside the blueprint enables the programme to select the most cost-effective combination of projects and activity workstreams. This helps the design of the programme's blueprint to focus on a target capability that will be the basis for realizing the expected benefits within justifiable costs.

Throughout the programme, the integrity of information included in the business case and the related documentation should be maintained and kept current – thus providing an auditable trail between it and the progress of the programme.

The business case will provide leaders with key information to convince stakeholders to give support and commitment.

### 10.3.1 Net benefit line

The business case is where a trade-off is made between:

- The costs associated with delivering the new capability and embedding changes, and
- Realizable benefits and the value to the organization of having those benefits.

The concept of 'net benefit' is represented by the net benefit line in Figure 10.3. During the early stages of a programme the cumulative costs of delivery and embedding might outweigh the cumulative benefit to the organization(s). As the programme continues, more benefits are realized, thus providing greater value, so the cumulative net benefit increases.

Of course, the analysis illustrated in Figure 10.3 can only meaningfully compare cashable (financial) benefits against financial cost. Other benefits that are listed in the benefit profiles and benefits realization plan may have non-financial measures; however, best practice is to express benefits in financial terms wherever possible.

The programme is usually planned to close:

- Some time after complete delivery of the full capability (also shown in Figure 10.3)
- When sufficient transition is deemed to have been achieved from the old capability to the new
- When changes are so embedded that the target outcome is achieved.

This means that arrangements to continue benefits management and tracking of net benefits (costs and benefits) after the programme close should be made while the programme is still live. Business change managers (BCMs), who will continue in their operational roles, will be central to achieving this post-programme continuity.

**Tip**

The net benefit line has a value in engaging many stakeholders. For example:

- The very credibility of the programme may be in the balance for some stakeholders, until there is demonstrable evidence of early realization of financial benefits.
- The moment the net benefit line rises above zero it could be managed as a communications milestone, with the message that the programme has already achieved its break-even in investment and is now moving into the black.
- As the programme draws to a close, expectations are managed by the message that the benefits still need to be realized.
- Compliance programmes may need to express their benefits as avoided costs (e.g. legal penalties) or forgone reputational damage.

The full business case is developed during Defining a Programme. Even though there should be an ongoing review by the programme manager, BCM and the programme office, it should also be

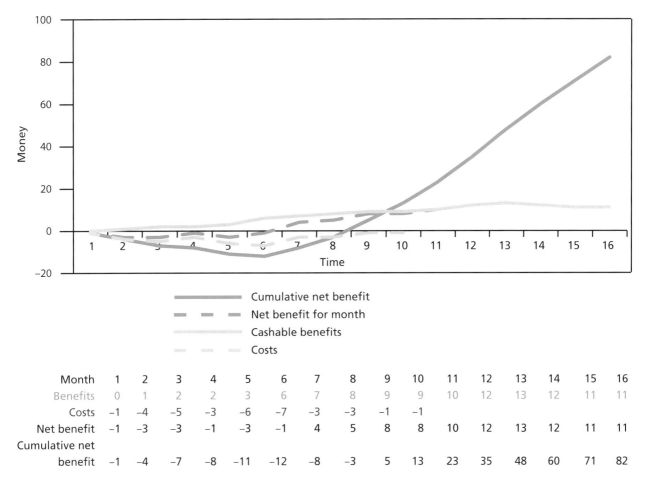

| Month | 1 | 2 | 3 | 4 | 5 | 6 | 7 | 8 | 9 | 10 | 11 | 12 | 13 | 14 | 15 | 16 |
|---|---|---|---|---|---|---|---|---|---|---|---|---|---|---|---|---|
| Benefits | 0 | 1 | 2 | 2 | 3 | 6 | 7 | 8 | 9 | 9 | 10 | 12 | 13 | 12 | 11 | 11 |
| Costs | -1 | -4 | -5 | -3 | -6 | -7 | -3 | -3 | -1 | -1 | | | | | | |
| Net benefit | -1 | -3 | -3 | -1 | -3 | -1 | 4 | 5 | 8 | 8 | 10 | 12 | 13 | 12 | 11 | 11 |
| Cumulative net benefit | -1 | -4 | -7 | -8 | -11 | -12 | -8 | -3 | 5 | 13 | 23 | 35 | 48 | 60 | 71 | 82 |

*Figure 10.3 Cumulative net benefit*

formally validated (reviewed and re-accepted) at the end of each tranche (see Figure 10.4 and section 10.4) by the programme board and SRO.

## 10.3.2 Costs

Programme business case management means budgeting for the programme's costs; these may be quite varied. Examples of cost categories are set out in Table 10.1.

Please note that because the programme plan can contain other plans (such as resource management, benefits realization etc.), it could also include cost information for those plans.

In addition to these programme costs, it is also important to consider within the business case the whole-life costs of operating/maintaining new products/equipment. For example, the benefit 'increased sales' may require more sales people to service the increased volumes. Some organizations might manage this as a dis-benefit, while others may factor the information into their longer-term business planning.

Where there is uncertainty about costs, this should be reflected as a risk, with appropriate contingency in place.

## 10.4 REVIEWING THE BUSINESS CASE

As a minimum, the business case should be reviewed at the end of each tranche to assess the continued viability of the programme and any need for realignment. In the UK public sector, such reviews are often undertaken as part of OGC Gateway reviews. It is good practice to formally review the business case at least every six months, particularly if tranche ends are spaced over longer periods.

Reviewing the business case should provide answers to the following questions:

- Is the programme (still) affordable – is there sufficient funding?
- Is the outcome (still) achievable – is there a realistic assessment of the organization's ability to cope with the scale of change envisaged?

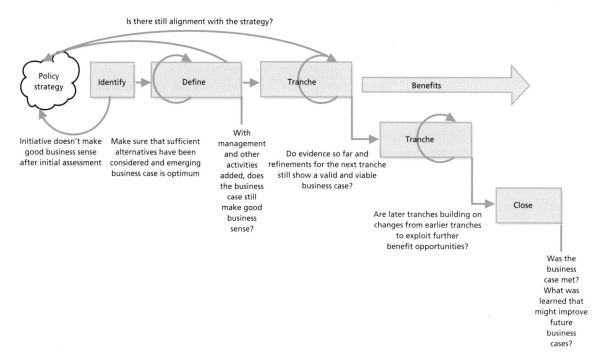

**Figure 10.4 Validating the business case**

- Does the programme (still) demonstrate value for money – are the benefits and the costs of realizing them in the right balance?
- Have options been considered – is the programme's dossier of projects (still) the appropriate or optimum way of achieving the desired outcome(s)?
- Is the programme still justifiable in terms of its ability to meet strategic objectives?
- Is there an up-to-date contingency plan and are there arrangements in place to ensure that there is sufficient financial cover for risks and uncertainties?

However, the business case is not just refreshed and updated. As a learning organization (see section 2.2.7), the programme management team will seek ways of building in new learning and observations where these can improve the business case even further. In effect, the end of each tranche becomes another mini Defining a Programme process resulting in an update for the business case document. It is tuned and optimized, taking advantage of both data on recent trends and a growing understanding of the possibilities by the management team.

## 10.5 MANAGING THE BUSINESS CASE

Information presented in the business case will serve many purposes during the life of the programme – all focused on ensuring successful delivery and strategically aligned outcomes.

The key questions here are:

- To what extent can the programme realize the expected benefits?
- Will changes to the cost-benefit profile (as in the net benefit line) alter the status and relative priority of the programme in relation to meeting the corporate strategic objectives?

The business case will be used to assess the impact of:

- Accommodating any strategic change or any changed business driver
- Proposed revisions to the programme's boundary and blueprint
- Revised benefit and cost estimates from the BCMs and the projects
- Any major new issue identified
- Any significant new risk identified.

Delivering the business case should not end with the programme. The SRO should continue to champion:

**Table 10.1 Types of programme cost**

| Type | Description | Possible information source |
|---|---|---|
| Project costs, sometimes referred to as investment or development costs | Project costs in acquiring and delivering the enabling outputs<br>For project and programme contingency and change budget | Projects dossier<br>Programme plan<br>Project business cases |
| Benefits realization costs | Setting up and implementing measurement, monitoring, and reporting on benefits realization<br>Other costs incurred in achieving the benefits, which can be attributed to benefits – for example, compensation packages for staff | Benefits management strategy<br>Benefit profiles<br>Benefits realization plan |
| Business change and transition costs | Cost of preparing, training, moving and supporting an operational unit until new practices are embedded. This could include interim operational resources required to embed the change<br>Costs of activities defined in the Realizing the Benefits element of the tranche, including the costs of the BCM and business change teams. | Programme plan<br>Resource management plan<br>Benefit profiles |
| Programme management costs | Some programme roles will be full-time: for example the programme office and the programme manager<br>Associated costs for these roles and for programme management activities: for example office space, programme tools for tracking and reporting progress<br>Contingency budget for dealing with risk and change<br>Assurance and review costs | Resource management plan<br>Information management strategy<br>Programme communications plan<br>Quality and assurance strategy<br>Programme plan |
| Capital costs | Capital costs are normally for fixed assets which can often be found under the 'technology' heading in the blueprint. In accountancy terms the impact of these costs will often be spread over a number of years | Blueprint |

- Values and principles that underpinned the change initiative
- Desired outcomes
- Continued leveraging of the benefits after the programme closes.

## 10.6 BUSINESS CASE WITHIN THE TRANSFORMATIONAL FLOW

This section covers how the business case governance theme is applied in each of the processes in the transformational flow. The business case provides the organization with a reasoned justification for why the programme should be established and should continue to exist. As it moves through the transitional flow processes, the programme should refer to, challenge and revise the business case to ensure that the programme remains a valid and good use of corporate resources.

### 10.6.1 Identifying a Programme

This is the genesis of the business case. The programme mandate is an input to Identifying a Programme. It might contain a suggested business case and should at least provide much of the raw material for outlining one. If the programme mandate is flawed, this should be revealed during the development of the programme brief. The programme brief is created in this process and provides an outline business case.

More guidance is available in sections 14.2, 14.5 and 14.7.

### 10.6.2 Defining a Programme

This is where the full business case is created and developed, using input from all the other work undertaken in Defining a Programme. This process provides guidance on how to develop the business case by iteration so that it presents the optimum way forward, selected from a range of alternatives.

More guidance is available in section 15.6 and particularly section 15.15.

### 10.6.3 Managing the Tranches

The business case is the key control document. It will need to be updated and reviewed throughout each tranche to ensure proper control. At the end of each tranche, it is reviewed, validated and re-accepted. The programme's plans may need to be refined, based on lessons learned so far, so the business case may need to be adjusted to reflect this. At the end of each tranche, as part of the review that takes place, the business case needs to demonstrate that the programme is still affordable, outcomes are still achievable and it still represents value for money. The business case must also continue to be aligned to corporate strategy.

More guidance is available in section 16.7.

### 10.6.4 Delivering the Capability

There will be individual project business cases as well as the business case for the programme. The programme's business case is broader than a project business case and is more than a summation of the project business cases. It will also include the cost of business changes required in the programme and additional benefits realization costs, showing how these integrate with the project outputs to achieve the corporate strategic objectives. Reporting from the projects to the programme should include the provision of updated project business cases.

### 10.6.5 Realizing the Benefits

Benefits are an important part of the business case, the other parts being cost, time and risk. If the programme fails to realize its planned benefits, then the business case will fail to be achieved. Benefits reviews will provide an important input to reviewing the business case.

More guidance is available in section 18.2.2.

### 10.6.6 Closing a Programme

If all has gone well, the business case will have been achieved. The business case is finally updated from all the programme plans and the business cases of the constituent projects. In many programmes there are still benefits to be realized after the programme has closed. Further updates of the business case may be required.

More guidance is available in sections 19.3 and 19.5.

## 10.7 THE KEY ROLES

In the case of programmes involving more than one sponsoring organization, each organization will have its own business case. The sponsoring group may find it difficult to select the SRO of the overall programme and its business case. One approach to resolving this issue is to consider the financial input to the programme. Since the financial investment underpins the viability of the programme, the organization with the largest financial stake usually nominates the SRO to be responsible for the overall business case.

The development of the business case and the input of specific information will inevitably require expertise from other members of the programme management team and, in some cases, input from external specialists. On larger programmes, it may be necessary to appoint a programme accountant to carry out this responsibility on behalf of the programme manager.

Table 10.2 contains a summary of the key roles and typical areas of focus.

There is no specific guidance for the two main control boards (sponsoring group and programme board) because they are forums where decisions are made and direction set with input from the four key roles. Therefore, guidance has been restricted to individuals rather than broadened to groups.

This in no way weakens or undermines the roles of the sponsoring group or the programme board, which are essential for any essential programme and have their responsibilities set out in Chapter 4.

**Table 10.2 The business case and the key roles**

| Role | Area of focus |
|---|---|
| Senior responsible owner (SRO) | Answering to the sponsoring group for the successful delivery of the programme and achievement of the business case |
| | Securing investment for the programme |
| | Ensuring that the business case is controlled and audit trails are in place to account for changes as the programme develops |
| | Scanning the business horizons surrounding the programme for issues that will lead to realignment of the programme in some way |
| | Ensuring that the progress of the programme remains aligned with the business case |
| | Consulting with the sponsoring group to identify any early-warning indicators of change that may undermine the business case or cause it to lose strategic alignment |
| | Initiating independent assurance reviews of business case viability |
| Programme manager | Preparing the business case |
| | Supporting the SRO in the ongoing validation and review of the business case |
| | Managing the programme's expenditure against the overall investment defined in the business case |
| | Identifying opportunities to optimize the business case |
| Business change manager(s) (BCM) | Profiling the benefits and dis-benefits and their associated costs |
| | Ensuring that benefits continue to be valid through regular business case reviews |
| | Ensuring that the full cost of change is being captured in the business case |
| | Identifying operational risks to the business case and ensuring that they are controlled |
| | Measuring benefits at the start of the programme and tracking throughout to inform the net benefits |
| | Managing business change costs |
| | Managing benefits realization costs |
| | Realizing the profiled benefits |
| Programme office | Supporting the SRO and the programme manager in compiling and updating the business case |
| | Collecting and maintaining business case information |
| | Facilitating business case reviews |

# Risk and issue management

11

# 11 Risk and issue management

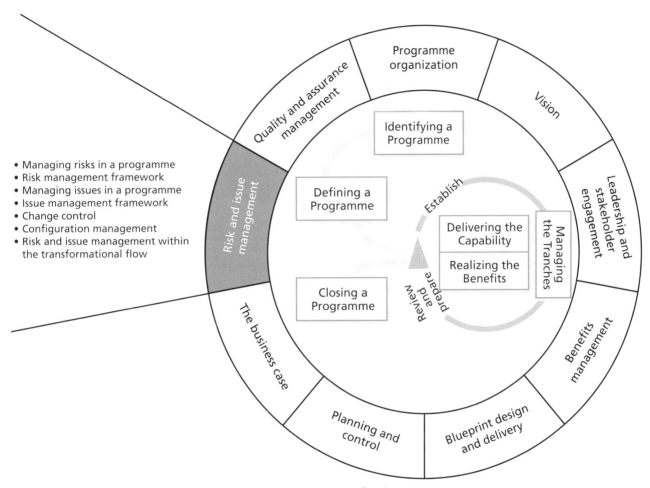

- Managing risks in a programme
- Risk management framework
- Managing issues in a programme
- Issue management framework
- Change control
- Configuration management
- Risk and issue management within the transformational flow

*Figure 11.1 Overview of how risk and issue management fits into MSP*

## 11.1 INTRODUCTION

At any point during a programme, there may be events or situations which can affect the direction of the programme, the delivery of its outputs and capability, the achievement of outcomes or the realization of expected benefits. These events or situations are the risks and issues that the programme has to manage and resolve.

Successful programme management has at its core the need to both manage and tolerate uncertainty, complexity and ambiguity. Risk and issue management are the vehicles for achieving this, where:

- A **risk** is an uncertain event (or set of events) which, should it occur, will have an effect on the achievement of objectives. This effect

need not be detrimental. A risk can be either a threat (i.e. an uncertain event that could have a negative impact on objectives or benefits) or an opportunity (i.e. an uncertain event that could have a favourable impact on objectives or benefits).

- **Issues** are events that have happened, were not planned and require management actions. Risks, should they occur, become issues.

The aim of programme risk and issue management is to support better decision-making through a good understanding of risks and issues and their likely impact.

*Management of Risk: Guidance for Practitioners* (M_o_R) is the well-established standard guide that explains risk management concepts and approaches in detail. This chapter builds on the proven concepts that are relevant and specific to successful risk and issue management within a programme. It includes a section on configuration management (see section 11.7) to support effective change control over the programme's assets where they have been affected by issues.

Figure 11.1 provides an overview of how the risk and issue management governance theme fits into MSP.

### 11.1.1 Sources and perspectives

Risks and issues can emerge from a variety of sources – for example:

- Benefits management, transition activities, costs, scope and timescales
- Dependencies, constraints, assumptions, quality of operations, resources and programme deliverables
- Anything that cannot be resolved by the project, or issues common to more than one project
- Stakeholders, organization and programme staff, and third parties
- Degradation of operational performance beyond acceptable levels
- Ambiguity or lack of knowledge about the 'as-is' state, interim state and the desired end state
- Other projects and programmes under way within the organization.

Programmes also interface with other organizational perspectives as can be seen in Figure 11.2. In order to anticipate risks at an early stage and tackle issues appropriately, it is important to understand these perspectives and continuously evaluate them during the programme's life.

#### 11.1.1.1 Strategic level

Changes at the strategic level can affect the programme, its interdependencies with other initiatives and ultimately its outcomes and benefits realization. Areas to consider include:

- Changes that are driven by external political, economic, social, legislative, environmental and technical factors
- Other programmes, including inter-programme dependencies
- Cross-organizational initiatives, including working with third-party suppliers or partners
- Internal political pressures.

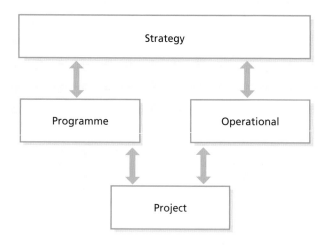

**Figure 11.2 Interrelationships between different organizational perspectives**

#### 11.1.1.2 Programme level

Programmes focus on delivering benefits to the organization and often affect a wide variety of stakeholders both internally and externally, positively and negatively. Risk management for a programme must be designed to work across organizational boundaries in order to accommodate these differing interests and ensure that stakeholders are engaged appropriately.

Typically, the principal areas of risk and issues within a programme relate to:

- Aggregating threats from projects
- Lack of consensus within the steering group or programme board
- Lack of clarity about the expected benefits and the buy-in from key stakeholders
- The complexity and complications associated with working across organizational boundaries, which also tend to lead to a larger and more diverse group of stakeholders
- The management of interdependencies between the programme and its projects, and between the programme and its wider context
- Lack of certainty about funding
- Unrealistic timescales resulting from poor planning

■ Availability of suitable resources to deliver the programme.

### 11.1.1.3 Project level

The project outputs within a programme are the vehicles for delivering the programme outcomes and benefits; therefore, much of the focus of risk and issue management within a programme is from the project perspective. The programme should set the risk and issue management standards for the project and then give staff the authority to manage their risks and issues within these parameters.

Areas where project risks and issues arise include:

■ Lack of clarity of customer requirements
■ Timely availability of resources with the right skills and expertise
■ Realism about timescales
■ Quality expectations
■ Lack of visibility of the blueprint and the context of what the project is delivering
■ Procurement and acquisition
■ Scope creep and scheduling
■ Lack of visibility of programme risks at the project level.

To manage the risks to projects well, the programme needs to ensure that each project brief outlines the risks from the perspective of the programme and then to request the project to provide regular feedback to the programme's risk management activities.

### 11.1.1.4 Operational level

As projects deliver their outputs, the transition to new ways of working and new systems can lead to further sources of risk. For example, during a handover process, risks and issues could arise from the need to maintain operational stability as well as the integrity of the systems, infrastructure and support services. Transition must hence be properly planned, managed and resourced.

Areas to consider include:

■ The quality of the benefit-enabling outputs from the projects within the programme
■ Organizational and cultural issues and the increased likelihood of changes to the organizational environment because of the naturally longer timescales under which programmes operate

■ Business continuity and survival
■ Transfer of outputs to operations and ability to cope with the new ways of working
■ Commitment from business operations
■ Stakeholder support
■ Industrial relations
■ Rate and amount of changes
■ Availability of resources to support the changes
■ Organizational track record of managing change.

### 11.1.2 M_o_R risk management principles

The key principles for risk management at programme level are that it:

■ Aligns with objectives
■ Fits the context
■ Engages stakeholders
■ Provides clear guidance
■ Informs decision-making
■ Facilitates continual improvement
■ Creates a supportive culture
■ Achieves measurable value.

Application of these principles is essential for the development of good programme risk management practices. They are informed by proven corporate governance principles and the international standard for risk management, ISO 31000: 2009. They recognize that programme risk management should be aligned to the organization's internal controls, adapted and applied to the context of the programme. Adherence to these principles enables programmes to tailor the organization's risk management practices to meet their specific needs.

## 11.2 MANAGING RISKS IN A PROGRAMME

Before the risk management cycle can operate, the specific arrangements for managing risk need to be specified.

### 11.2.1 Risk management strategy

The risk management strategy is created and approved in Defining a Programme, and it describes an approach to risk management which reflects the programme's unique objectives. This guide describes the specific management activities that will be undertaken within the programme.

The strategy should reflect the organization's risk policies and process guidance (where these exist). These may define the risk management process to be followed and the priorities to be observed by the programme to ensure it is compliant with the organization's risk governance arrangements.

Building on these corporate standards, the programme will set its own appetite and culture for managing its risks in the programme's strategy documents.

In a portfolio environment, much of the strategy may be prescribed, and a key role of the strategy is to prescribe to the projects how they will manage their risks.

The risk management strategy should clarify how opportunities will be managed, and describe how the interface with the benefits management approach will be handled as defined in the benefits management strategy.

The risk management strategy should be clear about how information flows will work in the programme. One of the dangers is that programme, projects and operations manage their risks in isolation from one another, so the full picture cannot be seen (or, conversely, all the risks are captured in one place, which can result in key details being buried in the volume of information).

### 11.2.2 Risk appetite

Risk appetite is the amount of risk that the organization, or subset of it, is willing to accept. Understanding corporate risk appetite is essential for a programme to devise a successful risk management strategy, steer project risk activities and define aggregation and escalation rules. Properly defined and communicated, risk appetite helps to insulate a programme from unwelcome surprises and provides it and its projects with clear tolerances in which to operate.

### 11.2.3 Tolerance thresholds

Thresholds translate risk appetite into a guideline that steers programme and project behaviour. Thresholds define the exposure to risks on one level that, if exceeded, requires escalation and reaction from the level above. This applies to projects and their programme (as well as the programme and the organization to which it reports).

When setting tolerance for projects, it is important that the programme manager sets tolerance in line with the objectives of the programme. There may be certain requirements from a project that have no tolerance: for example, risks that may affect the dependencies on benefits activities. Setting generic tolerance thresholds may hide aggregating threats from the programme board and senior responsible owner (SRO). The same applies to operational risks; for example, delays in one area may have a domino effect across the programme that goes beyond tolerance thresholds, but they are only discovered when they are triggered.

### 11.2.4 Assumptions

When a programme's business case (or the business cases of the projects within the programme) is created, 'assumptions' are often used to define the boundary of the programme and provide for uncertainties outside its immediate area of influence.

Assumptions are the result of uncertainty, and the likelihood of a particular event (or sequence of events) having a result on which the programme is depending. A false assumption can have a serious effect on the programme, and it is therefore recommended that programme assumptions are treated as sources of risk; each should be recorded in the risk register and managed accordingly.

Project assumptions should be reviewed at programme level to see if they should be viewed as sources of risk to the programme and managed accordingly. The project should then manage the assumption as a risk.

### 11.2.5 Early-warning indicators

Risk management needs to be proactive to anticipate potential problems. Early-warning indicators can be used to provide information on the potential sources of risk, or as a way of tracking sensitive risks, triggering further corrective actions if predefined levels are reached. Whilst these early-warning indicators could measure a number of diverse wide-ranging monitors, they are only of value if they:

- Are measuring valid indicators
- Are reviewed on a regular basis
- Use accurate information
- Reach decision makers and are acted upon.

Early-warning indicators are vital for a programme, as they provide measures that give advanced warning of trends or events that could adversely affect the programme's outcomes. Key early-warning indicators relating directly to the programme's objectives might include:

■ Requests to change key programme information, such as the vision statement and blueprint, that set the agenda for the programme
■ Reduction or delays in the delivery of expected/planned benefits on time and on budget
■ Increase in the level of aggregated risk resulting from project and operational risks
■ Changes to organizational structures
■ Changes to services or products
■ Changes to processes.

## 11.2.6 Risk register

The risk register is a repository used to capture information about risks in a consistent and structured manner. It is created during Defining a Programme; any existing risks at that point will be described in the programme brief. Each organization will need to decide on the specific layout of its register. The programme's risk management strategy defines in detail the content and purpose of this repository. The programme's projects will also maintain their own repositories, and the programme will coordinate its activities with a separate register. In addition, the risk management strategy defines how risks are reported and escalated. Finally, the strategy determines how accountability for certain types of risks, those that pose an aggregated threat on programme level or span beyond individual projects, will change between the projects and the programme if required.

Appendix A provides a description of a typical risk register.

## 11.2.7 Threat and opportunity

Most people define risks as threats to the programme, but some risks actually provide opportunities to improve a programme's outcomes and benefits. What constitutes a threat or an opportunity can vary, and the same event can have very different impacts on individual projects;

furthermore, once these threats or opportunities are aggregated at programme level, the resulting effects change again.

Whether a threat or an opportunity, it is important to remember that there may be one or more events that will trigger the threat and cause the risk to be realized. Differentiating between the threat/opportunity and the event will help the programme to focus its risk response. It may not be possible to remove the threat or opportunity, but it might be possible to avoid or remove events that will trigger the risk.

### Tip

There is the potential for overlap between risk management and benefits management best practice when an opportunity becomes a potential benefit.

Organizations can achieve effective opportunity management by categorizing all opportunities as benefits, and only including threats in the risk register. There is no right or wrong way of handling this, as long as opportunities are managed through one of the two approaches. Each organization needs to confirm its approach in its risk and benefits management strategies.

## 11.2.8 Evaluating risks

The uncertainty associated with risks is expressed as the probability of their becoming issues. A risk will potentially impact the programme in a number of ways: for instance, cost, time and benefits. These may be shown in the form of a probability impact grid, giving the criteria for each level within the scale, e.g. for very high, high, medium, low and very low. Probability and impact values can be attributed to these ratings so that ranking values can be calculated for each cell of the grid.

'Expected value' is a way of estimating the financial exposure of risks by discounting the total cost of their impact against the probability of their occurrence. It is calculated by multiplying the estimated average risk impact by the estimated probability to give a weighted risk.

For example, if a risk has a probability of 60% with the estimated cost of the impact of the risk occurring at £5,000, the expected value of the risk is 60% of £5,000 = £3,000.

This is not meaningful for an individual risk, as the cost of the risk occurring is its full cost. However, it does help to provide an understanding of the total risk exposure faced by the programme by totalling the expected values for all the risks identified for the programme.

When evaluating risks, the programme manager can mandate the use of several techniques to understand the net effect of the identified threats and opportunities on a programme when aggregated. This may include preparing, for example:

- An estimated monetary value (EMV) calculation, which records the weighted average of the anticipated impact
- A risk model, which aggregates the risks together using a simulation technique
- A net present value (NPV) calculation using an accepted discount rate.

### 11.2.9 Risk aggregation

Individual threats can have an aggregated impact, where the net effect of threats (and opportunities) changes when they are combined. At project level, a small risk can have limited impact. But if the risk is combined with other risks in adjacent projects, it can produce a significant impact at programme level. An identified risk can be of concern for a project, but there might be an opportunity in another project that cancels or compensates for the effect. This aggregation is particularly important when evaluating risks across the programme. Dependencies between risks need to be taken into account as well as the distinction between threats and opportunities.

As an example, consider currency exchange rates: the future movement of these rates can have an impact on individual projects, but the accumulated effect is often only visible at the higher programme level.

At programme level, project and operational risks can therefore:

- Accumulate to a critical mass
- Grow (where the sum of the risks is bigger than the individual parts)
- Reduce (where the sum of the risks is smaller than the individual parts).

Risks can also be interdependent. The appearance of one risk can lead to a cascade of other risks materializing with either aggregated or individual effects. When crafting a response, identifying such relationships can save significant effort for the programme: instead of spreading activities between all risks, focusing on the mitigation of the root cause risk in the relationship can also help to avoid all the other risks.

There are also risks that affect a number of programmes. Intra-programme risks may involve any aspect of the programme: for example, internal or external resources, suppliers, stakeholders, changes to blueprints or budgetary changes.

All of these aggregated risks require attention from the programme manager. One of the reasons that programmes are conceived in the first place (as opposed to running independent projects) is that they add the required management layer that allows such issues to be detected and adequately addressed. The value of a programme is hence not only in the realization of benefits that individual projects cannot achieve, but also in the management of risks that individual projects cannot deal with.

All the critical risks across the programme, and the interactions between them, can be shown using a summary risk profile (see Figure 11.3), which expands the concept of the individual probability impact grid. The grid provides a useful visual explanation of aggregations and interdependencies. This shows how risks of a certain impact and probability for individual projects (white circles in the diagram) can have a very different effect on the programme (coloured circles): an example would be interest rate effects that cancel each other out, or environmental effects of individual projects that could multiply at a programme level.

To manage aggregation, the programme manager will need to know details of:

- The major threats and opportunities
- When specific risks could manifest themselves in operations/projects
- The level of impact in each operation/project
- The overall level of impact across the programme
- The cost of contingency to meet the impact

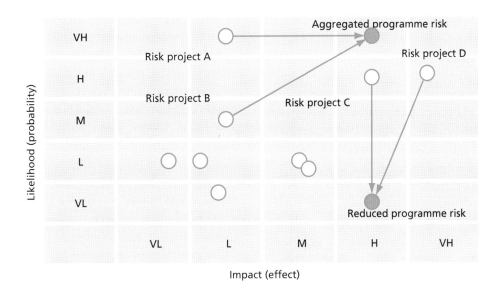

*Figure 11.3 Summary risk profile*

- The mitigation plan to contain the impact locally
- The mitigation plan to minimize the impact on the programme.

The programme office should play a central role in building and maintaining efficient, effective and consistent two-way flows of information between the programme and its projects. Using risk checklists can simplify the process and establish consistency.

## 11.2.10 Proximity

'Proximity' reflects the fact that risks will occur at particular times in the future and the expected value will vary according to when they occur. Whereas an understanding of a risk's probability and impact informs management of the priority of a risk, understanding a risk's proximity informs management of its impending urgency. Knowing the proximity also helps to identify the appropriate response and the required trigger and timing of the response.

## 11.2.11 Progress reporting

Programmes need to monitor the evolution of their overall risk exposure. A progress report, whether as a separate document or incorporated within other progress reports, is a useful tool to maintain oversight. Programmes should use progress reports to monitor overall risk and issue trends across the entire programme, risks at their own level, aggregated and escalated projects risk,

and key project risks if required. A well-defined and maintained progress report is the main control for programmes to manage their risks and issues.

The programme's strategies will define how progress reports are composed. Typical content of a progress report includes:

- Progress of planned risk management action
- Effectiveness of implemented actions
- Trend analysis of closed and new risks and issues
- Spend against contingencies
- Numbers emerging in the different categories
- Numbers emerging in the different projects
- Anticipated emerging or aggregated risks that will require specific management attention
- Movement of risk against key programme objectives and benefits.

## 11.3 RISK MANAGEMENT FRAMEWORK

This section describes a risk management framework, which comprises a cycle of steps that are repeated through the life of the programme and additional activities that apply to each of the steps (see Figure 11.4). The cycle of steps is:

- Identify
- Assess
- Plan
- Implement.

These steps are supported by activities to:

- Communicate
- Embed and review.

> **Tip**
>
> The cycle is applicable to both the programme and its constituent projects, and it is described in detail in *Management of Risk*. Risk cycle activities will be repeated throughout the transformational flow as described later. During Managing the Tranches, Delivering the Capability and Realizing the Benefits, the programme must continue to constantly scan for new risks, assess them, plan and implement the responses.

### 11.3.1 Communicate

Rather than being a distinct element, communication is an activity that is carried out throughout the whole risk management cycle. Effective communication is key to the identification of new threats and opportunities or changes in existing risks. Horizon-scanning in particular depends on the maintenance of a good communications network, including relevant contacts and sources of information to facilitate the identification of changes that may affect the programme's overall risk exposure.

The implementation of risk management is dependent on participation, and participation, in turn, is dependent on communication. It is important for management to engage with staff across the programme as well as with wider stakeholders.

### 11.3.2 Embed and review

'Embed and review' ensures risk management is being appropriately and successfully handled within the programme and across the organization. It should ensure that the risk management strategy is being followed.

It looks at each individual step of the framework to determine its contribution to the overall quality or risk management. The use of health checks and maturity models support organizational efforts to gain maximum value from investment in risk management.

### 11.3.3 Risk management cycle

#### 11.3.3.1 Identify step

Programme risk management starts with the identification of uncertain events articulated as threats and opportunities. Thus:

- Good practice for a first activity is to explore the programme context: understanding what are the programme's objectives and scope, what assumptions have been made, who the stakeholders are, where the programme fits inside the organization and the current environment. Knowledge of the context enables the programme to search for risk methodically and later devise the most appropriate responses.
- The second activity is the identification of actual risks, both threats to the programmes objectives as well as opportunities to overachieve on outcomes and benefits. Once identified, the risks will be entered into the risk register.

#### 11.3.3.2 Assess step

The assessment of risk can be broken down into two activities:

- Estimate the threats and the opportunities to the programme in terms of their probability, impact and proximity
- Evaluate the net aggregated effect of the identified threats and opportunities on the programme.

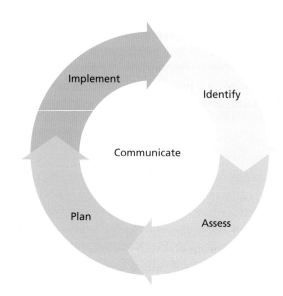

***Figure 11.4 Programme risk management cycle***

Evaluation is especially important for programmes where individual smaller project risks can quickly aggregate to a substantial risk at programme level.

The assessment should also help to form a view of the aggregated level of risk that the programme is facing as it progresses.

### 11.3.3.3 Plan step

The primary goal of the plan element is to prepare specific management responses to the threats and opportunities that have been identified, ideally to remove or reduce the threats and to maximize the opportunities. Attention to this process ensures as far as possible that the business and its staff are not taken by surprise if a risk materializes.

For each risk that has been identified and appropriately assessed, the project or programme has a series of responses available that it can use individually or in combination to deflect a threat or help to realize an opportunity. Table 11.1 lists these responses.

It is common for risk responses not to be fully effective, in that they do not remove the risk in its entirety. This leaves a residual risk. If the original risk was significant and the risk response was only partially successful, the remaining risk can be considerable.

### 11.3.3.4 Implement step

The primary goal of the implement element is to ensure that the planned risk management actions are implemented and monitored as to their effectiveness, and corrective action is taken where responses do not match expectations.

An important part of this is to ensure that clear roles and responsibilities are allocated, so that someone is responsible for the management and control of the risk, and that risk actionees are identified to implement the response action allocated to them. The key roles are:

- **Risk owner** Responsible for the management and control of all aspects of the risks assigned to them, including managing, tracking and reporting the implementation of the selected actions to address the threats or to maximize the opportunities
- **Risk actionee** Responsible for the implementation of risk response actions. They support and take direction from the risk owner.

## 11.4 MANAGING ISSUES IN A PROGRAMME

Issues can occur at any point from the launch of the programme at the beginning of Identifying a Programme to when the programme closes. Some issues may be unresolved at the end of the programme, and responsibility for these may need to be transferred to operational management.

The governance arrangements for managing issues are developed and approved in Defining a Programme. These are documented in the issue management strategy. During Defining a Programme, issues are managed according the governance arrangements that are part of the programme preparation plan, which is produced and approved in Identifying a Programme.

### 11.4.1 Issue definition

An issue is a relevant event that has happened, was not planned and requires management action. The action required may be to fix a problem or to change the boundary of the programme. An issue generally emerges from one of a number of sources, for example:

- Constraints identified at the outset of the programme
- Within the programme itself
- In operational areas to be changed by the programme, where these have a consequential impact on the programme
- From an escalation of a programme's constituent projects
- As generated by stakeholders
- Other sources external to the programme (e.g. changes to corporate strategy or conflicts with other concurrent change initiatives).

Issues that occur in a project may need to be escalated if they fall outside the project's tolerance levels set by the programme. Issue management in a programme needs to cover all of these circumstances.

A common cause of overload in a programme is when it tries to manage the project issues directly and does not effectively manage escalation and delegation. However, the programme manager does need to be satisfied that the project teams are managing issues to a satisfactory standard and

**Table 11.1 Threat and opportunity responses**

| Response options | Use |
|---|---|
| Avoid a threat<br>Exploit an opportunity | This option is about making the uncertain situation certain by removing the risk. This can often be achieved by removing the cause of a threat, or by implementing the cause of an opportunity. This option may be adopted for no extra cost by changing the way the work is planned. More often though, costs will be incurred in order to remove all residual risk for threats and opportunities. Where costs are incurred these must be justified, i.e. the cost of response is warranted to make the situation certain. |
| Reduce a threat<br>Enhance an opportunity | This option chooses definite action now to change the probability and/or the impact of the risk. The term 'mitigate' is relevant when discussing reduction of a threat, i.e. making the threat less likely to occur and/or reducing the impact if it did. Enhancing an opportunity is the reverse process, i.e. making the opportunity more likely to occur and/or increasing the impact if it did. Again, because this option commits the organization to costs for reduction/enhancement now, response costs must be justified in terms of the change to residual risk. |
| Transfer the risk (threat or opportunity) | Transfer is an option that aims to pass part of the risk to a third party. Insurance is the classic form of transfer, where the insurer picks up the risk cost, but where the insured retains the impact on other objectives, e.g. time delay. Transfer can apply to opportunities, where a third party gains a cost benefit but the primary risk taker gains another benefit, but this is not a commonly used option whereas transfer of threats is commonly used. Once again, the cost of transference must be justified in terms of the change to residual risk – is the premium you pay worth it? It is important to note that some elements of risk cannot be transferred, although an organization may choose to delegate the management of the risks to a third party. |
| Share the risk (threat or opportunity) | 'Share' is an option that is different in nature from the transfer response. It seeks for multiple parties, typically within a supply chain, to share the risk on a pain/gain share basis. Rarely can risks be entirely shared in this way (for example, the primary risk taker will always need to protect its brand and reputation), but this can be a successful way of encouraging collaboration on risk management activities, particularly in programmes and projects. |
| Accept the risk | The 'accept' option means that the organization 'takes the chance' that the risk will occur, with its full impact if it did. There is no change to residual risk with the accept option, but neither are any costs incurred now to manage the risk, or to prepare to manage the risk in future. An example would be the risk to profitability as a result of currency fluctuations. An organization may decide to take the chance and not engage in any hedging or other provision to protect margins from wide variation in rates. This option would not be appropriate if the risk exposure exceeded the risk tolerance threshold for the organizational activity in question. Note that in a case such as currency fluctuations where the impact could be positive or negative, this is actually two risks, because a risk is the relationship between the uncertain event and the impact of that event. There is a risk leading to loss and the risk leading to gain. Framing the uncertainty as two risks allows for different responses to each part. |
| Prepare contingent plans | This option involves preparing plans now, but not taking action now. Most usually associated with the accept option, preparing contingent plans in this instance is saying: 'We will accept the risk for now, but we'll make a plan for what we'll do if the situation changes.' This option applies equally to other responses and is often referred to as a 'fallback' plan, i.e. what we will do if the original response doesn't work. Fallback plans apply to all other strategies, even avoiding a threat and exploiting an opportunity, because the plan to avoid/exploit may not be successful despite good intentions.<br><br>This option is important because it builds in future managerial flexibility for a smaller committed cost than investing in more proactive strategies. This does not mean that investing now to respond to a risk is wrong, but such investments do need to be cost-justified as previously mentioned. |

that the aggregated impact on the programme from all issues in all its projects is understood and acceptable.

Issues can typically be classified into one of the following three types:

■ A previously identified risk that has now materialized and requires appropriate issue management action
■ A request for change to some aspect of the programme, an operation or a project
■ A problem affecting all or part of the programme in some way.

### 11.4.2 Issue management strategy

The issue management strategy describes the programme's approach to issue management and is similar to the way risk management is described in the risk management strategy.

The issue management strategy outlines how issues will be identified, categorized, severity-rated and then managed, and how change control will be applied, and it includes any specific reference to other strategies that support it.

The issue management strategy should contain clear guidance on how issues will be managed across the programme, projects and operations. This will require clear routes through which issues can be escalated to the programme or delegated from the programme to projects or operational areas.

A key element to be defined by the issue management strategy will be the change control procedures. One of the dangers faced by a programme is the lack of control of minor changes that may happen at project or operational levels and which may seem inconsequential in themselves. These can aggregate and eventually deliver significant deviation from what is needed to fulfil the requirements defined in the blueprint, undermining the achievement of benefits (see section 11.6).

Appendix A provides a description the contents of a typical issue management strategy.

### 11.4.3 Issue register

Issues are recorded in the issue register, which is created in Defining a Programme. Any existing issues at that time will be stated in the programme brief. The issue register is similar to the risk register

and is a repository that focuses on all identified issues that have occurred; it includes former risks if these have materialized. The shape, content and purpose of this register are defined in the issue management strategy. Appendix A provides a description of a typical issue register.

The programme office should play a central role in building and maintaining efficient, effective and consistent operation of issue management. The programme office manages and coordinates the information and support systems, and provides support and advice on the issue management cycle.

## 11.5 ISSUE MANAGEMENT FRAMEWORK

This section describes an issue management framework which is similar to the risk management framework as it describes a cycle supported by ongoing activities. The issue management cycle (see Figure 11.5) comprises five steps:

■ Capture
■ Examine
■ Propose course of action
■ Decide
■ Implement.

And the ongoing activities are:

■ Monitor and control
■ Embed and review.

### 11.5.1 Monitor and control

Issue management actions, like other activities in the programme, need to be actively monitored and controlled. This is to ensure that:

■ The resolution can be achieved within the estimates of time and cost
■ The impact on the overall risk profile of the programme is not greater than anticipated
■ The impact on the planned capability is acceptable
■ Benefits are not adversely impacted more than estimated in the initial assessment
■ Progress or changes in other parts of the programme don't render these resolution actions inappropriate
■ The impact on the organization's performance is managed.

More information on monitoring and control can be found in Chapter 9.

### 11.5.2 Embed and review

'Embed and review' ensures that issue management is being appropriately and successfully handled within each programme and ultimately across the organization.

It looks at each individual step of the cycle to determine its contribution to the overall quality of issue management. Health checks and maturity models can be used to support organizational efforts to gain maximum value from their investment in issue management.

A key review point for all aspects of managing the programme is at the end of each tranche. The results from such reviews and the characteristics of the programme for the next tranche may mean that the issue management strategy needs to be refined.

### 11.5.3 Issue management cycle

#### 11.5.3.1 Capture step

The first step is to undertake an initial analysis to determine the type of issue that has been raised. The issue management strategy provides the 'rules' on how this and all other issue management work will be carried out. All issues are recorded in the issue register as soon as they are identified.

When capturing the issue, it should be categorized, its severity and impact assessed, and it should be allocated to an individual or group for examination.

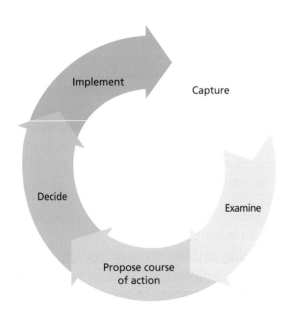

**Figure 11.5 Issue management cycle**

The initial decision might be to direct the issue to where it can most appropriately be managed. Some issues will be managed by the programme. Major issues may need to be escalated to the sponsoring group if the issues are outside the authority of the programme, and smaller issues can be delegated to an appropriate project.

#### 11.5.3.2 Examine step

The next step is to examine the issue by undertaking an impact analysis. The analysis should consider the impact that the issue and the options for its resolution will have on:

- The programme's performance, especially how benefits realization will be affected
- The programme business case
- The programme risk profile, i.e. the impact on the overall risk exposure of the programme
- The programme blueprint
- The projects dossier and the programme dependency network
- The programme's stakeholders, differentiating between those directly impacted and the wider range of stakeholders
- The operational performance of the organization and existing transition plans
- Supplier contracts and service level agreements.

The uncertain nature of some programmes means that the approach for future tranches is unclear. In such cases the impact analysis may be more appropriately conducted on the current tranche rather than the whole of the remaining programme. Where ongoing and future tranches are unclear, the review at the end of the current tranche will use the lessons learned so far to develop the approach for the rest of the programme. Whilst this might mean substantial changes for future activities, it might not be appropriate to manage these as issues, rather to re-visit Defining a Programme. See section 10.4.

Impact analysis in a programme must cover the broader view: the programme, its projects, operations and strategic objectives. In cross-organization programmes, the impact on the separate businesses will need to be considered; section 4.14.2 provides more information on this. Having undertaken the impact analysis, the severity and priority of the issue should be evaluated.

As a minimum, an issue should always be assessed against the impact on the projects, the blueprint and the benefits.

The issue register should be updated.

### 11.5.3.3 Propose course of action step

Alternative options should be considered before proposing a course of action to take.

The action chosen should maintain an acceptable balance between the advantage to be gained (benefits), and the impact on time, cost and risk. Where there are concurrent change initiatives affecting the same operational areas, this acceptable balance may require an assessment across these other programmes and projects.

Some changes may be mandatory, for example to comply with new legislation. The focus might then be to achieve compliance with minimum impact. However, in such cases the analysis work should explore where the mandatory change opens up other opportunities to improve the programme's performance and benefits.

The issue register should be updated.

### 11.5.3.4 Decide step

The issue management strategy will define who has the authority to make decisions about issues. The programme manager may be able to resolve or delegate minor issues without reference to any other role for a decision.

Other issues may need to be referred to the SRO. In some cases the proposal may need to be referred to a specialist role such as the design authority to ensure that the actions to be implemented do not result in further issues. Where the response action impacts an operational area, it may be appropriate to involve the business change manager (BCM).

If a decision is made to make a change, then this change should be planned, with appropriate recognition of the need for contingency, additional resources and a fall-back plan should the change cause unexpected problems.

The programme change procedures as defined in the issue management strategy should be triggered to gain authority and control the change. When a decision is made there will be an issue owner, issue actionee and a response action plan. The issue register should also be updated.

### 11.5.3.5 Implement step

The programme manager will communicate the decisions and response action plan to appropriate stakeholders for several reasons:

- So that personnel, especially each issue actionee, are aware of changes to their work schedules and can undertake their assigned tasks to fix the problems or implement the changes
- To inform those who raised the issue what course of action is being pursued
- To inform other stakeholders who may be affected by any changes
- To demonstrate effective management of the programme and maintain the confidence of the broader range of stakeholders.

The issue register is updated, and all other documents are revised where the decision affects their content. In particular, some of the programme's plans will almost always need to be updated. During the analysis of the issue in the 'examine' and 'propose' steps, the relationship between the issue and specific benefits will have been identified. The appropriate benefit profiles may now need to be updated. The programme's business case may need to be updated, as time, cost, risk and benefits may be affected by the decision. However, it might not be sensible to do this for every issue.

The change is then applied and the impact of the change monitored and lessons learned from its introduction. The impact of these should then be used for the assessment of future changes.

The configuration management information should be updated to reflect the change and impact on dependent assets related to the change.

The business case may need to be reviewed and updated.

## 11.6 CHANGE CONTROL

Programmes are inherently about delivering change, but they do not work in isolation, and changes are happening to the environment they are delivering to all the time. This can result in changing business requirements, reactions to unplanned events or failures, and loss of stakeholder confidence, all of which can affect the ability of the programme to deliver its objectives. There is a particular risk that small changes across a number of projects may conflict, and because of their apparent insignificance they may pass through unnoticed.

If good governance is in place, it is likely that the major issues will be under control, but it is important to ensure that rigour and control processes are applied to all changes at the project and programme level. Many small changes can have a serious aggregated effect on the overall programme and may go totally unnoticed. The issue management strategy sets out how issues and change control within a programme should work.

The basic steps of change control are:

- Capture the change and define why it is needed
- Allocate a priority so that the urgency is understood
- Assess the impact across the programme
- Analyse the options and test the potential solutions
- Authorize the resolution that is agreed (which could include no action)
- Implement the change and monitor the effects of the change for deviations from what is anticipated
- Review the effectiveness and update associated documentation.

All changes should undergo an assessment that considers their impact on at least the following:

- Programme plan
- Blueprint
- Benefits
- Projects dossier.

Programme changes are processed via issue management. Configuration management provides the control for managing these changes, as it not only helps to assess the impact of proposed changes but also recognizes that a change in a particular configuration item may necessitate a change in other items.

## 11.7 CONFIGURATION MANAGEMENT

The purpose of configuration management in a programme is to control the development of, and changes to, items that are important to the programme. These items include programme management documentation as well as the assets, products and services created by the programme. Configuration management covers the programme's dependencies on items outside of its control as well as those within the programme. All assets that are created by the programme are recorded as programme configurations and separate programme configuration items. Configuration management enables the function and physical characteristics of a configuration item, a particular configuration, a product or a service to be identified and recorded.

Configuration management specifies how the individual configuration items fit together into configurations. Important information about the desired configurations can be derived from the blueprint. Each item and configuration describes a programme's products or services; thus, it is possible to recognize how changing one configuration item will affect the way the product or service works. This is invaluable in change control as it facilitates impact analysis and reduces the risk of change having an adverse impact on the programme.

Configuration management provides information about items that need to be tested, independently and collectively with other items. The results of testing will be an indication of the status of each item, and eventually the entire configuration. Configuration items only become baselined when they have passed their quality controls.

Configuration management will be necessary in the programme's projects. The arrangements for configuration management at the programme and project levels must be carefully designed to ensure that they operate effectively together, as the quality of the products delivered by the programme will in part depend on quality at the project level.

Inclusion of the configuration management arrangement in the programme's information management strategy assists with both quality assurance and quality control.

### 11.7.1 Configuration management steps

There are five basic processes involved in programme-level configuration management:

1 **Planning** Based on the blueprint and the organization's approach to configuration management, decide what level of configuration management is appropriate for the programme and plan how it will be

achieved. The programme will then set out the requirements for configuration management that all its projects should adopt.

2  **Identifying**  This includes all of the programme-level configurations of assets created during the programme and any dependencies. A system for describing configuration items must be set up.

3  **Controlling**  Once the programme definition document is agreed, the configuration of the programme is baselined. Most programmes will change over time, and it is crucial that any changes to the configuration are properly version-controlled following procedures described in the information management strategy. Version control also includes managing all of the programme's management information. The programme should set out how dependencies on external assets will be managed in the event of external assets being revised. Control over an asset passes to business as usual when that asset is agreed to be no longer the responsibility of the programme.

4  **Status accounting**  This involves maintaining current and historical information concerned with each configuration, the configuration items (assets) and all dependencies – those external to the programme as well as inter-project dependencies.

5  **Verifying**  This includes auditing the programme to ensure that there is conformity between the documented configuration and the actual status of products and configuration items before delivery to operations. The dependencies are also verified as part of this audit, as these may have moved over time.

The programme's approach to configuration management is set out in the information management strategy, which is covered in Chapter 12 and Appendix A.

## 11.8  RISK AND ISSUE MANAGEMENT WITHIN THE TRANSFORMATIONAL FLOW

This section covers how the risk and issue management governance theme is applied in each of the processes in the transformational flow.

The programme should dedicate specific effort to describe and communicate the usefulness of risk and issue management along with the steps required to achieve this value.

The programme's risk culture should encourage innovation as well as allowing for timely responses to threats. Issues benefit from being shared as early as possible. To gain the most value from risk and issue management, the programme should look into creating an environment of trust where information about risks and issues is willingly shared and discussed.

### 11.8.1  Identifying a Programme

Risk management in this early phase of the programme is focused on identifying and clarifying ambiguity. The programme brief will include an initial set of programme risks and issues identified so far. It should also include possible response actions. Emergent programmes will in addition have to deal with current issues and risks inherited from its pre-existing projects, and consider them thoroughly during the identification phase. These will also be described in the programme brief.

By the end of Identifying a Programme, the risks and issues should be summarized in the programme brief. Failure to recognize key risks or issues at this point could have a serious impact later. More guidance is available in sections 14.5, 14.7 and 14.8.

### 11.8.2  Defining a Programme

The risk management strategy and issue management strategy are created during this process. They describe the principles, practices, tools and information that the programme will use to identify, analyse, monitor and control risk and issues. The risk register and issue register are set up to record risk and issue information and actions required. The initial risk and issue entries in the programme brief should then migrate into their appropriate registers.

This process will include collecting any updates for risks and issues already identified, and capturing new risks and issues. The decision to continue with the programme will be influenced by the risks and issues that surround the vision, blueprint, benefit profiles, programme plan and business case, and risk and issue management supports this decision-making with vital information.

More guidance is available in sections 15.13, 15.17 and 15.18.

### 11.8.3  Managing the Tranches

Following the definition of the programme, Managing the Tranches implements the defined governance arrangements for risk and issue management. Active management of risks and issues continues through every tranche with both risk and issue cycles active, with an assessment of the management processes effectiveness being part of each end-of-tranche review. The key focus of the management will be managing the aggregated risk exposure, monitoring for early-warning indicators of trouble and maintaining alignment of the programme and any threats to its achievement. The proactive and pragmatic resolution of issues will help to keep tranches on track. It is unwise to let issues sit unactioned on the issue register.

More guidance is available in sections 16.3 and 16.4.

### 11.8.4  Delivering the Capability

The programme provides the individual projects with their initial brief. This should include guidance on risk and issue management, which will pre-determine how a project will operate and interact with the programme.

Projects have to pay particular attention to the escalation rules established by the programme and to report any risks and issues that could have potential cross-programme or aggregated effects. The programme must pay attention to aggregated risk and issues, as the total impact of all risks and issues in the programme and its projects can be greater than the sum of their individual parts.

Risks and issues are most likely to be the source of the majority of escalations to the programme and cascade down to projects during delivery, as they will affect the achievement of project objectives and the business case. More guidance is available in sections 17.3 and 17.6.

### 11.8.5  Realizing the Benefits

The purpose of risk and issue management is to help avoid failure. Should any of the tranches deliver below expectation, then this constitutes an issue for the following tranches and needs to be managed accordingly.

During the three stages of this process – pre-transition, transition and post-transition – risk and issue management provides the BCM(s) with the means to anticipate and manage any deviations from the expected benefits realization progress. Any unforeseen events or changes in circumstances can pose a risk to benefits realization.

More guidance is available in sections 18.3.3 and 18.4.3.

### 11.8.6  Closing a Programme

Programmes close for two fundamental reasons:

■ The programme has successfully achieved its set end goals
■ It is not sensible to continue with the programme because one of several possible circumstances has occurred.

When a programme is closed prematurely without having achieved its goals, this is often caused by major issues or risks which the programme cannot effectively overcome. As soon as it becomes evident that the programme might significantly fail to achieve the outputs, outcomes or benefits that it was launched to deliver, it is sensible to consider closing it. Risk and issue management will contribute to the necessary evaluation of the situation and analysis of possible response options.

Whatever the reason for Closing a Programme, the risk and issue management strategies and respective registers need to be reviewed and updated prior to closure. More guidance is available in section 19.6.

## 11.9  THE KEY ROLES

Table 11.2 provides a summary of the key roles and typical areas of focus.

There is no specific guidance for the two main control boards (sponsoring group and programme board) because they are forums where decisions are made and direction set with input from the four key roles. Therefore, guidance has been restricted to individuals rather than broadened to groups.

This in no way weakens or undermines the roles of the sponsoring group or the programme board, which are essential for any essential programme and have their responsibilities set out in Chapter 4.

**Table 11.2 Risk and issue management and the key roles**

| Role | Area of focus |
|---|---|
| Senior responsible owner (SRO) | Authorizes the risk management strategy and issue management strategy and its adjustment, improvement and enforcement |
| | Intervenes to control risks and issues that affect the alignment of the programme with organizational objectives |
| | Initiates assurance reviews of risk and issue management effectiveness |
| | Ownership of strategic risks and issues, ensuring mitigation actions are dealt with at the appropriate senior level |
| Programme manager | Develops and implements the strategies for handling risks and issues |
| | Designs and manages the risk and issue management cycle |
| | Manages the aggregated level of risks and issues |
| | Assures programme adherence to the risk management principles |
| | Allocates risks and issues as appropriate |
| | Ensures that change control is undertaken by individuals with the correct authority |
| | Ensures that the impact of individual and aggregated risks is understood by the relevant stakeholders. |
| | Defines clear rules for escalation, cascade and thresholds |
| | Ownership of programme-level risks and issues |
| | Deploys a consistent language for risk management across the programme and its projects |
| | Communicates the progress of the resolution of issues in a clear and timely fashion across the programme |
| | Escalates items that cross programme boundaries to the SRO for resolution where necessary |
| | Designs and implementation of the configuration management system |
| Business change manager(s) (BCM) | Manages and coordinates the resolution of risks relating to operational performance and benefits achievement |
| | Ensures that the risk management cycle includes operational risks |
| | Manages risks that impact on business performance and transition |
| | Identifies operational issues and ensures that they are managed by the programme |
| | Identifies opportunities from the business operations and raises them for inclusion in the programme |
| | Contributes to impact assessments and change control |
| | Monitors and reports on business performance issues that may require the attention of the programme during transition |
| Programme office | Manages and coordinates the information and support systems to enable efficient handling of the programme's risks and issues |
| | Maintains the programme risk register |
| | Maintains the programme issue register |
| | Establishes, facilitates and maintains the risk management cycle |
| | Establishes, facilitates and maintains the issue management cycle |
| | Provides support and advice on the risks and issues to projects |
| | Coordinates risk and issue management interfaces with projects |
| | Maintains the configuration management system |
| | Facilitates the change control steps |

.

# Quality and assurance management

12

# 12 Quality and assurance management

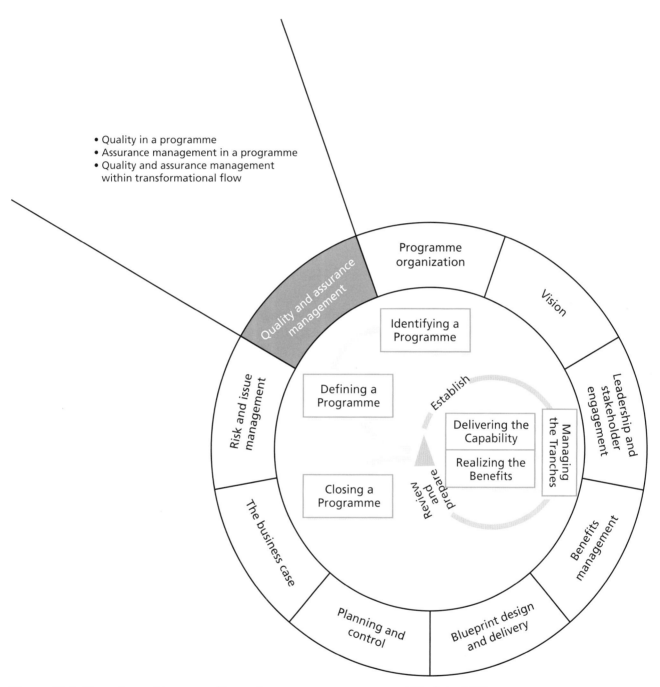

- Quality in a programme
- Assurance management in a programme
- Quality and assurance management within transformational flow

**Quality and assurance management**

**Programme organization**

**Vision**

**Leadership and stakeholder engagement**

**Benefits management**

**Blueprint design and delivery**

**Planning and control**

**The business case**

**Risk and issue management**

**Identifying a Programme**

**Defining a Programme**

**Closing a Programme**

**Establish**

**Review and prepare**

**Delivering the Capability**

**Realizing the Benefits**

**Managing the Tranches**

*Figure 12.1 Overview of how quality and assurance management fits into MSP*

## 12.1 INTRODUCTION

The purpose of quality and assurance management is to ensure that all management aspects of the programme are working appropriately and that it stays on target to achieve its objectives. If a programme does not apply quality and assurance effectively to its management activities, then it is less likely to achieve its objectives and deliver the anticipated value and benefits. Figure 12.1 provides an overview of how the quality and assurance management governance theme fits into MSP.

Quality and assurance are defined as follows:

- **Quality** is defined as the totality of features and inherent or assigned characteristics of a product, person, process, service and/or system that bears on its ability to show that it meets expectations or stated needs, requirements or specification.
- **Assurance** is the systematic set of actions necessary to provide confidence to the senior responsible owner (SRO) and stakeholders that the programme remains under control and on track to deliver and that it is aligned with the organization's strategic objectives.

Quality and assurance management must run continuously throughout the life of a programme; achieving the right level of quality must be an integral part of all the day-to-day activities of the programme.

Delivering programmes successfully is challenging because of their vagueness and the uncertain environment in which they have to operate. Where, for example, an IT project can ensure that an e-service system functions correctly through technical testing, the programme has to judge whether a sufficient number of the target customers will find the project deliverables sufficiently useful to make the investment worthwhile. That is to say, the programme should evaluate whether the users will eventually enjoy adequate benefit value after bringing the outputs into business as usual. Quality and assurance management at the programme level is different from that within a project:

- In a programme, the focus is on management, processes and alignment with the environment within which it exists. These may change during the life of the programme to reflect the organization's changing strategic priorities. Quality and assurance management in a programme must ensure that there is a full understanding of these corporate priorities, and that the programme's blueprint and plans remain aligned to them.
- By contrast, the management of quality within a project is focused on ensuring that the outputs will meet acceptance criteria (in a PRINCE2 project environment this includes meeting specifications as given in product descriptions) and that they are fit for purpose.

Programme-level quality must take into account the need to ensure that the project-level quality is delivering fit-for-purpose capabilities which enable the programme to deliver the outcomes and benefits.

The example provided of an IT supplier shows how it is possible for a project to be a success even though, in reality, the programme turns out to be a failure.

### Example

A large IT supplier was contracted to deliver an IT system to support a mission-critical programme. Because the contract was for a substantial fixed price, the supplier appointed a highly experienced project manager, who employed best-practice project management methods. The completed system was delivered on time and fully in accordance with the contract and specification.

All had not been straightforward, though. The final cost of developing the software was significantly higher than originally planned, but by delaying the procurement of hardware until the last possible moment, the project manager was able to make savings that almost exactly matched the cost of overruns on the software development.

The customer was less happy. During the development period one of the main programme sponsors had retired. His successor had different ideas. By the time the new system arrived, working procedures had changed and were no longer consistent with what was delivered. As a result, the new system was abandoned after six months of struggle.

The supplier was blamed for the failure, and a replacement IT system based on different technology was procured by the customer from elsewhere. The supplier did things right, but did not do the right things. The fault actually lay with the programme for not communicating the consequences of the sponsor's changes.

## 12.2 QUALITY IN A PROGRAMME

The programme's approach to quality is set out in the quality and assurance strategy. Quality in a programme is about identifying the right things to do, and doing them correctly. It is principally focused on process effectiveness, much of which is set out in the programme governance strategies. However, the programme principles are also an important contributor, as are the processes highlighted in section 12.2.2.

### 12.2.1 Quality and the programme management principles

The programme management principles describe the characteristics of a successful programme and act as critical success factors that apply to all programmes. Therefore, application of and adherence to the principles is essential for the programme to achieve a successful conclusion. To this end, the principles act as the focal point for establishing the critical things that the programme must do to be successful, and quality management makes sure that the programme is doing the right things to assure their achievement.

When planning for quality in the programme, the principles should be at the heart of the areas to be assured, as they represent the factors that will underpin whether the programme is successful or not.

The following points illustrate how the programme management principles can be tested to ensure that the programme is being delivered optimally:

- **Remaining aligned with corporate strategy** can be tested by checking the validity of the vision statement, blueprint, business case, benefits realization plan, having the right projects running and the currency of governance strategies.
  As the programme progresses, there will be changes to the environment within which the organization exists, which change priorities and potentially the scale or the timetable of what is required from the programme. This change should be actively managed to maintain the alignment between corporate strategy and the programme direction.
- **Leading change** can be tested by reviewing the quality of the leadership and behaviours exhibited by the people in the programme and the effect that they are having on the stakeholder landscape, in terms of levels of support and resistance. It is about having the right people in the right roles to provide the right solutions.
  The programme team should be well constructed and performing effectively, with the appropriate levels of ability and capacity and working as a team, rather than as a group of specialists or individuals.
- **Envisioning and communicating a better future** can be tested by the level of engagement that the programme is achieving, and the understanding of what it is intending to deliver and of the benefits which should be realized. The programme should be supporting the process with effective and innovative use of communications in order to maintain engagement and establish momentum.
- **Focusing on the benefits and threats to them** can be tested by checking that benefits are a permanent item on the programme board agenda, that all the benefits information is in place and current, and that the projects are clearly aligned with the benefits. The risk register illustrates the levels of sensitivity that are associated with benefits and focuses management attention on mitigating the risks.
  All too often, benefits are lost through uncontrolled changes to the operational environment from which the benefits are being sought, which undermine their realization. Key business performance indicators should be tracked to ensure that the business is remaining sufficiently stable to cope with the change and that the benefits are still achievable and desirable.
- **Adding value** can be tested by assuring that the programme is still justified in its current form. Changes in the corporate portfolio may lead to more optimal delivery configurations than existed at the outset. It may be that the programme has served its useful purpose and should close. Large programmes can almost take on a life of their own as they are as big as operational departments, so stopping one can be a significant task.
- **Designing and delivering a coherent capability** can be tested against the validity of the blueprint, ability of the projects to deliver that capability and the ability of the organization to adopt it. Compromises on project-level outputs

can fundamentally undermine the capability which is required for the outcomes, leaving organizations with a capability that is not fit for purpose – in effect, a waste of money. Compliance with this principle will be illustrated by effective management and control of project-level quality, testing of outputs and achieving their acceptance criteria. One of the challenges for the programme is not just ensuring that the outputs are those that were specified, but that the specification has evolved with the changing operational requirements to deliver a coherent capability that enables the realization of the benefits.

■ **Learning from experience** can be tested by how effectively reviews are being done, how well lessons from these and previous changes are utilized, and the effect that they are having on the programme and business performance metrics being used to measure internal effectiveness.

## 12.2.2 Scope of programme quality

Whereas the programme principles set out the areas that are critical to the success of a programme, the scope of quality is broader. In this section, eight process areas are identified that require management review of their effectiveness in supporting the achievement of the programme objectives.

A number of these processes are covered as part of the MSP governance themes and associated strategies; however, these are areas of particular importance that can cut across a number of themes and strategies, which is why they are being emphasized here in their own right. This is not an exhaustive list, but it provides useful scope for setting out the programme strategy for quality.

The emphasis is on management for all the topics, because good management requires good processes to be in place. The one exception is programme leadership, which is relevant across all the management areas.

Figure 12.2 summarizes the key elements to consider when developing and deploying quality and assurance management in programmes. As can be seen in section 12.4, quality and assurance management is an integral part of programme management throughout its lifecycle.

**Tip**

In organizations that have a portfolio office function, some of these quality management elements could be addressed by this central function. Programmes will then only need to adopt, adapt and amend the organization's approach to their own needs.

### 12.2.2.1 Communications management

Stakeholders directly affected by the programme can be considered as its customers. Quality management activities will need to focus clearly on testing the perceptions of (expected) success of the stakeholders, and the quality of the relationship with them, to ensure that there are no surprises for either side (see also Chapter 6). The term 'communications management' is used as we are referring to the management of the process and the quality of the application rather than the overarching need to engage stakeholders.

For effective communications with stakeholders and in order to understand their requirements for change and to be able to deliver them, programmes will need to:

■ Segment the programme's stakeholders and get to know and understand them by developing sound working relations
■ Anticipate what stakeholders' future needs and expectations will be and act accordingly in order to meet or exceed them
■ Monitor and review the experiences and perceptions of their stakeholders and, where deliverables do not meet the required quality, respond quickly and effectively to rectify the situation.

### 12.2.2.2 Supply chain management

Just as many operational parts of an organization depend on their suppliers providing goods or services that are fit for purpose, so too is a programme dependent on its suppliers.

Quality in a programme has to assure that suppliers apply quality management to their processes in order to ensure that they will deliver their obligations to the programme and that they are aligned effectively to the way the programme operates.

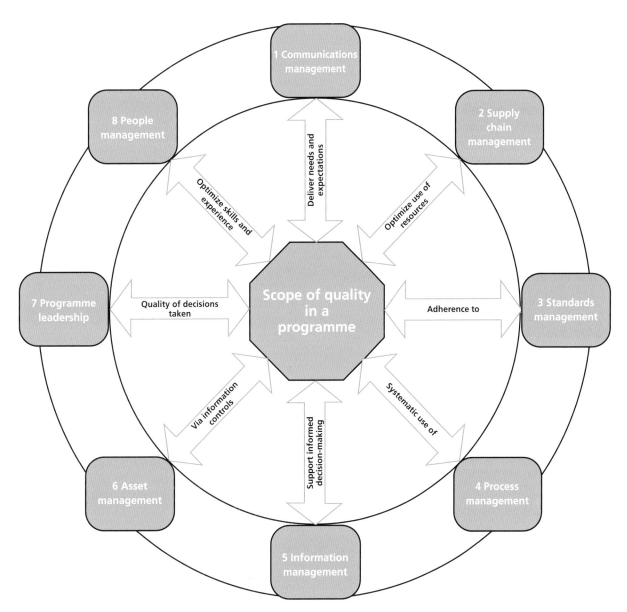

*Figure 12.2 Scope of programme quality*

Effective supply chain management will provide agility and flexibility through the provision of resources and services as and when the programme needs them. Effective procurement is essential to ensure that the right partners are selected, and the effective management of partners, once selected, is essential to good programme delivery.

The programme should seek to exploit the expertise of its supply chain to build its internal knowledge and abilities whilst ensuring that it does not become dependent or exposed to a level that leaves itself open to exploitation by the supply chain.

### 12.2.2.3 Standards management

Many organizations have a quality management system that supports operations to ensure that their products and services satisfactorily meet their customers' requirements. Consequently:

■ Programme management activities need to ensure that planned changes continue to be correctly aligned to the relevant parts of these corporate standards and policies

■ Quality management activities assure the suitability of these programme management activities.

It is particularly important to remember that most organizations review and change their policies and standards at intervals that are unlikely to coincide with a convenient review point in a programme. A monitoring and informing mechanism to alert programmes of pending policy or standards changes will help in two ways:

- The programme can provide input to the policy makers, to explain how well it is progressing in line with current policy and standards
- The mechanism enables programmes to assess the impact of proposals to change policies and standards. What might be gained and what will be lost can be fed back to the policy makers, so their decisions are made on an informed basis.

There are few business activities that are not subject to some aspect of legislation and/or regulation. Programmes need to be aware of which laws and regulations are relevant to ensure that their projects' outputs, and the changed operations, comply correctly. For example, if an organization advertises itself as complying with ISO 9001 or ISO 14001, then it must ensure that it can still comply after changes have been embedded.

### 12.2.2.4 Process management

To function effectively, a programme must deploy processes with the appropriate level of specification and rigour to get the job done. A process is a set of related activities that are carried out in a defined order. Quality in a programme needs to make sure that processes are appropriately adapted (see Chapter 15) and used effectively (see Chapter 17).

Applying quality to defining and managing processes will typically lead to:

- Achieving the programme's objectives in the most effective and efficient way
- Understanding the interdependencies inherent in a process
- Integration and alignment of the processes that will best achieve the desired results
- Structured approaches that harmonize and integrate processes
- Ability to focus effort on the key processes
- Taking into account resource constraints prior to action
- Continually improving systems through measurement and evaluation

- Establishing clear responsibility and accountability for managing key activities.

Good processes have in-built measurement and control to monitor against deviation.

The key to successful processes is their acceptance and understanding by the people who have to operate them. Education and training are a significant element of understanding why the process is needed and individuals having the competence to use it.

#### Tip

When teams do not follow a process, it is more likely that the problem is associated with their acceptance of the need for the process than the process itself. Organizations often waste money undertaking wholesale changes to programme and project processes, when investing in gaining commitment to use them would have been cheaper and quicker.

### 12.2.2.5 Information management

The core purpose of information management in a programme is to provide the right information, in the right format, to the right people at the right time. Programmes have access to and create large amounts of data, and good information management will stop the programme team being overwhelmed with irrelevant documents, templates and reports.

Critical success factors that underpin a successful information management system include:

- **Compliance** Information storage and retention should be compliant with organizational policies and applicable legislation. In particular, consideration should be given to data protection, freedom-of-information legislation and requirement in terms of length of retention for personnel and financial records.
- **Integrity** Information stored should be under change and release management control. This should ensure that the right versions of information are in circulation and use. Audit should be considered for checking that the distribution systems are working.
- **Availability** Decision makers should have access to the information and documentation they require when they need it.

- **Confidentiality** Levels of confidentiality should be set within the programme, documents allocated appropriate levels of sensitivity and their distribution limited accordingly. This may also require an audit trail and certification.
- **Currency** Information being used should reflect the current situation. Any gaps in reporting from projects or concerns about accuracy of business performance data should be acknowledged, together with limitations that this brings to decision-making.

Based on such factors, quality reviews should ensure that adequate, timely information is produced, correctly communicated and properly understood by the recipients.

The information management strategy sets out the approach of the programme and the information management plan sets out how this will be achieved. See Appendix A for more detail on the contents of the information management strategy and information management plan.

**Tips**

A major problem in many programmes (and projects) is incomplete and out-of-date information, which can severely compromise management and control.

Early in the programme (for example at the start of the first tranche) pay close attention to validating information flows to check that they are complete and up to date.

Establishing such a rigorous regime at an early stage will provide not just good information but reinforce the importance of quality.

### 12.2.2.6 Asset management

No organization can be fully efficient or effective unless it manages well those assets that are vital to the running of the organization's business. Assets come in many forms: they can range from the programme information used by MSP to software or the contents of a building.

The difference between asset management and configuration management is that configuration management tracks the interrelationships between the assets as well as the assets themselves.

The purpose of asset management is to identify, track and protect the programme's assets (i.e. anything that is of material value to its success). These can be grouped as follows:

- External assets – which exist outside the programme but changes to which could significantly affect the programme, e.g. legislation or corporate polices or strategies
- Programme assets that are originated by the programme itself, for example the blueprint and the programme plan
- Internal assets that interface between the projects and the programme, for example project progress reports or project initiation documents
- Project outputs, for example software, a building or a new organizational structure.

All assets of a programme will be subject to planned and unplanned changes and should come under change control and configuration management. Configuration management is covered in Chapter 11.

See Appendix A for descriptions of the information management strategy and information management plan and Appendix C for more on information management.

### 12.2.2.7 Programme leadership

Good leadership is critical to programme success. As with any other programme activities, the application of the quality and assurance plan must ensure that good, effective leadership is taking place.

The leaders of successful programmes provide clear direction and communicate that direction to people inside and outside the programme. The programme's leadership must establish a governance framework that provides adequate levels of control for the programme, including the delegation of unambiguous authority and responsibility (covered in Chapter 4), which quality review activities will evaluate regularly.

There is no guarantee that an effective business leader will automatically make a good programme leader. It is important that there is investment in building the skills and competency of the SRO to ensure that they are effective in their role as leader, especially if it is their first programme.

### 12.2.2.8 People management

Several of the principles for good programme management are particularly concerned with people (see Chapter 2):

- Leading change
- Envisioning and communicating a better future
- Learning from experience.

Quality activities should make sure that these are appropriately applied to get the best out of the people deployed on the programme. Individuals may be part of a programme for some years, and as such their welfare needs to be managed effectively. This should involve:

- Appropriate induction training when people join the programme
- Reward mechanisms linked to individual performance
- Career development plans and a recognized role in the programme
- Skills development and training linked to performance improvement
- Appropriate qualifications to benchmark and provide evidence of knowledge performance
- Appropriate contracts, terms and conditions to reflect their status as part of the programme rather than their normal role
- Exit plans to facilitate staff re-integration back into the business.

As people are assigned to their particular roles, they will need to understand the importance of their contribution to the programme and be told what will enable them to fulfil their role (within its constraints), for example:

- Their degree of accountability and level of authority and responsibility
- What the prevailing policy, processes and standards are to which they must adhere
- What resources are (or are not) available, including facilities, equipment and materials
- Their rights to create, access, use or delete data, information and records.

Reviews of individual and team performance will need to take place regularly and be reported to the SRO or programme board to ensure that all aspects of people management, including specific quality-related elements, are reviewed and the appropriate preventive or corrective action is taken.

## 12.3 ASSURANCE MANAGEMENT IN A PROGRAMME

### 12.3.1 Assurance management principles

If the SRO and stakeholders are to gain confidence that the programme is on track, then assurance management will have to demonstrate that it has followed an approach that is: independent of the programme; integrated across the programme; linked to major decision points; risk-based; and results in action as necessary. Such an approach should be based on the following five assurance management principles.

#### 12.3.1.1 Independence

The expectation is that assurance will have a level of independence from that which is being assured. Assessors should have no direct line management of the programme team. They should be disinterested in, and have no control over, project outcomes or service operations.

#### 12.3.1.2 Integrated

Integrated assurance is the planning, coordination and provision of assurance activities from the start of the programme through to delivery of benefits in a way which provides greater assurance with less effort. This is achieved through the provision of an agreed plan which will indicate how assurance reviews of all types will be scheduled to support decision-making and inform investment approvals, while avoiding duplication of activities that do not add value.

#### 12.3.1.3 Linked to major decision points

Assurance activity should be planned to support major events, outcomes, tranche ends or key approval points (e.g. funding decisions) throughout the end-to-end transformational flow from mandate through to the realization of benefits.

#### 12.3.1.4 Risk-based

Assurance activity should be:

- Based on an independent risk assessment
- Focused on areas of greatest risks to commercial, legal, regulatory, investment and performance requirements
- Cognizant of specific areas of financial, delivery, technical, social, political, programme, operational and reputational risks.

### 12.3.1.5 Action and intervention

Assurance is most effective when appropriate follow-up actions are taken to resolve any serious issues identified through planned assurance activity. These consequential assurance activities may involve further reviews, e.g. reviews of action plans, case conferences or more detailed reviews to ensure that appropriate action has been taken. This process should also include clear escalation routes that may be used if appropriate to the highest organizational levels for resolution of issues. (See also Chapter 11.)

## 12.3.2 Assurance management techniques

There are a number of techniques that can be used to help assure that the programme is being delivered optimally, that is to say in the most appropriate and effective way for the achievement of its purpose and objectives.

This guidance describes some of the ways in which a programme can ensure that it maintains control over itself and remains relevant to the environment within which it operates. When considering which practices to use, you should remember the need to establish and maintain an integrated assurance approach that provides reviews which may encompass some or all of the practices.

The benefit of taking an integrated approach is that reviews from different perspectives will ensure that a holistic approach maximizes the opportunities for improvements as the programme progresses.

### 12.3.2.1 Audit

Audit is a generic term, not confined solely to the audit of financial accounts, and is often used to assess the management and conduct of a programme. Audit involves examination of the activities of a programme with the aim of determining the extent to which they conform to specified criteria. The criteria may be internal standards and procedures or external codes of practice, accounting standards, contract conditions or statutory requirements. Audits may be carried out by internal audit staff or by external audit bodies.

**Tips**

Audit is about ensuring that the programme is 'doing things right' as defined in its control framework (covered in Chapter 15). In other words, is it following its own rules?

However, it might be appropriate to expect an audit to also check evidence that the programme is 'doing the right things' (relative to its business case), that its progress so far is on track to achieve first outcomes, and that it will realize the benefits that are in alignment with its strategy.

It is not unheard of for the programme audit also to assess the way in which the inherent achievability of the business case was undertaken.

Make sure that the audit staff are briefed clearly.

Programme auditors should provide the programme with their particular information needs, and be able to assist the programme manager to build any specific audit requirements into the governance strategies and plans for the programme.

Programme audits will consider any or all aspects of the programme, its management and ability to deliver. A corporate portfolio office or, where it exists, the centre of excellence for processes in the organization is well positioned to supervise and conduct these audits as required.

### 12.3.2.2 Effectiveness of measurements

Effective decisions are based on the accurate measurement of data and the analysis of reliable information, which is why the information management strategy and plan are crucial. This is as true for programmes as it is for any part of an organization. In order for people in a programme to measure progress and assess performance, measures of inputs, resources, activities and outputs will need to be taken prior to any change and throughout the programme. The data and information from these measures will need to be analysed and reviewed at the regular meetings set out in the schedule in the quality and assurance plan. Contrary to many people's perceptions, this approach will enable the programme to be more flexible to changes in the business environment and prevent fire-fighting. This is because the programme's leaders will be responding to hard facts and figures, and relying less on intuition.

Measurements in a programme can be considered in two ways:

- Measurements concerned with the management and control of the programme, for example cost and budget reports
- The measurement of the programme's outcomes to assess whether acceptable benefits are materializing.

Unsuitable measures or misinterpreted analyses are likely to reduce the ability to control quality. Assurance should ensure that measurement, analysis procedures and systems are effective.

Each of the programme governance strategies should set out the individual success criteria for the topics within its scope.

### 12.3.2.3 Assurance reviews

While audits tend to focus on conformance and compliance, reviews may be used as a programme assurance tool by senior managers to determine whether a programme should continue. Health checks can also be used to provide an impartial view of a programme during its lifecycle to assess whether or not it will meet its objectives.

Review is an important activity that is often forgotten or ignored. Without review, the findings of audits or other forms of programme assessment cannot be evaluated properly by the programme's leaders. This will lead to ill-informed decisions about the real performance and direction of the programme and what actions are needed to keep it on course.

Key areas to consider within a review would be based on the quality scope elements and the programme management principles, but some specific areas to focus on are:

- How well is the programme controlling and enabling its projects – is the level of overhead appropriate?
- How well are the business change managers (BCMs) preparing the organization for change, and are the benefits being truly delivered?
- Are the internal processes and governance strategies working effectively and optimally for the purpose of the programme?

Review activities include inspection of information, meetings with key individuals or attendance at any meeting where decisions are taken that affect the effectiveness and efficiency of the programme. It will be useful to set out these key meetings in the quality and assurance plan.

Health checks can also be used to provide an impartial view of a programme during its lifecycle to assess whether or not it will meet its objectives.

These reviews provide independent assurance that products or processes are fit for purpose – they meet the defined technical, quality or regulatory requirements.

Appendix D provides more information on the scope and content of health checks.

### 12.3.2.4 P3M3 maturity assessments

The level of organizational maturity in programme delivery will have a direct bearing on how well an organization is able to support its programmes. The Portfolio, Programme, Project Management Maturity Model (P3M3) has been developed to offer a specific Programme Management Maturity Model (PgM3) to enable organizations to assess their effectiveness.

The model views an organization's portfolio, programme and project management effectiveness through seven perspectives (see Figure 12.3), namely:

- Management control
- Benefits management
- Financial management
- Stakeholder engagement
- Risk management
- Organizational governance
- Resource management.

It uses a model with five levels of maturity, which will help to understand the context in which the programme is delivering. The five levels are:

1 Awareness (lowest)
2 Repeatable
3 Defined
4 Managed
5 Optimized (highest).

More details of P3M3 can be found in Appendix B, especially section B.6.

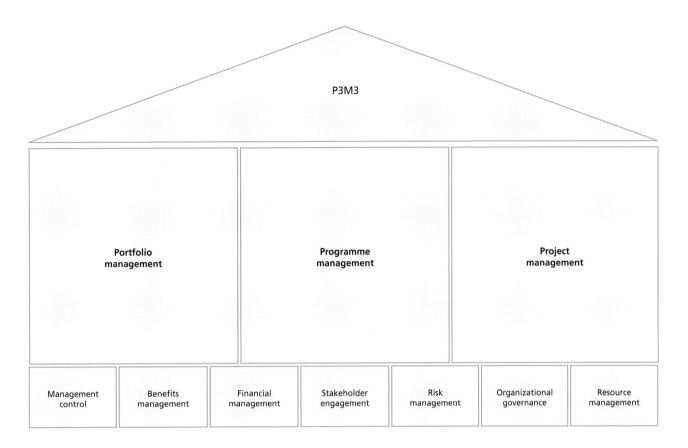

*Figure 12.3 P3M3 model*

Knowing the organization's maturity is important for individual programmes; less mature organizations will struggle with the processes and rigour associated with programme management, so the programme team will need to make more effort to communicate effectively and avoid jargon when engaging stakeholders. It also helps to set expectations within the team about what to expect from other parts of the organization, and vice versa.

A programme can use the maturity model to improve performance by using it to assess the maturity of the projects within the programme and also to measure itself against one or more of the perspectives to ensure that it is working consistently with its projects, for example risk management.

The outputs of a P3M3 review will provide an assessment of the organization's strengths and weaknesses and a rating against an international standard. This information can be used to build an improvement plan to increase the performance of the programme and its ability to deliver effective change.

### 12.3.2.5 Gated reviews

Gated reviews are an ideal way of applying assurance controls to programmes, as the programme is not allowed to progress to its next stage unless it has undergone a gated review. They can take place at the end of tranches, for example, and gated reviews check that the programme is under control and on target to meet the organization's needs. Gated reviews should also be applied to the projects to ensure they are properly under control and aligned to the blueprint and programme objectives.

In the UK, public sector programmes will be subject to one or more of the following assurance reviews:

- Starting gate
- Project assessment reviews (PARs)
- OGC Gateway.

*Starting gate*

Launching a major change project or programme has long-term consequences for an organization and its customers. In government, it may affect citizens, taxpayers, commercial suppliers and ministers. Experience shows that good planning, early on, enhances the prospects of achieving the intended benefits. OGC's starting gate is a short independent peer review at the early stages of the policy-to-delivery lifecycle. It offers departments the opportunity to gain independent assurance on how well practical delivery issues are being addressed in preparing for implementation through a programme or project. Starting gate is separate from the OGC Gateway review process for projects and programmes, but is highly relevant to it: most starting gate review topics are likely to be delivered through major programmes which will be subsequently subject to OGC Gateway reviews.

*Project assessment reviews*

These reviews have been developed for government projects to be more specific than the strategically focused OGC Gateway review. Using this more in-depth review and working in collaboration with the programme, they primarily give assurance that a programme's (or its projects'):

- Scope and delivery options are optimized and in line with strategic policy and achievable at optimal cost
- Financial viability is affordable, and that the value-for-money solution proposed is deliverable and in line with national strategies.

*OGC Gateway*

For programmes, the most used review is the OGC Gateway Review 0. This strategic-level review provides assurance to the SRO and key stakeholders, e.g. funding approval bodies and programme board, that there is a realistic chance of delivering the programme's overall objectives. It does this through ensuring that:

- The scope and purpose of the programme has been adequately researched
- There is a shared understanding of what is to be achieved by the main players
- There is a shared understanding of the timescales for delivery
- It fits within the organization's overall policy or management strategy and priorities
- There is a realistic possibility of securing the resources needed
- It is organized effectively to deliver the overall programme objectives, e.g. in tranches and projects
- The programme management structure, monitoring and resourcing are appropriate
- The risks affecting delivery have been identified and appropriate measures are in place to manage them.

In short, the first OGC Gateway Review 0 aims to test whether stakeholders' expectations of the programme are realistic, by reference to costs, outcomes, resource needs, timetable and general achievability. Subsequent OGC Gateway reviews revisit the same questions at appropriate points in the programme's life to confirm that the main stakeholders have a common understanding of desired outcomes and that the programme is likely to achieve them. There is high value in an organization subjecting its programme(s) to such rigour. The cost and effort saved by refocusing or cancelling a programme that is no longer strategically aligned far outweighs the cost and inconvenience of the activity.

### 12.3.3 Assurance management approach

The programme's approach to quality and assurance is set out in the quality and assurance strategy, and the associated plan defines how it will be deployed.

#### 12.3.3.1 Quality and assurance strategy

A key area of focus for the quality and assurance strategy is to ensure that there is integrated assurance of the programme to avoid having multiple overlapping reviews conducted by different interested parties. Relying on one type of assurance leaves the programme at risk of not seeing opportunities and threats from a more holistic approach. For high-profile programmes, there is also a danger that they suffer stagnation as a result of constant assurance reviews.

A strategy should be established by an organization to provide the strategic direction for its assurance regime. It applies to business change within the organization and its fundamental and integrated relationship with its financial approval and business decision-making system. If a portfolio-level assurance strategy is in place, this will provide much of the detail for the programme strategy. If it does not exist, the programme should develop its own with reference to the approach when the programme mandate is formulated. It must be approved by the sponsoring group and incorporated into the business case, as it is developed as a programme management cost.

The strategy should be reviewed periodically (e.g. in line with the business case developments) to ensure that it remains aligned with strategic requirements and business objectives, and that it monitors whether there are significant programme scope or risk changes.

The strategy should cross-reference the monitoring and control strategy, which covers the internal controls of the programme. Therefore, it is essential to explain how different aspects of assurance will be handled and avoidance of duplication achieved.

See Appendix A for more details.

#### 12.3.3.2 Quality and assurance plan

The plan identifies who will be responsible for quality, assurance, review and control. It describes how and when the programme will carry out audits, health checks and reviews; and describes the resources needed for the successful completion of specific quality activities. It also details how and when work will be monitored and reported.

The plan provides input to the planning of a programme to ensure that the required resources and time commitments are built into all relevant plans.

The plan should take into account the assurance coverage of its constituent projects and scheduling activities, to best avoid assurance overlap and overload. The plan should be endorsed by the sponsoring group and reviewed periodically in the light of any assurance activity undertaken, changes in risk potential or scope of the project. The plan should be developed using a risk-based approach to ensure that the assurance provision is proportionate and meets the needs of all those parties requiring assurance.

See Appendix A for more details.

## 12.4 QUALITY AND ASSURANCE MANAGEMENT WITHIN TRANSFORMATIONAL FLOW

This section covers how the quality and assurance management governance theme is applied in each of the processes in the transformational flow. Quality and assurance management will accompany a programme throughout its life. As each process in the flow follows on, a balance needs to be struck between over-engineering solutions and cutting corners. Quality management provides the yardstick against which to measure how acceptable the programme's outcomes will be. Quality assurance provides a consistent and documented method of checking whether the programme's processes are adequate to the task of meeting the targets set on the yardstick.

### 12.4.1 Identifying a Programme

Organizations initiate programmes in support of corporate strategic drivers for change. It is vital that these drivers are appropriately identified and understood at the earliest stage. The programme should specify its assurance approach and the critical success factors within the programme mandate. The programme brief is the first indication of whether the programme has understood its remit and is setting up to deliver the quality expected from it. During this phase the

SRO and programme board are appointed – key organizational resources that will influence the viability of the programme.

There should be independent assurance of the programme brief and the programme preparation plan.

More guidance is available in sections 14.5, 14.7 and 14.8.

### 12.4.2  Defining a Programme

Quality considerations are a key driving force behind this process. Corporate policies must be investigated and considered when developing the individual strategies. These strategies define how the programme will manage itself. They describe the management quality that the programme aspires to.

All the vital, initial directional decisions for the programme are made during this process. It will become increasingly more difficult to turn around a programme later if required, and utmost emphasis should hence be placed on quality. There should be an extensive formal review of the programme prior to approval to proceed into Managing the Tranches. Consideration should also be given to a review once the blueprint, benefits and projects dossier have stabilized and the direction and impact are emerging.

It is during this process that the strategies and then plans for both quality and assurance and for information management are created. More guidance is available in sections 15.3, 15.11, 15.12, 15.13, 15.17 and 15.18.

### 12.4.3  Managing the Tranches

Managing the Tranches requires embedding quality in the processes, tools and techniques that are described in the individual strategies being implemented. Quality and assurance measures are applied to the programme and regular audits and/or gate reviews are conducted as planned and appropriate. The production of adequate information is vital to monitor and control the programme; and communication with stakeholders becomes key to steering expectations and preparing for benefits realization.

Assurance reviews must be carried out as scheduled in the quality and assurance plan, and these should include reviews of the performance of internal and external partners. The end-of-tranche review provides an opportunity for an extensive formal review prior to commitment to further investment. Within Managing the Tranches many of the activities could be review points, but specifically those outlined in section 16.6.

More guidance is available in sections 16.2, 16.6, 16.8, 16.9 and 16.14.

### 12.4.4  Delivering the Capability

Projects are set up to deliver the outputs required to enable programme outcomes. For this, projects follow their own strict quality regime, focusing on product quality. Programme quality, focusing on management and outcome quality, needs to assure that projects deliver products that are adequate to meet the programme's objectives.

It is during this process that programmes will regularly engage with suppliers. Appropriate integration of suppliers into the programme organization, clear definition and management of responsibilities, exchange of information and communication with suppliers are activities which require the input of quality management.

The integrated assurance approach should ensure that a regime is in place to cover the programme and its projects, which is likely to include a gated review process for the larger projects. More guidance is available in sections 17.6 and 17.7.

### 12.4.5  Realizing the Benefits

During pre-transition there needs to be a focus on assurance that the business is preparing for and is ready for change during transition; that the transition will be handled optimally; and, critically, that the post-transition activities to embed the change and realize the benefits are actually happening.

The focus of quality and assurance reviews tends to be on project and programme performance. However, a regular cause of failure to achieve benefits is the lack of readiness of the organization to change; its inadequate review of preparations for transition; and its inability to re-stabilize and exploit the capability afterwards.

More guidance is available in sections 18.2.3, 18.3.3, 18.3.4 and 18.4.4.

**Table 12.1 Quality and assurance management and the key roles**

| Role | Area of focus |
|---|---|
| Senior responsible owner (SRO) | Consults with sponsoring group on approach to programme assurance |
| | Ensures that an adequate assurance regime is in place for all aspects of quality in the programme |
| | Signs off of the quality and information management strategies |
| | Initiates assurance reviews and audits |
| | Maintains focus on the programme management principles |
| Programme manager | Develops and implements the quality and assurance strategy, plans and then coordinates delivery of outputs from the projects that are fit for the purpose of achieving the desired outcomes and benefits |
| | Develops and implements the information management strategy and plan |
| | Initiates assurance reviews of project and supplier performance |
| | Ensures that lessons learned are implemented |
| Business change manager(s) (BCM) | Implements transitioning, realizing and reviewing of benefits from the outputs of the projects |
| | Initiates assurance reviews of business performance and change readiness |
| | Ensures that business change lessons learned are implemented |
| Programme office | Establishes and maintains the programme's quality and assurance plan and ensures the establishment of the appropriate audit, assurance and review processes for the programme in accordance with the quality and assurance strategy |
| | Establishes and maintains the programme's information management plan and ensures the establishment of the appropriate audit, assurance and review processes for the programme in accordance with the information management strategy |
| | Provides information to support assurance reviews |

## 12.4.6 Closing a Programme

Closing a programme engages quality management primarily from a review perspective. Formal reviews should be set up to look at whether the programme has achieved its objectives and if not, why not: there may be very good reasons.

Specifically, the strategies and plans for both quality and assurance and for information management should be reviewed and updated.

More generally, it should ensure that all programme documentation and information is updated and transitioned in accordance with the information management strategy. It will give adequate feedback on how corporate policies were applied in the programme and suggest any improvements if required.

More guidance is available in sections 19.5, 19.6 and 19.7.

## 12.5 THE KEY ROLES

Unlike the other theme chapters, the sponsoring group has a specific role to play. Members must ensure that they are satisfied that the appropriate reviews and governance are in place to maximize the likelihood of the success of the programme. This should be set out in the quality and assurance strategy.

The programme board will need to be satisfied that it can meet the needs of the strategy and will be willing to support it through the reviews, learning the lessons and leading improvements to performance.

Often, there are also specialist roles needed such as audit, compliance, design authority, business and systems architects, legal, procurement etc. These roles can be used to bench-test designs, prototypes etc. to predict whether the blueprint and project outputs will operate well enough to achieve the scale of improvement needed for the desired benefits. They are also important to help check that the new operations, its products and services will comply with relevant standards, regulations and legislation. Table 12.1 provides a summary of the key roles and typical areas of focus.

# PART 3

# The transformational flow

# Transformational flow overview

# 13 Transformational flow overview

## 13.1 INTRODUCTION

MSP programmes are all about delivering transformational change. This part of the guide looks at how the transformation is achieved through a series of iterative, interrelated steps. Figure 13.1 shows the transformational flow through an MSP programme with the main processes and key control documents involved in delivering an MSP programme. Each process may require more than one iteration before the next one begins. This is particularly true for the Delivering the Capability and Realizing the Benefits processes, as programmes often deliver their change through more than one tranche.

Typically, the programme mandate pulls together the high-level, strategic objectives of the programme from the organization's strategic drivers and relevant policies, plus the outline vision statement. This summary of the objectives is then developed into the programme brief.

Not all programmes start at the beginning of the process with a strategy/policy-driven mandate. Some programmes emerge as a result of a better understanding partway through the project(s) lifecycle (as discussed in section 1.6):

- The organization may discover a proposed change is bigger and more complex than originally thought, and decide that it should be converted into a programme to give a better chance of success.
- It may become apparent that several projects are trying to achieve similar changes to the same part of the organization, resulting in duplication and conflict. Combining the projects into a programme may well achieve focus and synergy, solve the duplication and conflict, and maximize benefits.

For emerging programmes, entry to the programme process is now much more than just a mandate. Consideration needs to be given to what has been achieved so far in each project, what will continue, and what will need to be stopped.

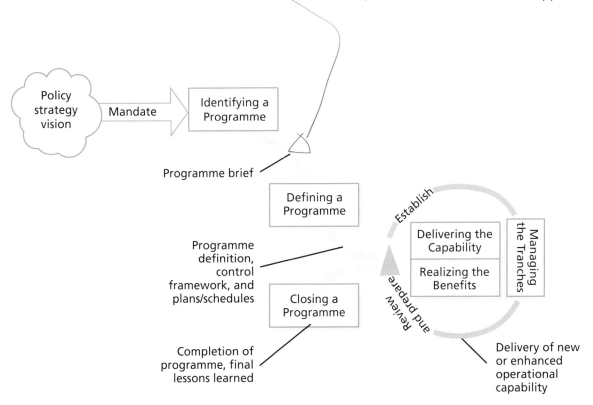

*Figure 13.1 Overview of the transformational flow*

The approved programme brief is the key input to the process of Defining a Programme. It provides the basis for development of the:

■ Programme outcomes and benefits
■ Plans/schedules
■ Control framework.

This document requires formal approval by the senior responsible owner (SRO) and sponsoring group before the programme moves into the next part of the flow, Defining a Programme.

The programme definition document can be used to assemble and summarize all of this information into one document. Programmes often produce substantial volumes of information during Defining a Programme, and the programme definition document can be useful for busy executives who only need an overview. As a form of consolidated summary, it can help to prepare the sponsoring group so that they are adequately informed before they are asked to authorize the programme.

The programme management strategies created in Defining a Programme are established in Managing the Tranches by implementing the associated plan. The programme definition, governance framework and plans are the basis for Delivering the Capability and Realizing the Benefits.

Early governance arrangements are developed in Identifying a Programme as part of the programme preparation plan for Defining a Programme, to manage and control the work in that process. They are developed further in Defining a Programme for Managing the Tranches. As the programme progresses, especially at the end of each tranche, it reviews the effectiveness of its governance arrangements and the continued viability of the programme's business case. As the programme moves to later tranches, its characteristics might change. For these reasons, governance arrangements are often refined as part of the preparation work for the next tranche.

The projects and activities are grouped into tranches. Each tranche delivers a step change in capability after which benefits realization can be assessed. The activities of Delivering the Capability and Realizing the Benefits are carried out for each tranche.

The end of each tranche provides a major assurance review point at which the programme can be formally assessed in terms of its progress

towards achieving the desired outcomes and measurable realization of benefits. Whilst all programmes should have clear vision, the precise route to that vision is often not clear early in the programme. Early tranches might be dedicated to exploring options and discovering a successful route to the vision.

A tranche formally comes to an end when the new capability has been delivered, transition is completed and the outcomes have been achieved. At this point there is formal authorization to continue with the programme into the next tranche. It also provides a critical stop/go decision about whether the programme is still valid and continues to meet the strategic needs of the organization. The programme principles 'remaining aligned with corporate strategy' and 'designing and delivering a coherent capability' are particularly relevant at this point (see section 12.2.1).

Throughout the programme, monitoring progress and the external environment provides continual assessment of crucial questions such as

■ Are we still on track?
■ Are the benefits still achievable?
■ Is the business case still valid and relevant?
■ Do we need to change anything to realign the programme, based on lessons learned so far, or because of changes external to the programme, such as strategy?

Closing a Programme is done after the blueprint is delivered, when the capabilities required to achieve the vision statement have been implemented, and sufficient benefits have been realized to:

■ Objectively judge whether the programme was successful
■ Be confident that the full benefits of the programme will be delivered in the business-as-usual environment.

Further reviews may be required following closure to assess and measure the continuing realization of benefits. These reviews should be initiated by the business change managers (BCMs), as the programme team will have been disbanded. If the programme was part of a corporate portfolio, the portfolio office may take over this responsibility.

Programmes close for many different reasons that can be considered from the following six groups:

- **Planned closure** because the programme has completed all planned work within its scope
- **External environment changes** dramatically and unexpectedly render the programme invalid and therefore it needs to close prematurely
- **Strategy changed** by the organization for internal reasons, not because of external environment changes; this renders the programme invalid and therefore it needs to close prematurely
- **Invalid business case** as evidence so far predicts that the business case cannot be achieved, corrective action is not practical, the programme is unrealistic and therefore needs to close prematurely
- **The 80/20 rule** shows that the cost of the remainder of the programme compared with additional benefits it will realize means that it does not make good business sense to complete the rest of the programme
- Evidence that the outcome is being achieved through **alternative actions/events**.

## 13.2 COLLABORATION WITH THEMES AND PRINCIPLES

The governance themes in Part 2 of this guide are used at specific points in the transformational flow and are illustrated at the end of the governance theme chapters. Within the transformational flow chapters, the governance themes are regularly referenced. Integration of the governance themes into the transformational flow is essential for understanding programme management and delivering effective programmes. The principles for good programme management are described in Chapter 2. These are universally applicable, at all times and for all types of activity.

## 13.3 STRUCTURE OF THE TRANSFORMATIONAL FLOW CHAPTERS

There is a chapter for each of the MSP transformational flow processes, with a diagram at the start of each chapter summarizing inputs, activities, outputs, controls and roles. Typical responsibilities are summarized in a RACI table at the end of each chapter. These need to be adapted and extended for each programme.

In the RACI tables, the sponsoring group is only referenced in the Identifying a Programme chapter (Chapter 14). This is because once the SRO is in place, that person is accountable for the programme but would be consulting and gaining endorsement from the sponsoring group on a regular basis.

The RACI tables are a simple way of seeing what level of responsibility each role has. The headings stand for:

- Responsible
- Accountable
- Consulted
- Informed.

The sponsoring group would be expected to authorize the programme and the SRO's recommendations at the end of Identifying a Programme, Defining a Programme and for each end of tranche as a minimum. The sponsoring group has specific responsibilities defined in Chapter 4; these are in no way diminished by not being included in all of the RACI tables at the end of the transformational flow chapters.

The programme board is also not referenced because it is principally made up of the SRO, programme manager and BCMs, each of whom has specific responsibilities. The programme board supports the SRO in driving the rate of change for the programme and has a critical role in resolving challenges and maintaining focus. It has clear responsibilities, which are defined in Chapter 4, but these are in no way diminished by not being included in the RACI tables at the end of the transformational flow chapters.

# Identifying a Programme

**14**

# 14 Identifying a Programme

## 14.1 INTRODUCTION

The concept (corporate strategy, initiative, policy or emerging programme) and the resulting vision that is driving the change generate the programme mandate – the trigger for initiating the overall programme management process. The signing-off of the programme mandate allows the Identifying a Programme process to begin, where the programme brief is developed. Identifying a Programme (see Figure 14.1) is typically a short process, perhaps taking only a few weeks or less, which turns the idea into a tangible business concept.

The programme brief defines the outline vision, expected benefits, estimates of costs, timescales and risks, allowing:

■ Clarification of what can be achieved, and the desired benefits

■ A management decision to be made on whether the programme is desirable and appropriate

■ Commitment to the investment and resources required to proceed to the next process of Defining a Programme, as set out in the programme preparation plan

■ Confirmation that the change should be managed as a programme.

Where a programme has emerged from other change initiatives, work in Identifying a Programme can be used to quickly assess which of these current change initiatives could be practically merged into a programme. This may well reveal duplication, conflict and gaps in the current initiatives, leading to recommended initial actions. It may be necessary to act quickly to avoid further unnecessary expenditure.

## 14.2 SPONSORING THE PROGRAMME

A programme requires initial and ongoing top-level sponsorship to gain and maintain the necessary commitment to the investment, resources, timescales, delivery and operational changes that will be involved. Those senior executives who are responsible for delivering the strategic objectives or policy requirements form the programme's sponsoring group. The sponsoring group provides the programme mandate.

The sponsoring group is made up of those senior executives who:

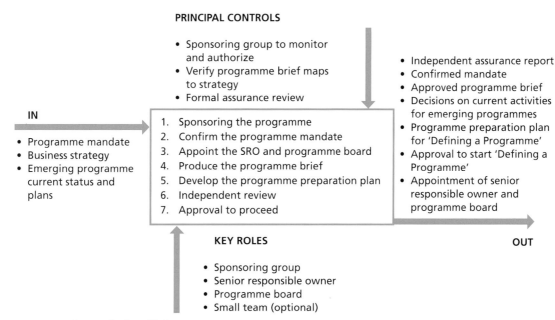

*Figure 14.1 Overview of Identifying a Programme*

- Have a strategic interest in the programme
- Have responsibility for the investment decision-making
- Will be significantly impacted by the programme
- Will be required to enable the delivery of the change.

Each member of the sponsoring group should:

- Clarify their perspective on the programme and particular interests
- Define the levels of engagement support they will be able to give to the programme
- Confirm their acceptance of, and commitment to, their roles and the programme.

Undertaking stakeholder analysis is necessary to understand who:

- Will be most impacted by the programme
- Can provide useful input when considering the composition of the sponsoring group.

The sponsoring group may be formed in any number of ways. It may be that the senior responsible owner (SRO) has already been nominated and takes a lead in forming the sponsoring group; alternatively, in some organizations where portfolio management has been adopted, the sponsoring group may be a corporate portfolio board, where a number of SROs sit.

See Chapter 6 for more on stakeholder analysis and Chapter 4 for the responsibilities of the sponsoring group.

## 14.3 CONFIRM THE PROGRAMME MANDATE

The programme mandate should articulate to the SRO (and the individuals who develop the programme brief) the direction, constraints, priorities and aspirations for the programme. This information sets the scene for a controlled start-up for the programme and should be confirmed at its outset. Appendix A provides the specific detail about what the programme mandate should contain.

The programme mandate will set out what will constitute success for the programme, identify these items as critical success factors, and outline the assurance regime that will be adopted to ensure that the programme achieves these.

The programme mandate may be a documented output from corporate strategic planning or policy development. However, it may not initially exist as a single, cohesive document. In this case, the information for the programme mandate will need to be drawn together into a single document derived from:

- Facilitated workshops
- Interviews and discussions with:
  - The sponsoring group
  - Key stakeholders
  - Members of the organization's executive
  - Senior management teams.

The consolidated programme mandate is reviewed and confirmed by the sponsoring group.

Information on the content of the programme mandate can be found in Appendix A.

## 14.4 APPOINT THE SRO AND PROGRAMME BOARD

The SRO will be personally accountable for the programme's success. The SRO, a peer and member of the sponsoring group, should be the individual with the most appropriate and relevant authority, credibility, experience and skills to lead and direct the programme.

The individual should be appointed by the sponsoring group at the earliest opportunity to be a focal point for the programme, providing leadership and direction, and bringing clarity where possible. It may well be that the SRO is already in place as a result of an executive decision, so in this case it will be simply a matter of endorsement.

A specific role definition should be prepared for the SRO, approved by the sponsoring group, and then the SRO should confirm understanding and acceptance of the role. Large programmes may impose a workload on the SRO that is too great; in such cases the SRO can be assisted by other persons with appropriate expertise.

This role definition should be included, with the other role definitions, as part of the organization structure document created during Defining a Programme; however, it is important that the SRO accepts and has clarity about their brief. This also applies to other programme board members and those to be appointed later.

The SRO will appoint and chair the programme board, which should be formed now to give the business early involvement and establish governance. It will undoubtedly evolve if the work to define the programme moves forward.

The terms of reference for the programme board should be drafted when it is initiated. See Chapter 4 for details of roles that should be covered by the programme board and examples of the responsibilities.

A small team may be appointed to assist with producing the programme brief and the programme preparation plan. It is important to identify and involve the likely programme manager and business change manager(s) (BCM) during this step if at all possible; if it is too early for this, then individuals with the skills and knowledge to perform these roles should be used in these initial stages.

Early involvement will help to build commitment from the individuals who will be tasked with implementing the programme and the associated business changes. See also section 2.2.2 for a discussion of the 'leading change' principle.

## 14.5   PRODUCE THE PROGRAMME BRIEF

The programme brief provides the formal basis for assessing whether the proposed programme is viable and achievable. Using the programme mandate, the programme's specific objectives, required benefits, potential risks, outline costs and timescales are defined. Options for delivery can also be developed.

It should restate 'where we are now', refining and expanding the input from the programme mandate. The assumptions about 'where we will be at a defined point in the future if we do nothing' should be re-examined, especially if some time has passed since the organization's strategy was approved.

The typical content of a programme brief is described in Appendix A.

All those involved in the programme will need to gain a summary understanding of the current change initiatives, identifying:

- Areas of potential overlap that may give rise to duplication or conflict

- Conflicts where activities in one initiative may diminish the outcomes of another
- Gaps where there are no (or insufficient) activities.

They also need to ensure that all these areas are directly related to the strategic objectives in the programme mandate.

The programme brief for an emergent programme will additionally need to clearly state what, if any, current work will be stopped (to resolve issues associated with duplicate/conflicting activities). It will also need to provide guidance for the re-shaping of the current change initiatives into a coherent programme.

The use of a programme brief (rather than a complete, highly detailed business case; see section 10.2.2) at this early stage of a programme helps to avoid futile, and often time-consuming, work on detailed cost analysis, investment appraisals, expenditure profiles and so on, when the overall concept of the proposed programme may not be viable for reasons other than financial justification. For example, if the initial expectations of benefits realization are unlikely to be achieved within a sensible timeframe, it may not be worthwhile taking the proposed programme any further.

The programme brief (once approved) provides the basis for development of the programme's full business case and other programme management information in the Defining a Programme process.

Tip

Within the programme brief there is reference to information that evolves into more detail once Defining a Programme begins. It may be more practical to have the risk register, issue register and benefits and stakeholder information organized in the appropriate formats that enable ongoing management rather than keep them in a specific template or format. The important point, as with all information, is that it exists and is available in a format that makes effective decision-making possible.

## 14.6 DEVELOP THE PROGRAMME PREPARATION PLAN

Defining a Programme involves the detailed planning and design of all aspects of the programme. A programme preparation plan for this work is produced, so that the sponsoring group are fully aware of, and willing to commit to, the cost, time and resource that will be required in the next part of the programme.

It is essential to plan sufficient time and resources, and to identify individuals with the right skills and experience, for the development of a detailed programme definition document.

At this point in the life of a programme there will be much uncertainty and ambiguity over the detail of what the programme will involve. Planning sufficient time and resources for Defining a Programme will help to clarify and reduce this uncertainty and ambiguity. The programme preparation plan will explain how the governance themes will be applied to manage the expected complexity of Defining a Programme.

During Defining a Programme, specific skills may be required – for example, market knowledge, procurement, technology or property expertise; in particular, consider the resources that will be required to develop the blueprint. This requirement should be identified in the programme preparation plan.

A key element of the programme preparation plan should be an explanation of how assurance will be applied during the often long and complex Defining a Programme process, when stakeholder engagement, in particular, will be very important.

The programme preparation plan will set out the governance arrangements, resources and anticipated timetable for the delivery of the Defining a Programme work.

See Appendix A for details of the content of the programme preparation plan.

**Tip**

When the programme moves from Identifying into Defining, there will be a step change in knowledge, skills and experience required. It is a common error for inexperienced programme teams to underestimate the resource requirements; developing blueprint and benefits information are skills rarely found among project and programme practitioners.

## 14.7 INDEPENDENT REVIEW

It is highly advisable to conduct an independent formal review of the programme brief to assess the scope, rationale and objectives of the programme. The review should assess the extent to which the organization(s) involved have the capacity and ability to deliver and realize the expected benefits. The reality, impacts, possible mitigations of identified risks and assumptions should be challenged.

Who will be involved and how the review will be conducted should have been outlined in the assurance arrangements in the programme mandate. For UK public sector programmes, this may take the form of an OGC Gateway review 0. The assurance arrangements for this review should be defined in the programme mandate.

## 14.8 APPROVAL TO PROCEED

The programme brief and programme preparation plan set the context and direction for the programme during Defining a Programme.

Formal approval of these means that:

- The SRO confirms that the programme meets the business requirements
- The programme board commits to supporting delivery
- The sponsoring group authorizes and commits to resource and support the SRO to undertake the process of Defining a Programme as specified in the programme preparation plan.

This approval is based on a confirmed understanding of, and commitment to, the proposed programme's vision, and the preliminary view of its expected benefits, risks, issues, timescales, resources and costs. There must be clear justification for the investment of resources in the programme, including:

- Estimated benefits outweighing the sum of costs and dis-benefits
- The expected outcomes and end state outweighing the expected risks and challenges.

## 14.9 RESPONSIBILITIES

Typical responsibilities for Identifying a Programme are summarized in Table 14.1. For more information on the roles of the sponsoring group and programme board, and their responsibilities with regard to the RACI tables, see Chapter 4 and section 13.3.

**Table 14.1 Typical responsibilities for Identifying a Programme**

| Flow steps | Sponsoring group | SRO | Programme manager | BCMs | Programme office |
|---|---|---|---|---|---|
| Sponsoring the programme | A | | | | |
| Confirm the programme mandate | A | | | | |
| Appoint the SRO and programme board | A | | | | |
| Produce the programme brief | | A | R | R | |
| Develop the programme preparation plan | | A | R | R | |
| Independent review | A | R | C | C | |
| Approval to proceed | A | R | C | C | |

R = responsible (gets the work done); A = accountable (answerable for the programme's success); C = consulted (supports, has the information or capability required); I = informed (notified, but not consulted)
R reports to A. Where there is only an A, then A assumes R as well.

# Defining a Programme

# 15 Defining a Programme

## 15.1 INTRODUCTION

The Defining a Programme process (see Figure 15.1) provides the basis for deciding whether to proceed with the programme or not. This is where the detailed definition and planning for the programme is undertaken.

The programme brief is used as the starting point for developing the programme definition information in more detail. See Appendix A for content of the programme brief.

The business case and governance for the programme will now be developed. The governance defines the strategies for quality and assurance, monitoring and control, information management, stakeholders, risks and issues, benefits and resources. The various programme approaches are contained in the strategies, and plans and schedules are developed to provide information on the resources, dependencies and timescales for delivery of capability and realization of benefits. This framework will be further developed and applied in Chapter 16 (Managing the Tranches).

The inevitable trade-off between resources, costs, quality, timings and benefits requires agreement between the sponsoring group and senior responsible owner (SRO). At the completion of Defining a Programme, formal approval is required from the sponsoring group and SRO to proceed with the programme.

The programme preparation plan will set out the governance arrangements, resources and anticipated timetable for the delivery of the Defining a Programme work.

## 15.2 ESTABLISH THE INFRASTRUCTURE FOR DEFINING A PROGRAMME

It is important to establish a programme infrastructure at the beginning to give the team the means to successfully conduct the necessary activities.

This infrastructure might cover items such as:

■ Office accommodation

■ Configuration management
■ Software tools
■ Computers and other office equipment.

At this stage in the programme the information volumes are relatively small. As Defining a Programme progresses, these volumes will increase significantly. Many documents produced in this process are dependent on information in other documents. Some parts of Defining a Programme iterate through more than one cycle, as described in the sections that follow. Document content will be frequently changing as the programme is designed and prepared. It is essential to have a mechanism to keep these co-dependent documents synchronized, otherwise the programme team and stakeholders may be misled. Configuration management facilities and processes provide this control and are an important tool in establishing an effective infrastructure.

## 15.3 ESTABLISH THE TEAM TO DEFINE THE PROGRAMME

The SRO will typically require the support of a small team. The programme preparation plan produced in Identifying a Programme is used to identify the skills and resources, and select and appoint the team.

The team will need appropriate skills, knowledge and experience in areas relevant to the programme and its management. Members of the team may subsequently fulfil formal roles, such as programme manager or business change manager (BCM), within the programme organization structure. See Chapter 4 for more detail on programme organization, roles and responsibilities.

At this point, specialist skills (for example, business and market analysis) to help with the construction of the blueprint, benefits or options analysis should be put in place.

For an emergent programme, careful consideration should be given to making best use of the resources on the current change initiatives relative to the new demands that the emergent programme will place on these projects. Some of

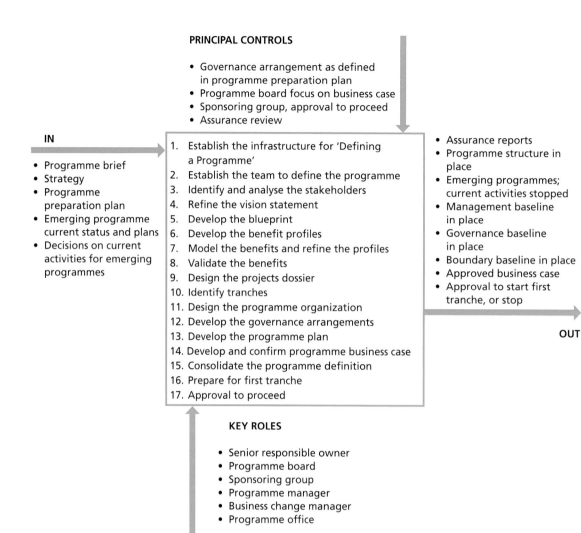

**PRINCIPAL CONTROLS**

- Governance arrangement as defined in programme preparation plan
- Programme board focus on business case
- Sponsoring group, approval to proceed
- Assurance review

**IN**

- Programme brief
- Strategy
- Programme preparation plan
- Emerging programme current status and plans
- Decisions on current activities for emerging programmes

1. Establish the infrastructure for 'Defining a Programme'
2. Establish the team to define the programme
3. Identify and analyse the stakeholders
4. Refine the vision statement
5. Develop the blueprint
6. Develop the benefit profiles
7. Model the benefits and refine the profiles
8. Validate the benefits
9. Design the projects dossier
10. Identify tranches
11. Design the programme organization
12. Develop the governance arrangements
13. Develop the programme plan
14. Develop and confirm programme business case
15. Consolidate the programme definition
16. Prepare for first tranche
17. Approval to proceed

- Assurance reports
- Programme structure in place
- Emerging programmes; current activities stopped
- Management baseline in place
- Governance baseline in place
- Boundary baseline in place
- Approved business case
- Approval to start first tranche, or stop

**OUT**

**KEY ROLES**

- Senior responsible owner
- Programme board
- Sponsoring group
- Programme manager
- Business change manager
- Programme office

*Figure 15.1 Overview of Defining a Programme*

these resources may be appropriate for the newly defined needs of this programme and others may be better deployed elsewhere.

Assurance arrangements should be put in place to support and monitor the direction of the programme.

## 15.4 IDENTIFY AND ANALYSE THE STAKEHOLDERS

All the programme's stakeholders (internal and external) should be identified, together with their particular interest in the programme. It is also important to identify any stakeholders who are likely to be worse off as a result of the programme, as their interests and influence may prevent the programme's successful outcome.

The input of the BCM is critical to identifying operational stakeholders and engaging at an early stage those who will have a high impact.

The analysis of stakeholders will identify the various information needs and communication flows that should be established as part of programme communications. The results of this analysis are contained in the stakeholder profiles (see Appendix A). It contains information such as:

- Stakeholder map
- Impact assessment
- Analysis information.

This work needs to be started at the beginning of Defining a Programme, as the programme team will need to engage stakeholders in these activities. The manner in which this early engagement takes place can have a critical effect on stakeholders' attitude to the programme. It is important that the engagement of stakeholders does not create early barriers to the progress and development of the programme (see Chapter 6 for more details).

## 15.5 REFINE THE VISION STATEMENT

The outline vision statement contained in the programme brief is refined into the programme's vision statement. It provides the basis for communicating and encouraging the buy-in and commitment from stakeholders.

The purpose is to communicate the transformed, beneficial future state to the programme's wide audience of stakeholders. When any organization goes through transformational change, different stakeholders will not necessarily understand the big picture without such a vision statement. The vision statement is written as a future state (not as an objective, trend or mission, all of which are commonly written beginning with the word 'To').

This is an important step as the feedback from initial stakeholder engagement will provide information on where the vision can be adapted to meet the needs of different stakeholders and avoid unnecessary conflict, whilst also making courageous statements that set the agenda for the programme.

### Example

A simple vision statement for a higher education institution could read as follows:

*When this programme is completed we will be able to offer our students a greater range of higher education courses than our competitors, enhancing our reputation as the foremost school for language studies in the world. A student will be able to choose from traditional courses, as well as IT-supported distance learning from anywhere in the globe, all leading to internationally recognized qualifications. Our students will also have the flexibility to progress through their chosen course at a speed to suit themselves.*

For further details on the vision statement, see Appendix A.

## 15.6 DEVELOP THE BLUEPRINT

Developing the blueprint involves many concepts of organizational design. It may encompass all dimensions of the organization or business – its cultural aspects as well as its structure, processes and activities – and how they need to change. Business analysis and design techniques may also be required to explore fully the opportunities and options for achieving the capabilities described in the vision statement. There are typically many options for achieving the required changes, with associated costs and impacts. Exploring these options and assessing the implications on the investment required is an important aspect for designing the optimum blueprint for the programme.

Designing the blueprint to realize the required benefits needs to be balanced against the costs of realizing those benefits. The programme's business case is developed in parallel with the blueprint to ensure consistency across the proposed changes to the organization, the costs of doing the changes and realization of the benefits being achievable.

The blueprint, benefits maps, projects dossier and programme plan are designed together, with the emerging business case acting as the moderator.

Some organizations have an overall blueprint for the entire business (sometimes referred to as the 'target operating model'). In these contexts, where each programme is briefed to deliver a discrete part of that corporate blueprint, ensure that work isn't duplicated elsewhere.

The gap – the difference between the 'as-is' and 'to-be' organization – will need to be analysed. It provides a critical input to designing the projects dossier and programme plan. The blueprint does not normally need to be expressed in detail. It will be the responsibility of the projects to develop more detailed designs and specifications to meet the requirements for the 'to-be' model. The programme must take responsibility for the integration and cohesiveness of the project-level designs, assuring that the blueprint is achieved.

The first benefits maps can be developed from the first cut of the blueprint. They will need to be enhanced when estimates of the time and cost are available from the programme plan. The merging of this information into the business case provides the control to judge if the developing programme designs are good enough in terms of an acceptable balance between time, cost, risks and benefits.

Figure 15.2 is an example showing how the blueprint, benefits maps and projects dossier might be developed together until an acceptable business case emerges. Through each iteration, the SRO will judge whether the developing business case is likely to be good enough for formal approval by the sponsoring group at the end of Defining a Programme (see Chapter 8 for more details).

Involving the target business operations (i.e. who will be part of the future organization) in the development of the blueprint is a powerful method for improving the quality of the information and increasing the understanding and buy-in to the change.

Further details on benefits maps can be found in Chapter 7.

Tip

One of the dangers that a programme blueprint faces is that the operational structures are changed from the 'as-is' state without reference to the programme, thus removing the basis of the anticipated outcomes. The more the business operations are involved in the development, the more they are likely understand the effect of these changes.

For further details on the blueprint, see Appendix A.

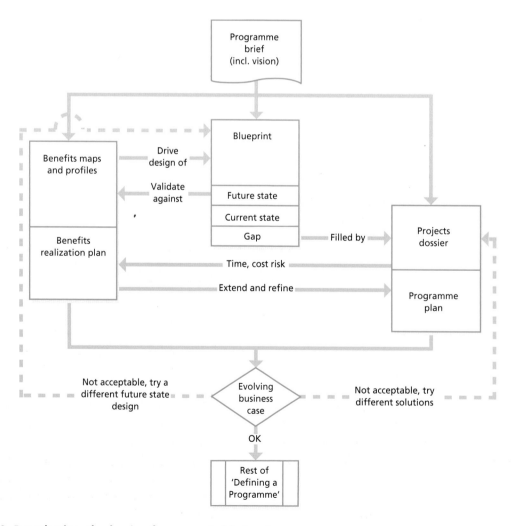

*Figure 15.2 Developing the basis of an acceptable business case*

For inexperienced programme teams, developing the blueprint is one of the toughest tasks, as the skills and experience needed may not be available within the organization. Not knowing what the programme has to create will significantly increase the risk of failure. Business performance and modelling teams may have expertise to help with the activities involved in developing the blueprint.

## 15.7    DEVELOP THE BENEFIT PROFILES

The vision statement and programme brief identify the required benefits from the programme. Each benefit (and dis-benefit) requires a complete definition, known as a benefit profile.

The total set of benefit profiles provides a planning and control tool to track progress on the delivery and realization of the benefits. The benefit profiles will be further refined as the detailed definition of the programme is developed.

Each benefit needs to have a baseline measurement. As the business prepares to go through the change cycle, it is important for it to understand its starting point. To do this it will have to establish KPIs that reflect the overall performance of the organization at this time. The baseline measurement for the benefit may be drawn from the 'as-is' information in the blueprint; the 'to-be' information may include the performance measure which will indicate that the benefit has been achieved.

These indicators will be tracked to assess the business stability during the lifetime of the programme and the delivery of benefits resulting from the changes being applied.

It is tempting for a programme to select indicators that are directly related to the outcomes that it will enable. However, it is important that a holistic range of relevant indicators is used for monitoring. It is no use cutting the costs of products if customers leave because of poor quality, and it is counterproductive to adopt mechanistic processes that cause creative staff to become disillusioned and leave.

The following should be considered when selecting benefit measure and performance baselines:

- Some KPIs may not be suitable for measuring benefits.
- Some KPIs may need to be adjusted as a result of operational changes. The programme may have an obligation to define new KPIs and provide processes and tools to support them.
- Current KPIs may need to be supplemented by other measures to assess the benefits realized.
- Performance criteria from contracts, service level agreements, compliance targets etc. may also need to be taken into account and re-negotiated, particularly to understand any penalties that could occur because of performance deterioration.
- Some measures may be subject to deviations as a result of normal process variation (e.g. seasonal trends). It is important this is understood and defined, otherwise actual benefit measures may be misunderstood.

For further details on benefit profiles, see Chapter 7.

Much of the business performance information that will enable the calculation of the benefits will be available from the blueprint in the 'as-is' state. Without such a business model, benefit calculations can only be guesstimates, and this should be reflected as a risk.

## 15.8    MODEL THE BENEFITS AND REFINE THE PROFILES

The first benefit profiles for end benefits are initially created from information in the vision statement and the programme brief. As the blueprint is designed, these can be extended and refined. Benefits maps are initially modelled (driven by the blueprint) and then extended by information from the projects dossier and programme plan. The mix of benefits, dependencies on project outputs, and other benefits becomes clearer. Benefit profiles are refined as a result.

Having too many benefits defined will increase the cost and complexity of achievement; using the benefit categories will help to rationalize the benefits and identify the priorities and coherent ways of grouping them. For further details see Chapter 7.

## 15.9 VALIDATE THE BENEFITS

A realistic assessment of the inevitable trade-off between the cost of realizing and measuring a benefit against the value of having that benefit should be made, in order to avoid wasting time on trying to realize unrealistic benefits.

Each benefit should represent some aspect of the programme's desired outcomes. Benefits that are not linked to strategic objectives may actually be unhelpful. Furthermore, they may distract from achieving the major benefits. Chapter 7 explains the tests that should be applied to validate a benefit.

The first validation of benefits is via the test of the emerging business case, as described in section 15.6 on developing the blueprint and in Chapter 8, which covers the design and delivery of the blueprint.

All benefits should ultimately pass the benefits validation test outlined in Chapter 7.

## 15.10 DESIGN THE PROJECTS DOSSIER

The vision statement, blueprint, benefit profiles and benefits maps provide the basis for designing the projects and any other activities necessary to deliver the new capabilities. These projects and activities form the programme's projects dossier, which represents the programme's approach and describes how it will deliver the future organization, the operation of which will result in the desired outcomes and benefits. It is used as the basis for developing the programme plan.

There may be different options for achieving improvements to business operations, in which case these should be explored in terms of timing, content, risks and benefits. Some projects and activities may be existing ongoing work that will need to be adopted into the programme as part of the projects dossier; others may be new initiatives that will require commissioning by the programme at the appropriate point.

## 15.11 IDENTIFY TRANCHES

The outcome(s) described in the vision statement and expressed in the blueprint can rarely be delivered in a single pass, but will typically be reached through progressive refinements or step changes in the capabilities of the organization.

These step changes can be used to define the ends of successive tranches, where formal reviews can be carried out.

The projects and activities in the projects dossier are scheduled together showing their relative timescales and dependencies. The delivery is built into tranches reflecting the step changes in capability. It may not be possible to define all of the required projects fully at this point. Further analysis may be required to complete the scoping of later projects after the results from early tranches have been assessed.

Early in the programme, the route to the vision is often unclear. Early tranches may be designed to explore and prove (or disprove) different approaches to achieve the vision. The most valuable output of these types of early tranches will be the information that enables the sponsoring group to decide whether to continue with the programme, and if so, to have confidence that the best route has been identified. If the results of early discovery work show that the vision is not attainable at reasonable cost, time and risk, the programme must be stopped or significantly changed. Failure to do this will almost certainly result in significant expenditure being wasted.

For further details on scheduling and tranches, see Chapter 8.

Tip

Once the blueprint has become stable, benefit profiles have been created, tranches defined and the projects dossier developed, this is a good point to undertake an assurance review of the programme and confirm the sponsoring group commitment to proceed. It will now be clear what the future state will look like, the level and complexity of change anticipated, and the value that will be gained.

There is little value in continuing with the rest of Defining a Programme until the direction of travel has been confirmed; further work may be wasteful.

## 15.12 DESIGN THE PROGRAMME ORGANIZATION

The organization for directing, managing, controlling and supporting the programme has to be designed. Successful programme delivery requires sufficient resourcing of the programme and change management activities. The structure must enable effective decision-making and efficient communication flows among the various members of the programme team and stakeholders. The nature and size of the programme will influence the design of an appropriate programme organization. The structure will need to integrate with, and operate alongside, the existing management structures of the organization(s). The programme organization should reflect the management levels appropriate to the visibility and significance of the programme.

See also section 2.2.2 and Chapter 4; for more details on the contents of the organization structure document see Appendix A.

Each role within the organization should be defined with its specific accountabilities, responsibilities and tasks, together with the skills and competencies required. Individuals with the appropriate skills and experience to take on these roles should be identified. If they are not available, a plan for acquiring the resources, internally or externally, should be developed in the resource management strategy.

It is often not possible to assemble all the people required with adequate competencies from internal resources. This must be addressed, perhaps using those resources with greater skills and experience to coach and mentor others. This situation should be identified by the programme and project risk analysis. Where the lack of skills and experience is significant, this must be reflected in the programme plan, to allow people sufficient time to learn and develop. It may be necessary to supplement internal resources with external expertise.

Many individuals assigned to programme roles will also have operational responsibilities. Prioritization of workloads is an important consideration. The work required of each role needs to be balanced against the time the individual is able to commit. It is important that there is understanding and agreement between the programme and line managers about:

- How to allocate resource time (from, to, how long, which days of the week, percentage of working week etc.) to programme or project work
- Who will manage the resource when working on the programme or project
- How conflict will be resolved
- How time will be tracked and accounted for.

It may be necessary to procure external resources for the programme, providing specialist skills and experience to fulfil some of the roles. It is important to remember that procurement is typically lengthy, and sufficient time and resources should be planned for procurement. Routes to procure additional resources include secondment, contracting, delegation or subcontracting the work, and sharing with other initiatives.

For further details on programme organization see Chapter 4.

## 15.13 DEVELOP THE GOVERNANCE ARRANGEMENTS

The programme management governance strategies should cover how the programme is going to handle the inevitable complexity and interdependencies, and bring the different aspects together. These strategies must be designed to integrate with the corporate governance of the organization where this already exists.

The various strategies required are described in detail in the governance themes chapters in Part 2, and also in Appendix A. They are as follows:

- Benefits management strategy
- Information management strategy
- Risk management strategy
- Issue management strategy
- Monitoring and control strategy
- Quality and assurance strategy
- Resource management strategy
- Stakeholder engagement strategy.

The governance elements underpinning these strategies and the plans that implement them are discussed further below. It is important that all programme strategies are aligned with existing corporate strategies.

This information is considered when finalizing the business case and informs the Managing the Tranches process (see Chapter 16).

## 15.14 DEVELOP THE PROGRAMME PLAN

The programme plan is developed by bringing together the information on projects, resources, timescales, risk, monitoring and control. The amount of information available and the level of detail required will develop as the programme progresses. An outline programme plan showing the estimated relative timescales for the projects should be developed at this stage. It should identify where assurance reviews of progress and benefits realization can be carried out.

It is perfectly acceptable for the programme plan to incorporate and aggregate the other plans required to implement the governance strategies into the programme plan where this is optimal.

For further details on developing the programme plan, see Chapter 8.

## 15.15 DEVELOP AND CONFIRM PROGRAMME BUSINESS CASE

The business case will have started to emerge in Identifying a Programme and it is then developed further (see section 15.6). This emerging business case is transformed into the final business case as the arrangements for managing the programme are developed.

The business case brings together information about the programme covering the costs, benefits, timings and risks so that the overall value for money and achievability of the programme can be assessed and appropriate management decisions made about the viability of the programme.

The business case will need to be further refined as the programme proceeds, especially at the end of tranches where formal reviews objectively judge the success (or shortfalls) achieved so far.

For further details on the business case, see Chapter 10.

## 15.16 CONSOLIDATE THE PROGRAMME DEFINITION

All of the information produced in Defining a Programme can now be consolidated. This can be produced as a complete set of information, with an executive summary, or can just be a summary that references the other detailed documents. See Appendix A for more details on the programme definition document.

The full set of programme information should now have been produced and should be under configuration management and change control. These are assembled into information baselines. More details can be found on the baselined documents and the information that should be contained in them in Appendix A.

## 15.17 PREPARE FOR FIRST TRANCHE

As the programme now has more clarity about the way forward, it can prepare for the first tranche(s). It is usually not sensible to prepare in detail for later tranches until near the end of the first tranche, when there will then be greater confidence about the programme's approach to achieving the desired benefits. Activities include:

- Prepare to establish the programme's governance and organization
- Specify the physical environment and infrastructure required for managing the next tranche
- Develop plans to establish governance and the organization structure.

Similar preparations need to occur as the programme approaches later tranches. See Chapter 16 for more detail.

## 15.18 APPROVAL TO PROCEED

The programme definition is assembled and the information produced in Defining a Programme is summarized and consolidated into one document to enable easy assimilation by stakeholders.

Approval to proceed is a four-stage process:

1 **SRO (and programme board) approves**

The complete set of documentation describing the programme, its governance, plans and business case should be approved by the SRO as suitable to submit for review and formal sponsoring group approval and authorization.

2 **Sponsoring group endorses**

Formal endorsement is sought from the programme's sponsoring group to confirm that the programme is designed to meet their expectations and requirements.

3 **Independent review**

Reviews may involve independent assurance scrutiny as defined in the programme assurance arrangements, such as an OGC Gateway review. An unbiased objective independent assurance review of the programme may be a contractual obligation in partnership programmes where several organizations are sharing the investment and the risk and later hope to share the benefits. These may be internal assurance reviews or, in the case of UK government, they may additionally be external assurance reviews. See also Chapter 12.

4 **Sponsoring group authorizes the SRO**

The sponsoring group must give its approval on behalf of the organization to proceed with the programme, including commitment to the investment required for the programme. In many programmes it is not possible to clarify total investment requirements at the start. In such cases the SRO obtains further formal approval from the sponsoring group when more information becomes available or at the end of further tranches.

## 15.19  RESPONSIBILITIES

Typical responsibilities for Defining a Programme are summarized in Table 15.1. For more information on the roles of the sponsoring group and programme board, and their responsibilities with regard to the RACI tables, see Chapter 4 and section 13.3.

**Table 15.1 Typical responsibilities for Defining a Programme**

| Flow steps | SRO | Programme manager | BCMs | Programme office |
|---|---|---|---|---|
| Establish the infrastructure for Defining a Programme | A | R | I | C |
| Establish the team to define the programme | A | R | I | C |
| Identify and analyse stakeholders | A | R | C | C |
| Refine the vision statement | A | R | C | |
| Develop the blueprint | A | R | C | C |
| Develop the benefit profiles | A | C | R | C |
| Model the benefits and refine the profiles | A | C | R | C |
| Validate the benefits | A | C | R | |
| Design the projects dossier | A | R | C | C |
| Identify tranches | A | R | R | C |
| Design the programme organization | A | R | C | C |
| Develop the governance arrangements | A | R | C | C |
| Develop the programme plan | A | R | C | C |
| Develop and confirm programme business case | A | R | C | I |
| Consolidate the programme definition | A | R | C | C |
| Prepare for first tranche | A | R | C | C |
| Approval to proceed | A | R | R | I |

R = responsible (gets the work done); A = accountable (answerable for the programme's success); C = consulted (supports, has the information or capability required); I = informed (notified, but not consulted)

# Managing the Tranches

16

# 16  Managing the Tranches

## 16.1  INTRODUCTION

The purpose of the Managing the Tranches process (see Figure 16.1) is to implement the defined programme management governance strategies for the programme, ensure that the capability delivery is aligned to the strategic direction of the organization, and enable the release of benefits. This accepts that, as the programme progresses, this will need to be adapted and refined to assure the effective delivery of the tranches and the final outcomes.

A key principle of the Managing the Tranches process is to maintain the balance between the rate of change being offered by the Delivering the Capability process and the rate of change that the operational areas can cope with. This is managed through the Realizing the Benefits stage which aligns the programme with the evolving and changing strategic needs of the organization.

Unlike some of the activities in other processes, which tend to happen in a logical sequence, the activities in Managing the Tranches may recur or happen concurrently. Most of the activities are linked to the governance themes and are intended to trigger the cycles that are defined in Part 2. For example, you do not 'manage risk and issues' once: this is a day-to-day activity that occurs throughout the tranche.

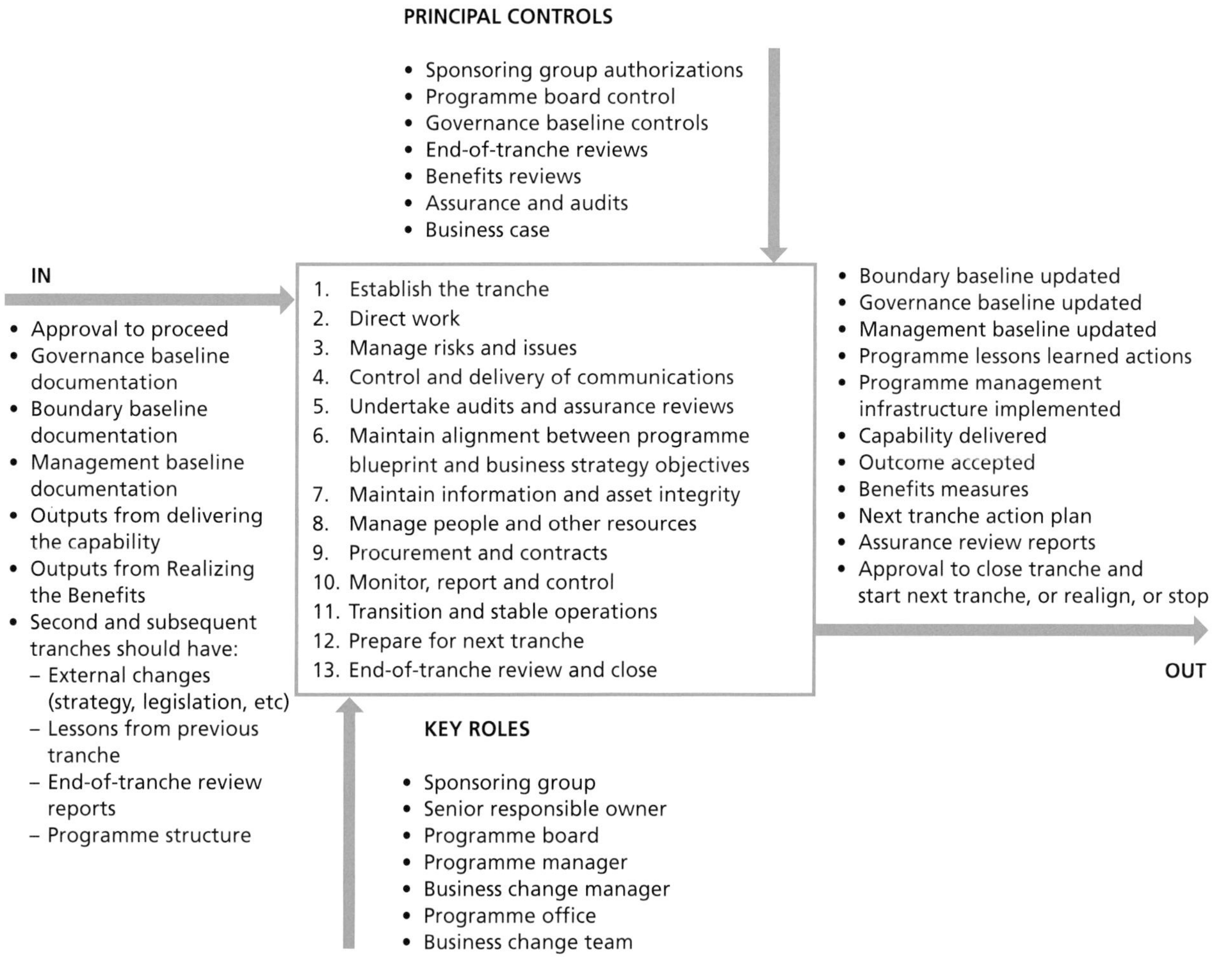

**PRINCIPAL CONTROLS**

- Sponsoring group authorizations
- Programme board control
- Governance baseline controls
- End-of-tranche reviews
- Benefits reviews
- Assurance and audits
- Business case

**IN**

- Approval to proceed
- Governance baseline documentation
- Boundary baseline documentation
- Management baseline documentation
- Outputs from delivering the capability
- Outputs from Realizing the Benefits
- Second and subsequent tranches should have:
  - External changes (strategy, legislation, etc)
  - Lessons from previous tranche
  - End-of-tranche review reports
  - Programme structure

1. Establish the tranche
2. Direct work
3. Manage risks and issues
4. Control and delivery of communications
5. Undertake audits and assurance reviews
6. Maintain alignment between programme blueprint and business strategy objectives
7. Maintain information and asset integrity
8. Manage people and other resources
9. Procurement and contracts
10. Monitor, report and control
11. Transition and stable operations
12. Prepare for next tranche
13. End-of-tranche review and close

- Boundary baseline updated
- Governance baseline updated
- Management baseline updated
- Programme lessons learned actions
- Programme management infrastructure implemented
- Capability delivered
- Outcome accepted
- Benefits measures
- Next tranche action plan
- Assurance review reports
- Approval to close tranche and start next tranche, or realign, or stop

**OUT**

**KEY ROLES**

- Sponsoring group
- Senior responsible owner
- Programme board
- Programme manager
- Business change manager
- Programme office
- Business change team

*Figure 16.1  Overview of Managing the Tranches*

## 16.2 ESTABLISH THE TRANCHE

### 16.2.1 Programme organization

The organization structure for the programme is now implemented, with the identified individuals appointed. Each role should have a clearly defined set of responsibilities that the appointed individual has understood and accepts, which should be based on the organization structure document described in Appendix A.

Plans should be put into place for development of the ability, capacity and performance of the team as the programme progresses.

See also Chapter 4 for structures and responsibilities, and see Chapter 12 for more detail about people management.

### 16.2.2 Business change team

The programme team delivers the means to change the operational part of an organization. The operational functions need to receive and effectively use the outcomes the programme delivers to achieve the benefits. A business change team represents the interests of the part of the organization to be changed, and will ensure that those parts are appropriately involved and thoroughly prepared for the transition. It will be especially active during transition when operational staff will need to be supported.

See also Chapters 6 and 7 and the organization structure document in Appendix A.

### 16.2.3 Programme office

The programme office should as a minimum provide an information hub for the programme and may also have skilled resources able to offer consultancy-style specialist assistance to the programme management team and the projects, as required. The programme office's functions and procedures are established and operated throughout the programme.

If the programme office is dedicated to the programme, its lack of independence means it cannot carry out audits or similar reviews of the programme. In such cases, arrangements need to be established with a different body that is independent of the programme and can therefore provide unbiased assessments.

### 16.2.4 Support for governance

The various governance strategies define the required arrangements, information and procedures that need to be put in place. The programme office provides support for the governance requirements of the programme, for example the collection, aggregation, analysis and reporting of detailed data, to enable the programme team to easily assess the overall state of the programme.

The appropriate governance strategy plans should now be activated to establish the governance. The assurance arrangements should be put in place to ensure that the programme is under appropriate controls (see also Appendix C).

### 16.2.5 Physical environment

The physical programme environment, including buildings, office space, office facilities and services, should be established, as defined in the resource management plan.

The technology and tools required to support the programme also need to be acquired and implemented, and staff trained in their use. Typical tools used to support the programme include:

■ Planning, estimating and scheduling tools
■ Tools to support risk management, quality and assurance management, financial management and change control
■ Document management and record management tools
■ Configuration management tools.

### 16.2.6 Communications

Now that the programme is moving into delivery, there will need to be activities to raise awareness of the programme and its impact on the organization in the widest sense. This could include launch publicity events and promotional articles if deemed appropriate.

The programme communications plan defines how the programme will inform the stakeholders about the programme and gives advice on encouraging feedback. The required mechanisms are set up.

## 16.3 DIRECT WORK

This is a catch-all activity, which covers much of the day-to-day work of the programme manager. Projects and other activities will need to be started according to the schedules and plans prepared in the Defining a Programme process. Starting the projects is managed in the Delivering the Capability process but it is triggered from here; other programme-level management activities that are carried out in this process include:

- Appointment of project delivery organizations
- Programme risk workshops
- Programme reporting
- Dealing with project exceptions
- Managing the programme and project teams.

## 16.4 MANAGE RISKS AND ISSUES

The steps in the risk management and issue management cycles will now be followed. Risks and issues are actively managed (added, assessed, reviewed, updated and closed) throughout the programme, and the overall risk and issues profiles continually monitored.

Managing risks and issues in a programme has three perspectives:

- The programme's internal risks and issues
- Those that arise outside the programme (e.g. from a change of strategy) and those that arise from outside the organization (e.g. change of legislation)
- Risks and issues escalated from the programme's projects and operational areas.

As well as careful monitoring of the programme and its projects, the programme manager needs a mechanism to scan the environment external to the programme. It can be useful to get help with this from those who monitor the external environment as part of their day-to-day role – for example, legal and marketing staff (see also Chapter 11).

For any given tranche, after an initial risk assessment, the aggregated risk for that tranche should gradually decline. As transition is about to start, open risks will most likely only be related to transition itself (i.e. the embedding of the new operations, achievement of the outcomes and the benefits measurement arrangements). Issues will increase as quality assurance activities take

place. As transition approaches, the number of open issues should also be rapidly decreasing. Any patterns contrary to these are causes for concern and should be investigated.

## 16.5 CONTROL AND DELIVERY OF COMMUNICATIONS

Use the programme communications plan as early as possible by notifying the stakeholders of the individuals appointed to specific roles on the programme. Thereafter, the communication activities should ensure that the stakeholders are kept informed and engaged in the work of the programme, its projects and the benefits expected.

When stakeholders have received new communications, it is important to check that they have understood them in the way the programme team intended. Misunderstanding in programmes can give rise to significant problems. Communications are intended to generate and maintain support from stakeholders. Communications, formal and informal, will affect how people feel about the programme. Stakeholders' attitudes need to be continually assessed, and any significant decline in attitude will require attention.

It is essential to ensure that feedback channels between the programme and its stakeholders are working effectively.

Stakeholders will often change during the life of a programme. The stakeholder engagement strategy will provide guidance on how to detect stakeholder changes and how to assess new stakeholders (see Chapter 6).

## 16.6 UNDERTAKE AUDITS AND ASSURANCE REVIEWS

The programme must ensure that mechanisms are in place to assess the performance of its processes and projects. These must be used regularly to ensure that the actual performance is acceptable. Stakeholders will require reassurance of this, and may initiate an audit to verify and validate progress and performance so far.

These reviews should be extended to the business operations to ensure that they are preparing appropriately for transition, and once they have undergone transition to ensure that the new systems and working practices are being embedded and that the change is established.

This is the transformational flow activity which triggers the activities in the quality and assurance plan and the strategic approach to audit and integrated assurance (see Chapter 12 for more details).

## 16.7 MAINTAIN ALIGNMENT BETWEEN PROGRAMME BLUEPRINT AND BUSINESS STRATEGIC OBJECTIVES

As an organization's strategy changes, monitoring arrangements should detect pending strategy changes. An impact assessment should take place, with the results fed back to the strategy makers. When corporate strategy changes are approved, the programme may also need to change (possibly including the blueprint, business case and other dependent documents) to ensure strategic alignment.

Programmes and their projects sometimes drift off course. Regular assurance of strategy against the blueprint will be needed to maintain the ongoing alignment of the programme with the corporate strategy. If the programme becomes significantly out of alignment with the strategy, the consequential impact on the business case can render the programme invalid and lead to closure.

## 16.8 MAINTAIN INFORMATION AND ASSET INTEGRITY

As projects are started, information volumes will increase significantly. It is vital that configuration management is in place to track new items and changes to existing items. Configuration management plays an important role in supporting issue management by helping to assess the impact of change requests. These activities link closely with quality activities, the information management strategy and information plan.

Configuration baselines should be updated at the end of each tranche. See Chapter 12 for more detail on information management, and Chapter 11 for more information on configuration management.

## 16.9 MANAGE PEOPLE AND OTHER RESOURCES

The resource management strategy defines rules of engagement for acquiring and using resources.

Resources are often shared across programmes, projects and operational work. Issues can arise if the resource required is not going to be available. A corporate portfolio office can be helpful here, as it can provide a complete picture of the utilization of resources and the status of potentially competing activities.

There are critical points in a programme when careful attention needs to be paid to managing people. As a tranche end approaches, people typically get concerned as they are soon going to have to change the way they do their work. It might help, for example, to provide extra support for staff as they prepare for transition and as they start to take on their new roles and use new systems.

For further details, see Chapters 6, 8, 9 and 12 and Appendix C.

## 16.10 PROCUREMENT AND CONTRACTS

The resource management strategy identifies the requirements for procurement and contract management within the programme, which are consequently set up as defined in the resource management plan. Managing suppliers and maintaining the alignment of their activities with the overall direction of the programme require specific management attention and intervention if things go off track. Procurement and contract management activities must be aligned to corporate policies and standards, and may require tailoring to suit the particular needs of the programme.

As part of this activity, there should be regular scheduled reviews of suppliers and their performance against expectation and the contract.

## 16.11 MONITOR, REPORT AND CONTROL

Arrangements defined in the monitoring and control strategy are implemented and should be used to control progress. Regular progress reporting from the projects informs the formal progress monitoring, which keeps the programme on track. Monitoring progress may identify problem areas requiring management intervention. These issues should be escalated and actioned as soon as possible to prevent the programme losing momentum and moving off track.

This is likely to be the primary focus for the programme board, where much of the progress will be reviewed and issues considered and resolved.

A key aspect of control is ensuring that the blueprint and the delivery of new capabilities defined within it remain internally consistent and coherent.

The following list summarizes monitoring and control activities that are important enough to warrant the attention of the senior responsible owner (SRO) and programme board:

- Check that information is complete, timely, accurate and relevant for the control and decision-making it supports. Any significant gaps in information, or if it is out of date, will mean that the programme is out of control. Significant amounts of information come from the programme's projects. Reporting mechanisms from projects must be checked regularly to ensure that they are functioning correctly
- Ensure that decisions – for planned activities and exceptions, their definitions and instructions – are contained in the monitoring and control strategy
- Approve major exceptions from projects
- Approve outcome achievements, accepting deviations
- Approve benefits achievements, accepting deviations
- Deal with benefits realization exceptions
- Deal with capability delivery escalations
- Initiate additional activities that will be required as part of Delivering the Capability
- Authorize exceptional communications activities to address stakeholder issues
- Monitor benefits realization, tracking business performance, benefits achievements and instigating ad hoc benefits reviews.

The internal control mechanisms are defined within the governance strategies: the monitoring and control strategy is particularly relevant.

## 16.12 TRANSITION AND STABLE OPERATIONS

This is particularly focused on the activities in Realizing the Benefits and the progress towards benefits achievement. It is a key role of the programme board to maintain focus on transition and organizational stability whilst maintaining momentum towards achieving the benefits.

Transition plans prepared earlier in the tranche will be activated when the project outputs have been combined and tested, the capability is ready for transition and operations are ready to use them, changing their ways of working. Transition can sometimes be very disruptive, and these plans may need to be very detailed in order to minimize the impact on ongoing business operations. Consider providing extra support to people who may be legitimately concerned at this difficult time.

Transition ends when the outputs are implemented and the new capabilities established. Measurement of the performance of the current state of operations must have been completed before transition starts. Performance measures should be tracked during the preparation and during transition and after to make sure that operations progress to a stable state and do not drift back to the old ways of working. Such measures are also important during this period to help minimize dis-benefits and spot opportunities to realize additional benefits.

The start of transition is usually a clearly identifiable event authorized by the SRO. Moving from transition to a stable state is more of a grey area and requires the judgement of experienced senior management to agree when the outcomes have been achieved and the post-transition phase begins.

If everything and everyone are not thoroughly prepared, the change to the new ways of working will take longer and may be less successful. This can produce undesirable downsides such that:

- Disruption to operations will be more severe, leading to loss of output and/or quality
- Improvements resulting from the new operations might be less pronounced, and delivery of benefits will be reduced or delayed
- Operations may revert to the old ways of working and lose faith in the programme.

The SRO and the programme board should provide formal authorization to proceed into transition, and ensure that appropriate criteria are in place for speeding up or slowing down the transition rate based on the performance of the organization during this period. Fall-back and contingency plans should be in place if transition takes business performance outside the forecasted acceptable deviation.

This control encourages the programme team and business change teams to check that preparations are adequate, and helps to gain commitment from operational staff, which will be critical during this period. For more details on transition, see Chapters 9 and 18.

## 16.13 PREPARE FOR NEXT TRANCHE

As the programme progresses, there is increasing clarity about the way forward. This should occur at the end of each tranche. Changes to the programme's approach may now be needed as a result of lessons from the tranche now ending, for example:

- Learning from what this tranche has achieved to inform the next tranche, especially where the programme is designed for incremental delivery of change
- Adapting governance and the organization structure

- Different skills and experience might be needed; for example if the nature of the programme is moving from exploratory to more of a roll-out, this should be reflected in the resource management plan
- Specifying the physical environment and infrastructure required for managing the next tranche
- Refining and developing the blueprint, benefits maps, benefit profiles and projects dossier for the next tranche, building on and complementing the change already delivered by previous tranches
- Reviewing and refining information baselines (see Appendix A).

The programme's business case will need to be refined as the plans for the next tranche(s) unfold. The emphasis, as described in Defining a Programme, is to consider alternative approaches to develop the best business case. Ideally, the business case should be improved at each tranche end, with the programme concentrating on change that is working well and reducing that which is not.

The SRO consults with the sponsoring group, who will authorize the start of the next tranche.

## 16.14 END-OF-TRANCHE REVIEW AND CLOSE

Programme information is updated, refined and maintained as the programme progresses. In particular, this should be done at the end of each tranche, as preparations for the next tranche need

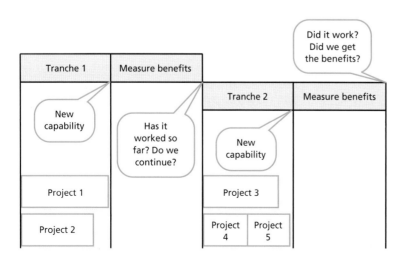

*Figure 16.2 Example of a programme where Tranche 1 is a pilot to test the strategy*

to be informed about what is working well and areas that need attention or adjustment. Successive refinements to the blueprint will highlight any adjustments that may need to be made to the projects dossier to keep the programme on track. The programme plan and benefits realization plan should be refined when completion and delivery dates from the projects are known.

The end of a tranche is reached when all the capability for that tranche has been delivered and transitioned into operational use.

At the end of each tranche there should be a full review to assess the ongoing viability of the programme and ensure that the delivery options and strategy remain optimal.

The end-of-tranche review provides a go/no-go decision point for the programme: it should only be allowed to continue to the next tranche if it is still viable. The SRO is accountable for ensuring that this review is undertaken formally, but will need authorization from the sponsoring group to support the recommendations.

The programme's business case, benefits and the benefits management approach must be reviewed at the end of each tranche. The business change manager(s) (BCM) should plan for at least one review after the tranche has closed, to assess the realization of post-tranche benefits. The end-of-tranche reviews may also include a formal assessment of the effectiveness of the programme management activities, including considering any programme lessons which have been documented during the tranche.

It may be useful to consider the assessment of benefits from both an internal and external perspective. The internal perspective will involve measuring reduction in costs, for example. The external perspective, for example via a programme audit function, will involve assessing whether the potential for realization of benefits remains on track and ensuring that all the possible benefit dependencies are considered.

If the tranche end has been designed to prove whether hypotheses embedded in the strategy can work satisfactorily, in order to collect and analyse sufficient benefit measures to reach a conclusion, there may be a planned delay before the next tranche starts. See Figure 16.2 for a diagrammatic example.

## 16.15 RESPONSIBILITIES

Typical responsibilities for Managing the Tranches are summarized in Table 16.1. For more information on the roles of the sponsoring group and programme board, and their responsibilities with regard to the RACI tables, see Chapter 4 and section 13.3.

**Table 16.1 Typical responsibilities for Managing the Tranches**

| Flow steps | SRO | Programme manager | BCMs | Programme office |
|---|---|---|---|---|
| Establish the tranche | A | R | C | C |
| Direct work | A | R | I | C |
| Manage risks and issues | A | R | R | C |
| Control and delivery of communications | A | R | R | C |
| Undertake audits and assurance reviews | A | R | R | I |
| Maintain alignment between programme blueprint and business strategic objectives | A | R | R | I |
| Maintain information and asset integrity | A | R | C | C |
| Manage people and other resources | A | R | C | C |
| Procurement and contracts | A | R | | |
| Monitor, report and control | A | R | C | C |
| Transition and stable operations | A | C | R | C |
| Prepare for next tranche | A | R | C | C |
| End-of-tranche review and close | A | R | C | C |

R = responsible (gets the work done); A = accountable (answerable for the programme's success); C = consulted (supports, has the information or capability required); I = informed (notified, but not consulted)
The Rs reflect responsibilities for different aspects of the programme: internal performance assurance for the programme manager, and business performance assurance and change readiness for the BCM.

Delivering the
Capability

17

# 17   Delivering the Capability

## 17.1   INTRODUCTION

The Delivering the Capability process (see Figure 17.1) covers the activities for coordinating and managing project delivery according to the programme plan. Delivery from the projects dossier provides the new outputs that enable the capabilities described in the blueprint. The activities of Delivering the Capability are repeated for each tranche of the programme.

Delivering the Capability and Realizing the Benefits (see Chapter 18) are distinct processes, but they do work closely together to harmonize the programme objectives with project delivery and benefits realization through transition to operations. The Managing the Tranches process (see Chapter 16) is used for overseeing these two processes, providing the high-level direction, guidance and control.

This process delivers the capability defined in the blueprint through the projects defined in the projects dossier. The detail in the blueprint provides the input requirements for the projects, which adopt the strategic requirements and undertake

detailed specification and design to deliver the outputs that create the capability needed to achieve the outcomes and deliver the benefits.

## 17.2   START PROJECTS

The programme manager is responsible for commissioning the projects within the projects dossier and should ensure that appropriate individuals are appointed to the key project roles, such as project executive (or sponsor) and project manager. The project executive is accountable to the programme board for the project's successful completion within specified scope, risk, time, cost and quality parameters. Tolerance levels should be set to enable the project delivery teams to manage minor deviations independently from the programme.

As each project is about to begin, the programme manager should ensure that each project management team fully understands the project brief, its context to the blueprint, tranches and benefits, and the project management standards that must be observed, as defined in the monitoring and control strategy. This should

*Figure 17.1  Overview of Delivering the Capability*

include ensuring that the project manager(s) and project executive(s) understand their contribution to the blueprint and the benefit(s) their project will deliver, or contribute towards.

Project briefing should adopt the following sequence as shown in Figure 17.2:

1 Identify projects started by the programme
2 Confirm how the projects fit into the big picture by referring to, for example, strategy
3 Make sure that the projects are aware of and understand interdependencies with other projects
4 Explain how the projects' outputs will be used (perhaps combined with other project outputs) to build capability and enable transition, lead to outcomes and benefits realization, and define acceptance criteria for those outputs
5 Use information from Defining a Programme to provide projects with guidance on quality, reporting, exceptions and escalation.

## 17.3 ENGAGE STAKEHOLDERS

Maintaining the engagement of stakeholders and keeping them informed of progress and issues are important parts of successful programme management. The cooperation of stakeholders will be needed, as projects in the programme need specific input. For example, involving stakeholders in requirements analysis, reviewing designs, user acceptance-testing etc. will give them a better understanding of the programme, while ensuring that the project's outputs are designed to reflect their needs. Their contribution and input can give them a sense of involvement, leading to better engagement and a more positive outcome.

The programme manager may need to provide guidance on communication events at times when projects engage with critical stakeholders, and involve the business change manager (BCM) (see also Chapter 6).

## 17.4 ALIGN PROJECTS WITH BENEFITS REALIZATION

The BCM is responsible for ensuring that the particular benefits relevant to each project can be realized from implementing the outputs from those projects. When projects are initiated within the programme, the project briefs should be aligned with the relevant benefit profiles and the benefits realization plan, and be agreed with the BCM.

Responsibility for ensuring that the projects deliver capability in alignment with the benefits realization plan lies with the programme manager.

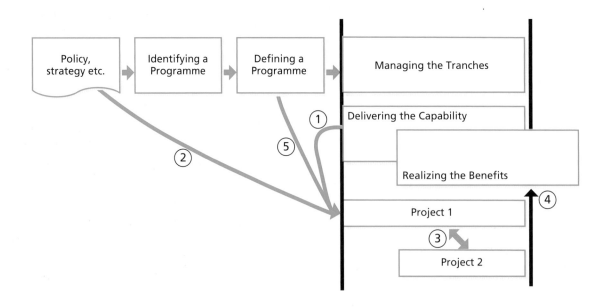

*Figure 17.2 Briefing projects*

The BCM has a key role to play in:

- The alignment of projects
- Ensuring the inputs, business requirements and time constraints
- Providing expertise from operational staff in assessing designs, prototypes and similar items
- Considering how well these proposals are likely to work in a full-scale operational environment.

If there is a business change team, then a member of the team may work alongside or as part of the project board representing the BCM in the day-to-day decision-making of the project.

The BCM must sign off that the project outputs will provide the capability to deliver the outcomes and benefits and that the project plan will deliver the capability in a timely manner to meet the transition arrangement being planned.

## 17.5 ALIGN PROJECTS WITH PROGRAMME OBJECTIVES

Aligning projects with programme objectives is a continual activity throughout the programme for all its projects. For projects started by the programme, the initial alignment is achieved via the project brief, and maintained through the reporting line between the projects and the programme.

The sign-off of the project plan by the programme manager should be based on assessing whether the proposed outputs and capability meet the strategic requirements from the blueprint and, if the project continues through more than one tranche, that the management stages are aligned as closely as possible with the tranche end to ensure that maximum control can be exercised by the programme on the direction of the project.

The programme manager would seek to ensure that dependencies that have been identified are understood and managed effectively.

In emergent programmes there will be projects that are already under way. Their progress and project information (such as the PID, or project initiation document) should be reviewed by the programme team. Any required amendments, re-scoping or re-planning in order to align with the programme's blueprint, programme plan and benefits realization plan should be agreed and actioned.

## 17.6 GOVERNANCE: MANAGE AND CONTROL DELIVERY

Overseeing projects is critical to success. When the programme starts projects, part of the brief explains the relationship between the project and its programme:

- When and how the project reports to the programme
- Reporting exceptions (including a definition of exceptions with stated tolerances for time, cost, quality, risk and issues) so that the project knows when circumstances are beyond its authority
- Acceptable tolerance within which the project can operate.

Governance in this process requires effective links to be formed between the programme team and the project boards. See Chapter 4 for examples of programme and project governance structures.

See also details on monitoring and control strategy in Appendix A.

### 17.6.1 Monitor and control progress

Projects should report in an agreed format to help aggregate the information at the programme level in line with the monitoring and control strategy. Progress against the programme's plans and schedules is monitored and tracked. Any departures (outside agreed tolerances) from previously published project plans are assessed for impact on the rest of the programme. The impact of any change within a project or on other parties within the programme needs to be recognized as early as possible in order to manage the change carefully. The programme manager will use information from projects to help update the programme plan (see Appendix A).

The live projects are monitored by focusing on the areas that are key to the programme, such as:

- **Outputs** Project outputs meet the requirements of their customers, which could be the programme itself
- **Timely completion** Adhering to delivery forecasts, and reporting exceptions as soon as possible to ensure alignment with the programme plan and other dependencies

- **Estimates, costs and benefits** Tolerance-tracking and estimating the contribution towards benefits realization, reporting exceptions quickly
- **Resources** Confirming suitability and availability, including supplier performance
- **Scope** Changes need to be formally managed to avoid insidious scope creep.

The programme manager, having initiated projects from the projects dossier, needs to oversee progress. This includes the following tasks:

- Review projects, and obtain information for benefit reviews and assessments
- Deal with escalations and exceptions from projects
- Manage dependencies and interfaces between projects with particular emphasis on making sure that projects understand how their outputs need to combine to achieve the desired outcomes
- Check alignment with the requirements of the blueprint
- Oversee quality with particular emphasis on making sure that project outputs will work well enough in a full-scale operational environment to achieve the benefits desired (in conjunction with the BCM).

### 17.6.2 Manage risks and resolve issues

The identified risks need to be regularly reviewed and challenged. New risks may be identified and responses planned or actioned.

As the programme progresses, there will be the inevitable delays, unforeseen situations and other situations that threaten the programme. The programme manager is responsible for recognizing and dealing with anything that could affect the successful delivery of the programme. This may involve escalating issues arising from individual projects to the senior responsible owner (SRO), liaising with the BCM(s) or working with the projects to manage risks and resolve issues that could affect delivery of project outputs, programme outcomes and therefore benefits realization.

Projects will also identify risks from their own perspective. They must be clear about when risks need to be managed at a project level and when

they should be escalated to the programme manager (and should then be defined in the risk management strategy).

For each project, this guidance on managing risks and issues should be described in the project brief prepared by the programme manager. For the programme overall, rules are contained in the risk management strategy and issue management strategy (see Appendix A for more details).

Circumstances that should require a project to escalate risks or issues to the programme manager include situations where:

- Dependent projects or programmes are impacted
- The project does not have sufficient authority for the action required
- The action required will exceed project tolerances for quality, time or cost
- The project does not have the necessary skills or experience and does not have the authority to acquire them
- The project cannot deliver its outputs in line with the benefits realization plan.

## 17.7 CLOSE PROJECTS

As each project prepares for closure, there should be a formal delivery of the project's outputs to the programme. In order for a project to successfully close all of its outputs, it must meet the acceptance criteria defined during project start-up, subject to any formal change control.

It is important that the closing of projects is carefully controlled by the programme manager. If the combined outputs from projects don't support effective transition and don't enable the required improvement to operational improvement, the expected benefits may not be realized. See also the discussion of managing transition in Chapter 18.

Part of project closure involves the planning of a post-project review to assess the realization of benefits from the effectiveness of the capability delivered and the outputs. These reviews should be scheduled to fit into the programme's review schedule and may require external independent scrutiny.

The process of project closure should include the dissemination of lessons learned across the programme to share knowledge and experiences with the other projects. It is often useful for members of the programme team to contribute to project evaluation review and lessons learned reports where successes and problem areas associated with the project and its project management process are captured. Throughout the programme, the projects need to be advised of any issues arising that may impact on benefit responsibilities. The lessons learned reports may be useful to inform this activity.

## 17.8 RESPONSIBILITIES

Typical responsibilities for Delivering the Capability are summarized in Table 17.1. For more information on the roles of the sponsoring group and programme board, and their responsibilities with regard to the RACI tables, see Chapter 4 and section 13.3.

**Table 17.1 Typical responsibilities for Delivering the Capability**

| Flow steps | SRO | Programme manager | BCMs | Programme office |
|---|---|---|---|---|
| Start projects | A | R | C | C |
| Engage stakeholders | A | R | C | C |
| Align projects with benefits realization | A | R | R | C |
| Align projects with programme objectives | A | R | C | C |
| Governance: manage and control delivery | A | R | C | C |
| Close projects | A | R | C | C |

R = responsible (gets the work done); A = accountable (answerable for the programme's success); C = consulted (supports, has the information or capability required); I = informed (notified, but not consulted)

# Realizing the
# Benefits

18

# 18 Realizing the Benefits

## 18.1 INTRODUCTION

The purpose of the Realizing the Benefits process (see Figure 18.1) is to manage the benefits from their initial identification to their successful realization. The activities cover monitoring the progress of the projects to ensure that the outputs are fit for purpose and can be integrated into operations such that the benefits can be realized.

Realizing the Benefits incorporates the planning and management of the transition from old to new ways of working and the achievement of the outcomes, whilst ensuring that the operational stability and performance of the operations are maintained. The activities of this process are repeated as necessary for each tranche of the programme.

Three distinct sets of activities are covered in this chapter:

- **Manage pre-transition** The analysis, preparation and planning for business transformation
- **Manage transition** Delivering and supporting the changes
- **Manage post-transition** Reviewing progress, measuring performance and adapting to change.

## 18.2 MANAGE PRE-TRANSITION

### 18.2.1 Establish benefits measurements

Benefits realization is what the programme is all about. It is important to ensure that this is made real by the implementation of relevant and reliable measurement processes. These measures are defined in each of the benefit profiles, and overall in the benefits management strategy.

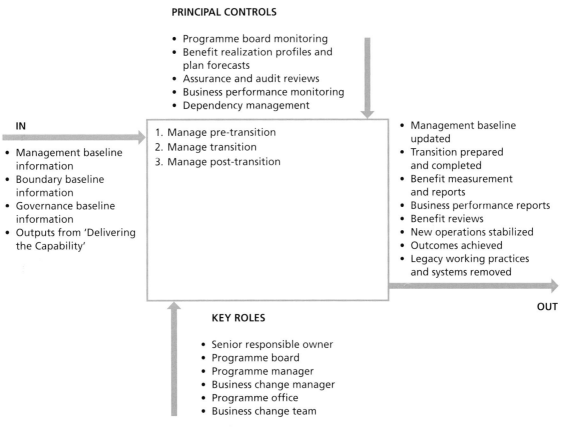

**PRINCIPAL CONTROLS**

- Programme board monitoring
- Benefit realization profiles and plan forecasts
- Assurance and audit reviews
- Business performance monitoring
- Dependency management

**IN**

- Management baseline information
- Boundary baseline information
- Governance baseline information
- Outputs from 'Delivering the Capability'

1. Manage pre-transition
2. Manage transition
3. Manage post-transition

- Management baseline updated
- Transition prepared and completed
- Benefit measurement and reports
- Business performance reports
- Benefit reviews
- New operations stabilized
- Outcomes achieved
- Legacy working practices and systems removed

**OUT**

**KEY ROLES**

- Senior responsible owner
- Programme board
- Programme manager
- Business change manager
- Programme office
- Business change team

*Figure 18.1 Overview of Realizing the Benefits*

### 18.2.1.1 Source data and set-up reporting

Business performance information will be needed for the current state and during the life of the programme. Whilst this is defined in benefit profiles, it is now that the actual collection of data starts, possibly in parallel with the activities in Defining a Programme (see Chapter 15). This can be challenging. Therefore, it is sensible to take a pragmatic approach, incrementally building on the information that is initially available.

Information produced to assist with managing benefits realization should pass the following tests:

- **Currency** It is no good using data that is out of date. Ongoing reporting must capture recent information.

- **Accuracy** If the information is based on unreliable or volatile data, invalid decisions may be made. There may be a need to look for a second indicator from another source to cross-check.

- **Relevance** Only report relevant information. It should be brief and effective; if there is too much information, critical evidence may be missed.

The business change manager (BCM) should regularly test the validity and authenticity of information being provided and reported upon to ensure that the basis for decision-making is correct.

### 18.2.1.2 Performance baselines

In order to measure the improvements resulting from benefits realization, the 'as-is' needs to be measured. Without this, there will be no way of assessing whether the 'to-be' measurements indicate an improvement or not. The identification of what measures are relevant is undertaken during Defining a Programme and details are recorded in each benefit profile.

**Tip**

Business performance baselines should be established as early as possible, preferably during Identifying a Programme as part of the 'as-is' state in the programme brief. This will be further developed during Defining a Programme within the blueprint. This 'as-is' information should be used, along with any other information that BCMs believe to be important for tracking the stability of business performance. Wherever possible, these should be measures already in use, or if they are being developed they should be relevant and of value to operations.

## 18.2.2 Monitor benefits realization

Throughout the programme, progress is monitored against the business case, programme plan, benefits realization plan and the blueprint to identify potential improvements to enhance benefit achievement or opportunities to minimize dis-benefits. Adjustments may be necessary to deal with a range of events or circumstances – for example:

- Business operations that will use the project outputs are unstable
- Forward plans are no longer realistic based on experience to date
- External circumstances have changed, affecting the future course of the programme
- The programme's objectives have changed or been refocused.

Monitoring and collaboration with projects needs to be benefits-focused. This could include, for example, assessing designs, prototypes and similar items to consider how well they are likely to work in a full-scale operational environment. This would be part of answering the big question 'Will the scale of the improvement be enough to produce the desired benefits?'

The benefits are managed and controlled throughout the programme with the same degree of rigour as the projects. Both benefits and costs are of primary importance to the success of the programme. During the programme, there may be change or opportunities for improving the benefits, and the benefit profiles will need to be reassessed and adjusted as necessary.

It is essential for the organization to establish change control in those parts of the business that are covered by the blueprint and which will have an effect on benefits realization.

Performance indicators that show changes at a corporate or strategic level include:

- Revenue
- Profitability
- Contract penalties imposed
- Lost bids
- Insurance premiums increases
- Legal actions
- Media coverage
- Regulator penalties

Performance indicators that show changes to operations include:

- Staff turnover
- Productivity
- Customer satisfaction
- Process performance
- Service/product quality
- Staff morale.

See also Chapters 7, 8, 10 and 11.

### 18.2.3  Plan transition

Change in an organization needs to be planned and managed carefully. Transition plans often contain considerably more detail than other parts of the programme plan.

In preparing the plan, consideration should be given to:

- Staff and their working practices
- Information and technology
- Temporary facilities for those managing the transition
- Levels of stakeholder support and engagement in the areas to be changed
- The cultural and infrastructural migration from the old to the new
- Integration with the programme plan to be aware that a tranche end approaches
- Maintaining business operations during transition
- Exit or back-out arrangements should the change fail badly.

### 18.2.4  Communicate the change

This is about taking the affected business areas, operating units and the individuals themselves through the engagement cycle for the planned changes, to raise awareness and interest, and to get engagement and involvement.

The programme communications plan provides the basis for effective communication. The risk register, plans, vision statement, blueprint and benefits provide key information for the communications required when reviewing and planning change activities.

Change must be carefully communicated well before actual transition. Late communication is likely to result in significant resistance. See also section 2.2.3 and Chapter 6.

### 18.2.5  Assess readiness for change

As preparation for implementing the change, it is a critical responsibility of the BCM(s) and the team involved in change to be fully engaged with the project teams and the business operations and to immerse them in the change that is coming.

This comes at a point where the project outputs have been or are being delivered to the BCMs, and they need to make the decision as to whether the capability meets the needs of the business and that the business is ready to transition. The recommendation is made by the BCM, but the ultimate decision sits with the SRO, who remains accountable.

Seeking out other organizations that have been through similar changes will help the organization to prepare and avoid some of the pain of pioneering change.

When assessing capacity of the organization to make the changes, consider the following:

- Recent track record and experience of change
- Past experience of implementing this type of change
- Availability of resources to support the change in terms of volume, competency and experience
- How the intended change fits with the organization's culture and values, i.e. whether it goes deeper than a change to a way of working
- Effectiveness of the supporting systems that could enable change – for example, communications channels, process maturity etc.

- Skills and mobility of the workforce
- Current status of service-level performance to customers and degree of satisfaction
- Third-party supplier performance and alignment with change plans
- Service management's ability to support the organization through transition and in its new operational state.

As part of assessing readiness for change, all benefits- and transition-related documentation, including plans and profiles, should be updated.

## 18.3 MANAGE TRANSITION

### 18.3.1 Initiate transition

As the projects approach completion, the relevant business operations need to be prepared for implementing the outputs from the projects. The transition plan is reviewed and updated to reflect the activities of transition. These activities need to be managed into the business environment, ensuring successful take-up of the new capability whilst maintaining the appropriate levels of business as usual.

The transition may be achieved in a single change to the operations, or it may be achieved through a series of incremental or modular changes. The transition plan should provide the route map for implementation.

### 18.3.2 Establish support arrangements

Managing the transition will often require careful consideration of individuals' personal concerns about their working environment, and what the changes will mean to them. The transition to achieve the programme's outcome may also affect individuals and organizations external to the organization delivering the programme. Support may be required from HR and system specialists.

To avoid unnecessary disruption, transition often involves very detailed plans. These transition plans are delivered now, and the BCMs and business change team must provide clear and concise direction, making and obtaining rapid decisions.

### 18.3.3 Enact transition

Transition can start as soon as:

- All the outputs from projects that are required for this transition are complete, ready for operational use and the programme has verified through quality assurance that they will function correctly together
- Operational staff are trained and briefed on their new roles, as well as on any temporary duties they may perform during transition
- There are no risks and issues outstanding that the new operations are not willing to take responsibility for
- Contingencies and back-out arrangements are in place should the changes fail
- Temporary transition management arrangements are in place
- The senior responsible owner (SRO), in consultation with the programme board, has given the approval to start transition.

As soon as the start of transition is approved, it is important to verify that staff understand the role they will play during transition, and that they know how the management structure for transition will operate.

Transition is the responsibility of the programme, but may well make use of project team members. Programme and/or project staff should enact the transition plan and monitor progress, react and adapt to events as they develop, and ensure that stop/go criteria for aborting the implementation are monitored and action taken where appropriate.

Monitoring of the performance indicators will be important to assess the overall level of business stability.

### 18.3.4 Review transition

When the new arrangements are in place, the transition should be reviewed, lessons documented and any follow-on actions and requirements captured. There should be broad engagement with the stakeholder community to guide their perception, interest and support for the programme. This may be a testing time for everyone concerned; it is therefore important to maintain measured and effective communications.

At this stage the project manager and teams can be disengaged. The process of embedding the working practices leading to the release of benefits then starts, under the control of the programme.

New ways of working will inevitably require a settling-down period. The BCM(s) should ensure that the programme provides sufficient support during this period.

### 18.3.5 Manage outcome achievement

It will take time for outcomes to be fully realized, working practices established and the business stabilized at the desired new state. When the outcomes have been achieved, it is critical that this is actively acknowledged through the programme communications plan.

However, beware of declaring victory too early. It is critical that the business has stabilized in the new state and the change is fully achieved. There is a danger that if the programme focus moves on to the next outcome too early, the operations may regress to the old ways of working without the support and rigour of the programme processes and procedures.

## 18.4 MANAGE POST-TRANSITION

### 18.4.1 Measure benefits

The benefit profiles define how each benefit will be measured. Reporting on benefits realized to date should be part of the end-of-tranche review and any other planned benefit reviews.

If the tranche ending has been designed to prove whether hypotheses embedded in the strategy can work satisfactorily, there may be a planned delay before the next tranche starts, in order to collect and analyse sufficient benefit measures to reach a conclusion.

Starting the next tranche prematurely before clear conclusions have been reached can significantly increase the programme risk. If the conclusions from benefits measures indicate that the programme should stop or change significantly, any projects running may also need to be stopped or changed, and much of the expenditure so far may be wasted.

Key performance indicators that were selected as measures and recorded in the benefit profiles will form the basis for comparison. It is important that as performance is monitored the consequences are understood. For example, you may be focused on headcount reduction, but if there is suddenly an upsurge in resignations or accidents then the cause and effect will need to be investigated.

It is wise to look at historic averages and seasonal trends to forecast expected performance averages over the life of the programme. For further details on measuring benefits and benefit reviews, see Chapter 7.

### 18.4.2 Remove access to legacy working practices and systems

One of the toughest aspects of delivering any change is stopping legacy practices that are embedded, and removing access to tools and systems that support these old practices will enable the new ways of working to be established.

The BCM must ensure that old working practices and systems are identified, the impact of removal is understood and that they are decommissioned as soon as business stability and resilience has been achieved. This reinforces and supports the new *modus operandi* and organizational culture.

This is a critical activity that is often overlooked. If old ways of working remain, there is a danger that the business will revert to using them once the pressure of the programme is removed. This, in turn, threatens the sustainability of the improvements and the realization of the benefits.

### 18.4.3 Respond to changing requirements

As part of embedding the new ways of working, ideas and problems will be highlighted and recognized. Many of these will not have been foreseen, and it is a natural part of the programme flow that the programme is able to respond to these changing requirements.

Once the additional requirements have been quantified, they should be provided to the programme manager for consideration and inclusion in the projects dossier via the programme's issue register, with an impact assessment on the blueprint, programme plan, benefit profiles and benefits realization plan.

### 18.4.4 Monitor and report benefits realization

Through the transition process, the benefit measures should be monitored and progress tracked for signs of deviation outside the anticipated parameters. Where the business performance moves out of tolerance, this should be escalated to the SRO and the sponsoring group.

Benefit profiles and the benefits realization plan should be updated and released in accordance with arrangements defined in the benefits management strategy.

BCMs will provide input to benefit reviews when the analysis of benefits measures is complete and conclusions have been drawn. Benefit reviews can also help the programme to understand the extent to which key stakeholders have been satisfied with the improvements.

It is not always possible or necessary for a programme to continue until the end of the benefits measurement period. If benefits realization results so far provide a clear indication of the final realization level and operational managers will take on the responsibilities for completing the measures, the programme can propose that it ends its responsibility.

## 18.5 RESPONSIBILITIES

Typical responsibilities for Realizing the Benefits are summarized in Table 18.1. For more information on the roles of the sponsoring group and programme board, and their responsibilities with regard to the RACI tables, see Chapter 4 and section 13.3.

**Table 18.1 Typical responsibilities for Realizing the Benefits**

| Flow steps | SRO | Programme manager | BCMs (and business change team) | Programme office |
|---|---|---|---|---|
| **Manage pre-transition** | | | | |
| Establish benefits measurements | A | C | R | C |
| Monitor benefits realization | A | C | R | C |
| Plan transition | A | R | R | C |
| Communicate the change | A | C | R | C |
| Assess readiness for change | A | C | R | I |
| **Manage transition** | | | | |
| Initiate transition | A | C | R | I |
| Establish support arrangements | A | C | R | I |
| Enact transition | A | C | R | I |
| Review transition | A | C | R | C |
| Manage outcome achievement | A | C | R | I |
| **Manage post-transition** | | | | |
| Measure benefits | A | C | R | C |
| Remove access to legacy working practices and systems | A | C | R | I |
| Respond to changing requirements | A | C | R | C |
| Monitor and report benefits realization | A | C | R | C |

R = responsible (gets the work done); A = accountable (answerable for the programme's success); C = consulted (supports, has the information or capability required); I = informed (notified, but not consulted)

# Closing a Programme

19

# 19 Closing a Programme

## 19.1 INTRODUCTION

Programmes tend to last for a significant period, typically years. There is a danger of allowing the programme to drift on, as if it is part of normal business. The purpose of the Closing a Programme process (see Figure 19.1) is to ensure the end goal of formally recognizing that the programme is completed. This is when the programme has delivered the required new capabilities described in the blueprint and has assessed the outcomes via benefit measures.

Some benefits will have been realized during the running of the programme; others may not be fully realized until some time after the last project has delivered. Closing a Programme identifies the need for future assessment of benefits realization outside the programme as well as a formal review by the programme of those achieved so far. If there are benefits realization activities which need to continue for a significant period of time after the capability has been delivered, then it may be impractical to maintain the whole programme management structure to control these last activities. It is conceivable that the programme may be closed and this realization activity managed as a separate piece of work, possibly a project. Alternatively, responsibility for the post-programme benefits realization activity may be taken on by the business-as-usual area receiving the benefit or by the corporate portfolio.

Closure comprises the final assessment of the programme and the decommissioning of its resources and infrastructure. Programme closure may be scheduled at any point after the completion of the last project within the projects dossier and the capability has been delivered. To a large extent, when the programme formally closes will depend on the amount of support required to ensure that the new operational environment delivered by the programme is fully embedded. Additionally, consideration also needs to be given to outstanding benefits realization activities.

Examples of tests for whether a programme can close include:

- Blueprint has been delivered

- Outcomes have been achieved
- Business case has been satisfied (thus far)
- Benefits are self-sustaining
- Last tranche has been completed as per the programme plan
- No risks or issues are outstanding that are unacceptable to operations.

It is not always sensible for a programme to continue to its planned end point. Indications that a programme should be closed prematurely include:

- Evidence so far indicates that the programme does not make good business sense, and it is not possible to change it sufficiently to produce an acceptable business case
- The organization is not able to secure adequate funding or sufficient resources to complete the outstanding work
- External circumstances have changed sufficiently to render the remainder of the programme irrelevant
- Strategy has been changed by the organization for internal reasons, not because of external environment changes; this renders the programme invalid
- The 80/20 rule shows that the cost of the remainder of the programme compared with additional benefits it will realize means that it does not make good business sense to complete the rest of the programme
- There is evidence that the outcome is being achieved through alternative actions/events.

## 19.2 CONFIRM ONGOING SUPPORT IS IN PLACE

Whilst the programme is running, it is able to support and facilitate the overall change process. The programme can act as a vehicle for resolving disputes and issues that have arisen during the transition. Careful consideration must be given to how the business will operate without the support of the programme. For example, programmes often establish new supply chain relationships, appointing and migrating to a new operator. When

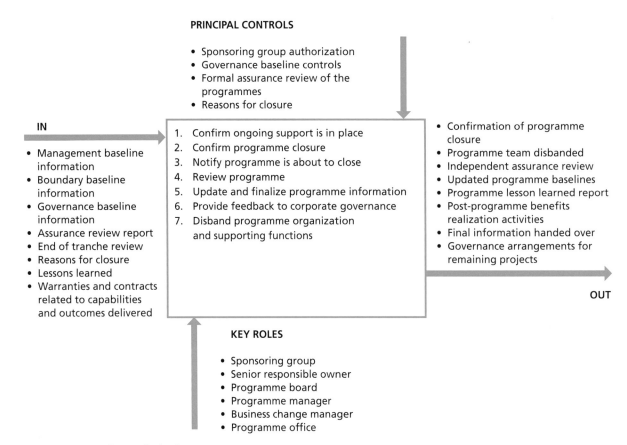

**PRINCIPAL CONTROLS**

- Sponsoring group authorization
- Governance baseline controls
- Formal assurance review of the programmes
- Reasons for closure

**IN**

- Management baseline information
- Boundary baseline information
- Governance baseline information
- Assurance review report
- End of tranche review
- Reasons for closure
- Lessons learned
- Warranties and contracts related to capabilities and outcomes delivered

1. Confirm ongoing support is in place
2. Confirm programme closure
3. Notify programme is about to close
4. Review programme
5. Update and finalize programme information
6. Provide feedback to corporate governance
7. Disband programme organization and supporting functions

- Confirmation of programme closure
- Programme team disbanded
- Independent assurance review
- Updated programme baselines
- Programme lesson learned report
- Post-programme benefits realization activities
- Final information handed over
- Governance arrangements for remaining projects

**OUT**

**KEY ROLES**

- Sponsoring group
- Senior responsible owner
- Programme board
- Programme manager
- Business change manager
- Programme office

*Figure 19.1 Overview of Closing a Programme*

the programme closes, gaps in communications and processes between the new operator and business operations can emerge because the programme has been providing the bridge and resolving issues up to this point. So there may be new post-programme risks that need to be identified and managed.

After closure, the embedded changes must be able to continue with smooth-running operations and working practices. For programmes where the outcome primarily affects those external to the organization running the programme, any ongoing support requirements should be established, separate from the programme, so that the programme can formally close.

All stakeholders should be informed of programme closure and its outcome.

## 19.3   CONFIRM PROGRAMME CLOSURE

Programme closure involves formal confirmation that:

- The business case has been satisfied
- All projects have been completed satisfactorily

- Business performance is stable
- Any remaining handover or transition activities required have been defined and assigned to relevant business operations.

If the programme is being closed prematurely (i.e. before the blueprint has been achieved), the remaining live projects that are still required by the organization need to be reassigned to business management or perhaps to another programme.

The senior responsible owner (SRO) will propose closure to the sponsoring group. If satisfied with the overall outcome, they will endorse the recommendation to confirm programme closure. If they are not satisfied, they must give clear direction about further work to be carried out.

## 19.4   NOTIFY PROGRAMME IS ABOUT TO CLOSE

Notify the programme organization, stakeholders and programme office that the programme is preparing to close. Produce instructions and a timetable for closing activities and the programme review. For a scheduled programme closure, this notification should have been built into the programme communications plan already. For a premature closure, it will require significantly more communication and stakeholder engagement to ensure that the early closure does not taint the previous good work of the programme.

## 19.5    REVIEW PROGRAMME

Throughout the programme, the end-of-tranche reviews will have been monitoring and measuring benefits realization. As part of Closing a Programme a formal review should be conducted to assess the delivery of the complete blueprint, realization of the overall benefits and achievement of the programme's business case. Benefits reviews should have already been carried out during the programme, so the final review may be a consolidation of their findings.

This review should also assess and evaluate the performance of the programme and its management processes to identify lessons learned that may benefit other programmes. The review may involve independent external scrutiny, such as a gated review.

A further review, following programme closure, may be required to provide a complete assessment of benefits realized as a result of the programme, including those benefits that may not have been ready for measurement and assessment when the programme closed.

## 19.6    UPDATE AND FINALIZE PROGRAMME INFORMATION

Programme information should be reviewed and updated to ensure that any residual issues, risks and outstanding actions have been dealt with appropriately.

Risks and issues for which operations have agreed to take responsibility are handed over. Note that the accountability for these remains with the SRO.

The strategies, plans and boundary documents should be reviewed to assess their effectiveness, appropriateness and what lessons can be learned for future programmes. Any corporate and legislative governance requirements affecting the storage of information should be complied with as part of the archiving of documents.

## 19.7    PROVIDE FEEDBACK TO CORPORATE GOVERNANCE

Programmes initiated to deliver corporate strategic objectives need to provide feedback to the strategists. No strategies are guaranteed to succeed, and good feedback from each programme will help the organization to develop more informed and therefore better strategic decisions. This may be handled via a portfolio office if one exists.

## 19.8    DISBAND PROGRAMME ORGANIZATION AND SUPPORTING FUNCTIONS

The programme's infrastructure and management processes are disbanded and individuals and resources released from the programme. Staff redeployment back into the organization should be planned in advance. Staff will have updated their skills as a result of their experiences on the programme, and it is important that this is reflected in their personal development information. Any contracts used by the programme should be finalized and closed, or responsibility for continued contract management handed over to the relevant business management function.

## 19.9    RESPONSIBILITIES

Typical responsibilities for Closing a Programme are summarized in Table 19.1. For more information on the role of the sponsoring group and programme board see Chapter 4.

The sponsoring group would be expected to authorize the programme and the SRO's recommendations at the end of Identifying a Programme, Defining a Programme and for each end of tranche as a minimum. The sponsoring group has specific responsibilities defined in Chapter 4; these are in no way diminished by not being included in the RACI tables.

The programme board is also not referenced. This is because it is principally made up of the SRO, programme manager and BCMs who have specific responsibilities. The programme board supports the SRO in driving the rate of change for the programme and has a critical role in resolving challenges and maintaining focus. It has clear responsibilities defined in Chapter 4; these are in no way diminished by not being included in the RACI tables.

**Table 19.1 Typical responsibilities for Closing a Programme**

| Flow steps | SRO | Programme manager | BCMs | Programme office |
|---|---|---|---|---|
| Confirm ongoing support is in place | A | R | C | C |
| Confirm programme closure | A | C | C | I |
| Notify programme is about the close | A | R | C | I |
| Review programme | A | C | R | I |
| Update and finalize programme information | A | R | C | C |
| Provide feedback to corporate governance | A | R | C | I |
| Disband programme organization and supporting functions | A | R | I | I |

R = responsible (gets the work done); A = accountable (answerable for the programme's success); C = consulted (supports, has the information or capability required); I = informed (notified, but not consulted)

# PART 4

# Appendices, further information and glossary

Appendix A:
Programme
information

# Appendix A: Programme information

## A.1 INTRODUCTION

This appendix provides an explanation of the information that is required to manage a programme successfully. It explains what documentation you should establish, where the information could be sourced from and what to consider including in the contents. You will also find details on who should be involved in creating the documentation and what their role should be in the process.

The format for the information is indicative and intentionally non-prescriptive. This enables organizations to structure, store and integrate information with their existing corporate governance frameworks; it is more important for organizations to identify and maintain the information to support their programme in a form that is appropriate to them. The following information descriptions should be seen as flexible checklists rather than rigid templates.

For example, the programme brief contains information that many organizations would also include in an outline business case. Therefore, the use of either term should be seen as acceptable. It is the process of developing, capturing, analysing and acting on the information rather than the title that is important.

## A.2 WORKING WITH PROGRAMME INFORMATION

A programme exists within a dynamic environment. As such it is likely that information will be changing constantly; the programme's knowledge will increase and this should be reflected in the information that is used to maintain context and manage delivery.

This appendix is not intended to provide templates; it is guidance on what should be included when constructing your documentation and when you should review and update the contents.

It is perfectly acceptable to integrate information into aggregated documents to make life easier; for example, governance strategy plans could be integrated into the programme plan if it is practical

or the governance strategies themselves could be consolidated into one, as much of the information is replicated. The level and structure of programme information should be appropriate to the needs of the individual programme or organization.

Bear in mind that there is core information within a programme that is cross-referenced in multiple documents; you may need to create an indexing system within your programme to enable cross-referencing of this core information. For example, the benefit profile states that you should identify risks to the achievement of the benefit. These risks should also be contained within your risk register, where the impact assessment should include reference to the implications of the risk on that benefit and contributing projects, which in turn could create a project-level risk. This necessary replication of information requires careful tracking to ensure that all instances of the same information are updated so as to maintain integrity throughout the programme documentation.

An example of a common structure that could be used for all the governance strategies (or to integrate them) could be:

- Roles, accountabilities and responsibilities
- Processes, tools and techniques to be used
- Standards to be applied and any subject matter expertise that is required, including legislation and policies
- Escalation routes and triggers for interventions
- Criteria for measuring success and assurance/review arrangements
- Definition of key terms.

## A.3 PROGRAMME INFORMATION EVOLUTION

Table A.1 outlines the information that is described in the section, when it is created and maintained, and to which information baseline it is allocated. There are three categories of information, which are reflected in their information baseline.

The following points should be considered with respect to information baselines:

- Baselines help the planning and development of the programme information
- The completion and approval of the set of documents in each baseline represents a step forward in the development of the programme
- Reviews of effectiveness can be scheduled – for example, the governance baseline could be reviewed as part of a health check
- Classification helps programme teams understand their purpose and maintenance regimes; for example, management information is in constant use, so the management baseline would be regularly updated, whereas the boundary baseline would be relatively stable, with a change potentially having a major impact on the programme's viability
- Baselines of documents interrelate; if one is changed, the impact on the others should be considered.

Table A.2 illustrates where and when documents are created and how they are managed over the programme lifecycle. Information will be continually changing; the programme information must be maintained to reflect the changing environment within which the programme exists and to maintain context. Section A.4 describes the individual documents in terms of their purpose and content, and Table A.3 shows who produces, reviews and approves each document.

**Table A.1 Information baselines**

| Information baseline | Description of purpose |
| --- | --- |
| Boundary | Those which set out the direction and the scope of the of the programme |
| Governance | Those that set the standards and frameworks within which the programme will be delivered; defines 'how' the programme will be managed |
| Management | Those that are created and used to manage the delivery of the programme; defines 'what' activities will be undertaken by 'whom' to deliver the programme. |

## A.4 DESCRIPTION OF DOCUMENTS

### A.4.1 Benefit profile

#### A.4.1.1 Purpose

Used to define each benefit (and dis-benefit) and provide a detailed understanding of what will be involved and how the benefit will be realized.

#### A.4.1.2 Typical content

- Reference number or identifier
- Description of the benefit (or dis-benefit)
- Programme or organizational objectives supported and the related observable outcomes from the programme implementation
- Category or categories that are appropriate to the benefits
- KPIs in the business operations that will be affected by the benefit, both immediately after realization and for the future
- Current or baseline performance levels, and improvement or deterioration trajectory anticipated
- Benefit realization and business change costs
- Capabilities required for the benefit to be realized: the project(s) within the programme directly related to the realization of the benefit
- Outcomes that will need to be in place to enable the benefit realization
- Business changes required for realization (to process, culture, people, policy)
- Related issues and risks to the full realization of the benefit
- Any dependencies on contributory events, programmes or projects outside the boundary of this programme
- Who is responsible for realizing this benefit (typically the BCM for this area of the business)
- Attribution: the benefit owner and the operations area that will receive this benefit
- Measurement (financial wherever possible)

### A.4.2 Benefits management strategy

#### A.4.2.1 Purpose

Defines the approach to realizing benefits and the framework within which benefits realization will be achieved.

**Table A.2 Document management over the programme lifecycle**

| Title | Identifying | Defining | Managing the tranche start | Managing the tranche end | Deliver capability | Realize benefits | Closure | Information baseline |
|---|---|---|---|---|---|---|---|---|
| Benefit profile | | CR | | RU | | IM | RU | Boundary |
| Benefits management strategy | | CR | IM | RU | | | RU | Governance |
| Benefits map | | CR* | IM | RU | | RU | RU | Boundary |
| Benefits realization plan | | CR | | RU | | IM | RU | Management |
| Blueprint | | CR | IM | RU | | | RU | Boundary |
| Business case | | CR* | | RU | | | RU | Boundary |
| Information management plan | | CR | IM | RU | | | RU | Management |
| Information management strategy | | CR | IM | RU | | | RU | Governance |
| Issue management strategy | | CR | IM | RU | | | RU | Governance |
| Issue register | | CR* | RU | RU | RU | RU | RU | Management |
| Monitoring and control strategy | | CR | IM | RU | | | RU | Governance |
| Organization structure | | CR | IM | RU | | | RU | Governance |
| Programme brief** | CR | | | | | | | Boundary |
| Programme communications plan | | CR | IM | RU | IM | IM | RU | Management |
| Programme definition document | | CR | | RU | | | RU | Boundary |
| Programme mandate** | RU | | | | | | | Boundary |
| Programme plan | | CR | IM | RU | | | RU | Management |
| Programme preparation plan | CR | IM | | | | | | Management |
| Projects dossier | | CR | RU | RU | IM | | RU | Boundary |
| Quality and assurance plan | | CR | IM | RU | | | RU | Management |
| Quality and assurance strategy | | CR | IM | RU | | | RU | Governance |
| Resource management plan | | CR | IM | RU | | | RU | Management |
| Resource management strategy | | CR | IM | RU | | | RU | Governance |
| Risk management strategy | | CR | IM | RU | | | RU | Governance |
| Risk register | | CR* | RU | RU | RU | RU | RU | Management |
| Stakeholder engagement strategy | | CR | IM | RU | | | RU | Governance |
| Stakeholder profiles | | CR | RU | RU | RU | RU | RU | Management |
| Vision statement | | CR* | | | | | | Boundary |

CR = create; IM = implement, manage and refine; RU = review and update
*This information is initially created as part of the programme brief.
**These are 'moments in time' documents that are no longer referenced once the information has been expanded in other documents as the programme develops. However, they are important for retrospective assessment; hence they are part of the boundary baseline.

### A.4.2.2 Typical content

- Scope and explanation of which areas of the business will be covered by benefits management and realization activity
- Measurement methods and processes that will be used to monitor and assess the realization of the benefits (including the level of granularity to be applied in the benefits realization plan)
- A description of the functions, roles, accountabilities and responsibilities for benefit planning and realization, aligned with the programme's organization structure
- Priorities for the programme in terms of benefit types to be sought (e.g. cashable direct), to inform and focus the filtering and prioritization process
- Processes to ensure that benefits are not double-counted and that cumulative benefits are achievable
- The relationships between capabilities and the benefits
- Clarity, if necessary, as to opportunities to be managed in relationship to risk management
- The relationship with other programme information
- Categories to be used by the programme or inherited from a portfolio
- Any organizational-specific information or headings that should be included in the benefit profiles
- Tools, systems and sources of information that will be used to enable measurement
- Critical success factors against which the effectiveness of benefits management should be measured
- Clarification of benefits-related terminology appropriate to the organization
- The review and assessment process for measuring benefits realization, covering who will be involved in the reviews, and how and when the reviews will be carried out
- Standards for identifying, mapping, monitoring and reviewing the programme's benefits.

### A.4.3 Benefits map

#### A.4.3.1 Purpose

Illustrates the sequential relationship between benefits.

### A.4.3.2 Typical content

- Benefits and dis-benefits, including short- and long-term benefits
- Outputs
- Capabilities
- Outcomes
- Strategic objectives
- Dependencies:
  - Between benefits
  - On project outputs
  - On capabilities and outcomes
- Additional business changes to enable realization of benefits
- Other external dependencies.

#### A.4.3.3 Notes

Can be adapted to be included within the benefits realization plan.

### A.4.4 Benefits realization plan

#### A.4.4.1 Purpose

Used to track realization of benefits across the programme and set review controls.

#### A.4.4.2 Typical content

- A schedule detailing when each benefit, dis-benefit or group of benefits will be realized (typically as a chart with benefits of the same measure aggregated over time intervals through the life of the programme's business case)
- Appropriate milestones for benefits reviews to take a forward view of the likelihood of ongoing success
- Estimated effort and costs associated with the plan
- Detail of transition schedules
- Benefit reporting schedule, which is submitted to the programme board
- Relationship between outcomes and benefits in the schedule
- Dates when specific outcomes that enable the benefits will be achieved
- Dependencies external to the programme
- Details of any handover and embedding activities, beyond the mere implementation of a deliverable or output, to enhance the process of

benefits realization after the capability has been delivered; this part of the benefits realization plan is also referred to as a transition plan

- Reference to how the benefits realization will be maintained after programme closure.

### A.4.4.3 Notes

This may be incorporated as part of the overarching programme plan and could include the benefits map.

## A.4.5 Blueprint

### A.4.5.1 Purpose

Used to maintain focus on delivering the required transformation and business change.

### A.4.5.2 Typical content

- Processes and business models of functions, including operational costs and performance levels, of the required vision of the future state; may be expressed in a number of ways, including flow and process graphics
- Organization structure, staffing levels, roles and skill requirements necessary to support the future business operations; any necessary changes to organizational culture or style may also be included
- Technology, IT systems, tools, equipment, buildings and accommodation required for the future business operations together with details of re-use of existing infrastructure or implementation of new infrastructure to support the vision of the future state
- Information and data required to effectively manage the future business operations
- The complete blueprint document may contain several sections: the current 'as-is' state, sections for the intermediate future state for each tranche, and the final future 'to-be' state for the end of the last tranche.

### A.4.5.3 Notes

The blueprint for a programme can, and should, take many different forms: prototypes, models and workshops can all assist in describing the future state. It describes the future capability that the programme is to deliver but may also include intermediate states aligned with tranches. It is sometimes referred to as the 'target operating model'.

## A.4.6 Business case

### A.4.6.1 Purpose

Used to validate the initiation of the programme and the ongoing viability of the programme.

### A.4.6.2 Typical content

- The strategic objectives for the programme, reflecting the vision statement, and aligning with the organizational context and business environment
- The expected benefits, with recognition of the organization's ability to achieve the necessary transformation and change
- The overall risk profile, indicating the major risks to programme delivery and benefits realization; detailed risk assessment will be part of the programme's risk register
- Estimated costs and overall timescales; detailed scheduling of programme milestones will be part of the programme plan
- Investment appraisal
- Forecasts of cash flow and expenditure over the programme timeline
- Options and approaches that have been considered, including likely costs, benefits and risks.

## A.4.7 Information management plan

### A.4.7.1 Purpose

Sets out the timetable and arrangements for implementing and managing the information management strategy.

### A.4.7.2 Typical content

- Timetable to achieve:
  - Information storage systems
  - Configuration management
  - Release management
  - Information change control
  - Naming conventions
  - Security controls
  - Information, filing and documentation structures
- Schedule for availability of templates to support the programme governance
- Estimated effort and costs associated with the plan

- Schedule for the extraction and delivery of information to support review, or similar procedures that are stipulated in activities in other plans
- How and when information management work will be monitored and reported, to include alert mechanisms that warn about serious violations of the programme's information assets
- Who will be responsible for the actions identified in the plan

### A.4.7.3 Notes

This may be incorporated as part of the overarching programme plan.

## A.4.8 Information management strategy

### A.4.8.1 Purpose

Describes the measures, systems and techniques that will be used to maintain and control programme information.

### A.4.8.2 Typical content

- Standards and processes to cover data and records management
- Naming conventions and versioning controls
- Use of terms, e.g. policy, strategy (could be a glossary)
- Systems that will be used to store information
- Responsibilities for management and maintenance of information
- Levels of confidentiality to be applied
- How information integrity will be maintained
- Criteria to assess effectiveness (cross-referenced with the monitoring and control strategy)
- Any information audit requirements which need to be met
- Release management arrangements for updated baselines or individual configuration items, and the relationship to the programme communications plan
- Approach to information availability
- Configuration management procedures, including:
  - Configuration management responsibilities and systems and storage arrangements
  - Configuration management naming conventions and policies that will be used; these may be adopted from broader organizational policies

- Explanation of how configuration management baselines will be implemented within the programme
- Information security arrangements to maintain confidentiality, integrity and availability of information within the configuration management arrangements
- Documentation standards and any relevant templates that will be used and in what circumstances.

### A.4.8.3 Notes

Quality and assurance may cover similar topics as the information management strategy, so it is worth considering combining them if it is more efficient.

## A.4.9 Issue management strategy

### A.4.9.1 Purpose

Used to describe the mechanisms and procedures for resolving issues.

### A.4.9.2 Typical content

- How issues will be identified, captured and assessed
- How issues will be managed across the programme, projects and operations
- Responsibilities for the effective management and resolution of issues within the programme and for authorizing changes
- How issue responsibilities will be allocated within the programme and between programmes, projects and operations
- Process and explanation of how change control will work in the programme
- Change control procedures for authorizing changes resulting from issues
- Procedures for implementing and controlling the changes
- How exceptions that may take the programme beyond its tolerances will be managed
- How the likely impact of exceptions will be assessed
- How responses to issues will be identified and by whom; who will carry out and manage the required responses

- Definition of what constitutes a project- or programme-level issue, and how issues will be escalated or allocated between projects and the programme
- Criteria for allocating severity ratings to issues; categories for severity might be 'critical', 'major', 'significant' and 'minor'
- Categorization mechanism for filtering issues, e.g. technical, business process, organizational, programme process
- How responses will be monitored and evaluated for their effectiveness
- Any organizational-specific heading information that will be required to be recorded within the issue register, other than the generic issue register template
- Criteria used to assess the effectiveness of issue management within the programme
- Other strategies used to support the issue management strategy.

### A.4.9.3 Notes

The information required for the issue management strategy and the risk management strategy is often very similar; it may make sense to include them in one document.

## A.4.10 Issue register

### A.4.10.1 Purpose

Used to capture and actively manage programme issues.

### A.4.10.2 Typical content

- Unique reference for each issue raised
- Date issue was raised (and resolved)
- Who raised the issue
- A description of the issue
- Description of the cause and impact of the issue
- Severity rating, for example 'critical', 'major', 'significant' or 'minor'
- Categorization of the issue, e.g. request for change, issue, stakeholder question
- A description of the issue response action to be undertaken, and by whom
- Issue owner – the named individual who is responsible for the management and control of all aspects of the issues assigned to them

- Issue actionee – the named individual responsible for the implementation of a given issue response action, the current status of the issue, and progress on its resolution, including providing feedback to the source
- Cross-reference to change control procedures where appropriate
- Description of how the issue was resolved and lessons learned from the actions taken.

### A.4.10.3 Notes

Headings must meet the needs of the issue management strategy and be coordinated with the risk register.

## A.4.11 Monitoring and control strategy

### A.4.11.1 Purpose

Defines how the programme will apply internal controls to itself.

### A.4.11.2 Typical content

- What controls will be in place, including project decision authority, change activities and tolerance
- Criteria to assess efficiency and effectiveness
- How projects will be started and monitored
- How the programme's internal process effectiveness will be monitored
- What standards will be applied to controlling the projects (e.g. PRINCE2)
- Information that will be required for monitoring
- Margins within which the programme will operate
- Escalation routes for managing exceptions
- How dependencies will be controlled
- Performance criteria to be used to assess effectiveness.

### A.4.11.3 Notes

This strategy is deployed as part of the programme plan and may also be referred to as the 'internal control strategy'. Can also be integrated with the quality and assurance strategy as it covers internal performance, so quality and assurance would be relevant.

## A.4.12 Organization structure

### A.4.12.1 Purpose

Description of the management roles, responsibilities and reporting lines in the programme.

### A.4.12.2 Typical content

- Programme organization chart; the programme organizational structure
- Description and responsibilities of individuals on the sponsoring group and programme board
- Role descriptions or terms of reference for the individuals within the programme's management team
- Business change management organization and responsibilities
- Expectations of responsibilities of organizational governance authorities, e.g. risk, compliance, accounting etc.
- Terms of reference for sponsoring group, programme board and any other bodies established to support the programme
- Allocation of assurance responsibilities within the programme
- How professional development and performance will be developed for the team.

## A.4.13 Programme brief

### A.4.13.1 Purpose

Used to assess whether the programme is viable and achievable.

### A.4.13.2 Typical content

- Outline vision statement for the programme, containing a clear statement of the end goal of the programme
- Outline description of the benefits or types of benefits that should be delivered by the new capability, an estimate of when they are likely to be achieved, and an indication of how they will be measured (also including significant dis-benefits). This could take the form of a benefits map
- Estimated costs, timescales and effort required to set up, manage and run the programme from initiation through to delivery and realization of the benefits

- Risks to the programme that can be recognized at this point in time, any current issues that may affect the programme, and any known constraints, assumptions or conflicts that may potentially affect the programme. These should also reflect levels of stakeholder support and engagement
- Options for delivery that are known about at this stage, including the potential impact of 'do nothing'
- An initial listing of the candidate projects or activities required, together with rough timescales and explanations for any projects that will be terminated
- Assessment of the current state, the current business operation and performance in the areas that will be impacted by the change.

### A.4.13.3 Notes

May also be referred to as the outline business case. The information initially referred to as the programme brief will evolve into a number of other documents, including the vision statement, issue register, risk register, business case and benefit profiles.

## A.4.14 Programme communications plan

### A.4.14.1 Purpose

Sets out the timetable and arrangements for implementing and managing the stakeholder engagement strategy.

### A.4.14.2 Typical content

- Schedule of communications activities
- The objectives of each communication
- The key messages of the communication, and the level of detail to be included
- Stakeholder audience for each communication, with an assessment of any sensitivities and their reaction
- Timing of the communication
- Description of channels to be used for each communication.
- Individual(s) responsible for undertaking the communication
- Feedback mechanisms
- Estimated effort and costs associated with the plan

- Reference to any supporting projects and business operations communications activity
- Information storage systems
- Possible stakeholder objections to the communication.

## A.4.15 Programme definition document

### A.4.15.1 Purpose

A document that is used to consolidate or summarize the information that was used to define the programme.

### A.4.15.2 Typical content

- Objectives for the programme
- Executive summary
- Justification and context for the programme
- Criteria against which it should be measured
- Vision statement
- Blueprint summary
- Programme roles and responsibilities
- Governance principles that have been applied
- Summary of the current state
- Explanation of tranche delivery structures
- Assurance arrangements
- Description of outcomes
- Summary of risks
- Summary of projects dossier
- Stakeholder summary
- Benefits map
- Timescales, milestones and tranches
- Information baselines, status and content.

### A.4.15.3 Notes

A programme may choose to have a single document that includes all the information developed during definition. This provides a single point of reference but may prove difficult to maintain under change control because of its size and complexity. Smaller programmes are more likely to find a single document more appropriate.

## A.4.16 Programme mandate

### A.4.16.1 Purpose

Used to describe the required outcomes from the programme, based on strategic or policy objectives.

### A.4.16.2 Typical content

- The strategic objectives of the programme
- The programme's context and the organizations that are likely be involved and affected (internal and external)
- Critical success factors against which the programme will be assessed
- What the programme is intended to deliver in terms of organizational improvements from new services and/or operational capability
- Boundaries within which the programme will work
- Possible strategies and approaches for delivery
- How the organization(s) involved will be improved as a result of delivering the new services/capability
- Initial assurance arrangements
- Expectations in terms of timescales and costs, benefits, potential constraints and deadlines that will need to be met
- Information on current or anticipated initiatives that will be included within this programme (for emerging programmes)
- Reference to any external drivers or pressures that may define the way in which the programme approaches the challenge: for example, where the driving force for change is coming from
- Summary of the 'as-is' state – the starting point at which the programme is being commissioned
- How the programme fits into the corporate mission and goals, and any other initiatives that are already under way or will be under way during the lifetime of the programme
- Initial budget.

### A.4.16.3 Notes

Some organizations may use terms like strategic or embryonic business case; this may have similar information, and as such could be used as an alternative to the programme mandate.

## A.4.17 Programme plan

### A.4.17.1 Purpose

Used to control and track the progress and delivery of the programme and resulting outcomes.

### A.4.17.2 Typical content

- An overall programme schedule showing the relative sequencing of all the projects in the projects dossier.
- Dependency network illustrating project input and output relationships
- Cross-reference to the risk register to explain any planned risk response activities
- Explanation of the grouping of projects and major activities into tranches, and the points at which end-of-tranche reviews will take place
- Risks and issues referenced during planning
- Transition planning information and schedules
- Programme-level management activities required to implement the monitoring and control strategy.
- Details of programme tranches
- Estimated effort and costs associated with the plan
- How the monitoring and control strategy will be deployed.

### A.4.17.3 Notes

Individual plans that can be consolidated into the programme plan include resource, quality and assurance information, benefits realization, and programme communications.

## A.4.18 Programme preparation plan

### A.4.18.1 Purpose

A plan that details how Defining a Programme will be undertaken.

### A.4.18.2 Typical content

- Resources required and where they will be sourced from. This should include key potential resources of the future programme management team, e.g. BCMs and programme manager
- Boundaries within which the team will work during definition
- Description of the deliverables from definition
- Governance and controls that will be applied to the defining team
- Assurance arrangements for Defining a Programme process
- Schedule of activities to achieve the outputs
- Membership of the programme board

- Estimated effort and costs associated with the plan.

## A.4.19 Projects dossier

### A.4.19.1 Purpose

Provides a list of projects required to deliver the blueprint, with high-level information and estimates.

### A.4.19.2 Typical content

- The list of projects, with descriptions and their objectives, which will be required to deliver the capability defined in the blueprint
- Outline information on outputs and resource requirements needed to deliver them
- Timescales and dependencies associated with each project, including dependencies on other projects
- Detail on initial requirements for each project, drawn from the blueprint
- High-level budgets allocated to individual projects that were used in the creation of the business case
- Links showing what contribution each project and major activity will make to the programme blueprint and benefits
- Issues and risks relating to the delivery of each project.

### A.4.19.3 Notes

This may also be referred to as a project register. The information in the projects dossier should provide the basis for the project brief that will be provided to the project team.

## A.4.20 Quality and assurance plan

### A.4.20.1 Purpose

Sets out the timetable and arrangements for carrying out the quality and assurance strategy.

### A.4.20.2 Typical content

- Schedule of activities required to implement the quality and assurance strategy
- Explanation of how the assurance arrangements will be deployed

- A description of who will undertake quality assurance, review and control activities aligned with those activities in other plans that produce items that require assurance or review
- A description of how and when the programme will carry out audits, health checks and reviews (or be subject to independent audit and review)
- Information on how and when quality of work will be monitored and reported, to include the collection, aggregation and analysis of quality-monitoring data from projects
- Estimated effort and costs associated with the plan
- Schedule for planned assurance reviews.

### A.4.20.3 Notes

This may be incorporated as part of the overarching programme plan.

## A.4.21 Quality and assurance strategy

### A.4.21.1 Purpose

Used to define and establish the activities for managing quality across the programme.

### A.4.21.2 Typical content

- Details of the processes that will be used to track programme performance against the principles and key areas; for example, people development
- Integrated assurance arrangements for the programme
- Aspects of the programme that will be subject to review and control and the quality criteria to be applied
- A description of the functions, roles and responsibilities for quality management, aligned with the programme's organization structure
- Any links to independent assurance such as gated reviews
- A description of what will trigger these activities (time-based, event-based, or associated with risk occurrence)
- A description of what actions will be taken depending on the results of quality checks and the thresholds for escalation
- Criteria for assessing programme success
- Explanation as to how continual improvement and lessons learned will be managed

- Interfaces with and dependencies on corporate management systems, including information requirements to support corporate quality management
- Interfaces with the monitoring and control strategy
- Responsibilities for assurance and quality
- Interfaces with the organization's internal audit functions
- Guidelines to ensure the appropriate use of audits and health checks
- Specific standards, regulations etc. that need to be adhered to, and which subject matter experts will be required to support quality management with regard to these areas
- Explanation of how the results of assurance reviews will be processed.

### A.4.21.3 Notes

Some organizations may refer to the quality and assurance strategy simply as the assurance management strategy.

## A.4.22 Resource management plan

### A.4.22.1 Purpose

Arrangements for implementing the resource management strategy.

### A.4.22.2 Typical content

- Schedule of activities to implement the resource management strategy
- Who will be responsible for resource management activities such as procurement, contract management, recruitment, budgeting, resource-sharing
- Tracking of use of resources (cross-referenced to the programme plan where appropriate)
- Timings of reviews and monitoring activities
- Explanation of how resources will be managed between the programme and projects; for example, will there be a pool or will each operate independently?
- Estimated effort and costs associated with the plan.

### A.4.22.3 Notes

This may be incorporated as part of the overarching programme plan.

## A.4.23 Resource management strategy

### A.4.23.1 Purpose

Used to identify how the programme will acquire and manage the resources required to achieve the business change.

### A.4.23.2 Typical content

- Funding requirements; accounting procedures for costs and expenditure; budgets for programme management resources and funding sources
- Procurement approach and reference to current contract frameworks or arrangements that will be used
- Cost and expenditure profile across the programme, expenditure approval procedures, financial reporting procedures
- Profile of resources that are shared across more than one of the projects within the projects dossier; should indicate the expected use by each project of the shared resource within time periods
- Explanation of how the resource requirements of the programme and projects will be achieved; consideration should be given to how the business operations capacity to resource the consequences of programme change will be managed
- Assets required, such as buildings and office equipment, to deliver the programme
- Technology and services required
- Which specialist skills and subject matter experts will be required and how they will be sourced
- Description of how the human resource requirements of the programme will be managed
- Explanation of how the mix of internal and external resources to the programme and projects will be managed
- How any necessary skills and knowledge will be transferred into business operations to establish the ongoing change
- Approach to dispute-resolution where resourcing conflicts occur with business-operational requirements, other initiatives and programmes.

## A.4.24 Risk management strategy

### A.4.24.1 Purpose

Defines the programme approach to risk management.

### A.4.24.2 Typical content

- Roles and responsibilities for managing risk in the programme, covering both threats and opportunities
- The process to be used and how it has been adapted from the organization's risk management standards, where they exist
- Any preferred techniques to be used for each step of the process described above
- The interface with the benefits management strategy for the approach to managing opportunities
- Scales for estimating probability and impact, giving the criteria to be used for each level within the scale
- Guidance on calculating expected value for all the risks associated with a programme
- Guidance on how proximity for risks is to be assessed
- Risk response categories, including threats and opportunities
- Any risk templates to be used, including the programme's risk register
- Relevant early-warning indicators
- Timing of risk management activities; when formal risk management activities are to be undertaken, e.g. as part of end-of-tranche reviews
- Information flows and reports that are to be produced, and their purpose, timing and recipients
- Criteria and processes for escalating risks in the programme
- Criteria to be used to assess the effectiveness of risk management within the programme
- The external or internal risk management standards to be applied.

### A.4.24.3 Notes

In some implementations, the information required for the issue management strategy and the risk management strategy may be contained in the same document. The content is derived from the organization's risk management policy and risk management process guidance.

## A.4.25 Risk register

### A.4.25.1 Purpose

Used to capture and actively manage the risks to the programme.

### A.4.25.2 Typical content

- Risk identifier – a unique reference for each risk; may need to be reflected in project risk registers when the risk could impact on one or more projects as well as the programme
- Description of the risk, including the cause of the risk, the event (description of the threat or opportunity) and its effect (summary of the likely impact on the programme and or its projects)
- Probability of the risk occurring; should be done for both the before and after state (i.e. before and after any risk response action has been implemented)
- Impact on the programme should the risk materialize, taken from the scales defined in the programme risk management strategy (where appropriate, this should show pre- and post-response action impacts)
- Proximity of the risk, which is an estimation of the timescale for when the risk might materialize
- Description of the proposed risk response
- Any residual risk after the response has been implemented
- Risk actionee – the individual responsible for the implementation of a risk response(s)
- Risk owner – named individual who is responsible for the management and control of all aspects of the risks assigned to them, including the implementation of the selected responses to address the threats or to maximize the opportunities. It should be noted that responsibilities for the probability reduction responses may be different from those of the impact reduction responses
- Response to the risk, which is dependent on whether the risk has been identified as a threat or an opportunity

- Current status of the risk itself and progress of any actions relating to the management of the risk
- Cross-reference to the programme plan to identify where risk response activities have been scheduled.

## A.4.26 Stakeholder engagement strategy

### A.4.26.1 Purpose

Used to define the framework that will enable effective stakeholder engagement and communication.

### A.4.26.2 Typical content

- Criteria on how stakeholders will be identified, grouped and tracked by the programme; it may be necessary to track specific key individuals and roles as well as groups
- Explanation of the process for adding to or changing the programme communications plan
- How the importance, influence, interest and impact of a stakeholder to a programme will be measured and assessed
- How stakeholder analysis information will be processed and stored, with reference to confidentiality of personal data
- Review cycle for stakeholder management information
- Explanation of how projects and the programme will interface on communications and stakeholder activities, including guidelines on where there is an overlap
- Responsibilities for delivering key messages and other information about the programme
- Process for identifying and handling objections, including the approach to managing negative publicity
- Description of how the programme will engage with all stakeholders, including appropriate channels and mechanisms for encouraging, receiving and responding to feedback from stakeholders
- Any policies on types of terminology and language that will be adopted within the programme
- Measures to determine the success of stakeholder engagement, including how well the communication process is engaging with stakeholders

- Description of the overall responsibilities for stakeholder engagement within the programme
- Explanations of the process for approving and integrating communications from the projects and business change teams to provide clarity and avoid overlap.

## A.4.27 Stakeholder profiles

### A.4.27.1 Purpose

Used to record stakeholder analysis information.

### A.4.27.2 Typical content

- Stakeholder map showing programme's stakeholders and their areas of interest
- Stakeholders' individual areas of concern/sensitivity
- Level of support for the programme
- Areas of the programme that stakeholders are interested in and why
- Levels of stakeholder influence on the programme and why, i.e. do we need them or do they need us?
- Any developing trends that are relevant to the programme
- Influence/interest matrix showing current and target positions for each stakeholder in terms of engagement
- Benefits distribution, showing which stakeholders receive which benefits, and which will experience dis-benefits
- Key influencers within the group, possibly those who have specialist knowledge or a relevant track record.

### A.4.27.3 Notes

A summary document illustrating the key information about each stakeholder could be referred to as a stakeholder register.

## A.4.28 Vision statement

### A.4.28.1 Purpose

Used to communicate the end goal of the programme; could be seen as providing an external 'artist's impression' of the desired future state.

### A.4.28.2 Typical content

- Clear statement of end goal of the programme; short and memorable

- Any imposed constraints
- Context for the programme and project teams
- Any relevant information to help set expectations and context within the broader business context
- Any information to support the justification for change; for example, a description of the current reality.

### A.4.28.3 Notes

Sufficiently flexible to remain relevant over the life of the programme. Terminology used should be suited to all stakeholders and the context of the programme.

## A.5 PROGRAMME INFORMATION RESPONSIBILITIES

The following list explains the levels of responsibility associated with the creation and maintenance of the programme information in Table A.3:

- **Approver** The individual accountable who signs off acceptance of the content, outcomes defined and fitness for purpose.
- **Producer** The individual who writes the document, or ensures that it is written, possibly consolidating information gathered from a number of sources.
- **Reviewer** Groups or individuals who would be given the opportunity to contribute to and approve the contents, but without executive responsibility.

The programme office will have an important involvement with all the documents, which will be dependent on its authority within the programme and broader organization. Its involvement could include:

- Advice on content
- Broader corporate governance that applies
- Provision of standards or templates
- Configuration management librarian
- Release management arrangements.

In addition there will be corporate functions that should also be consulted, in particular in the design of the governance documents.

**Table A.3 Programme information responsibilities**

| Document title | Approver | Producer | Reviewer |
|---|---|---|---|
| Benefit profile | SRO | BCM | PgM |
| Benefits management strategy | SRO | PgM | BCM |
| Benefits map | SRO | BCM | PgM |
| Benefits realization plan | SRO | PgM | BCM |
| Blueprint | SRO | PgM | BCM |
| Business case | SRO | PgM | BCM |
| Information management plan | SRO | PgM | BCM |
| Information management strategy | SRO | PgM | BCM |
| Issue management strategy | SRO | PgM | BCM |
| Issue register | SRO | PgM | BCM |
| Monitoring and control strategy | SRO | PgM | BCM |
| Organization structure | SRO | PgM | BCM |
| Programme brief | SG | SRO | |
| Programme communications plan | SRO | PgM | BCM |
| Programme definition document | SRO | PgM | BCM |
| Programme mandate | SG | | |
| Programme plan | SRO | PgM | BCM |
| Programme preparation plan | SRO | PgM | BCM |
| Projects dossier | SRO | PgM | BCM |
| Quality and assurance plan | SRO | PgM | BCM |
| Quality and assurance strategy | SRO | PgM | BCM |
| Resource management plan | SRO | PgM | BCM |
| Resource management strategy | SRO | PgM | BCM |
| Risk management strategy | SRO | PgM | BCM |
| Risk register | SRO | PgM | BCM |
| Stakeholder engagement strategy | SRO | PgM | BCM |
| Stakeholder profiles | SRO | PgM | BCM |
| Vision statement | SG | SRO | BCM |

SRO = senior responsible owner; BCM = business change manager; PgM = programme manager; SG = sponsoring group

# Appendix B: Adopting MSP

# Appendix B: Adopting MSP

## B.1 INTRODUCTION

Organization leaders will embark on transformational programmes for many reasons, but invariably there will be external drivers that are affecting the organization (see also Figure 1.3). They may choose to be on the leading edge of change and innovation by reacting first, or may prefer to have the benefit of learning from the experiences of others. Table B.1 gives examples of the sort of drivers that cause organizations to initiate a change programme.

**Table B.1 Drivers for change**

| | |
|---|---|
| Political | Change of chief executive officer |
| | Election results |
| | Changes to an industry regulator or watchdog |
| | Change to a major supplier or customer (e.g. a merger or acquisition) |
| | Changes within a partner organization |
| Environment | Global warming and increasing incidents of natural disasters |
| | Increased risk of pandemics |
| | Exposure to global terrorist threats, for example the World Trade Centre attack |
| | Focus on corporate governance stimulated by exposure of high-profile problems in global corporations |
| Societal | Increased demand for fair-trade products |
| | Awareness of local sustainability when buying food and other produce |
| | Attitudes to centralization or movement offshore |
| | Attitudes to drugs and alcohol |
| | Demographic and migration changes |
| Technological | Breakthroughs in cancer treatment drugs in the health sector |
| | Increasing demands on hardware technology from software suppliers |
| | Growth of global communications mediums – the internet being the obvious example |
| | Development of new production techniques (e.g. the increasing use of plastics to replace traditional materials) |
| Legislative | Health and safety |
| | Environmental protection |
| | Freedom of information |
| | Data protection |
| | Sarbanes-Oxley in the US |
| Economic | Public sector focus on procurement, efficiency and value for money |
| | Global interest rate changes |
| | Taxation policies and incentives |
| | Emergence of new markets and suppliers (e.g. China) |
| | Merger or acquisition changing the market balance |
| | Entry of a major new player |
| | Availability of alternative product technologies |
| | Changes to supply of raw materials |
| | Impact of government procurement policy and value-for-money initiatives on smaller enterprises |

## B.2 IS MSP THE CORRECT FRAMEWORK FOR THE CHANGE?

There is often debate about whether an initiative should be categorized as a portfolio, a programme or a project. It is critical to recognize that each is a tool for a purpose.

In principle, projects exist and thrive on certainty of outcome, whereas programmes exist and evolve in more ambiguous environments.

The decision on which toolset to deploy should depend on the scope of the change required; for example, if you were building a new road bypass around a town, it would be a large project; but if you extend the scope to include social or commercial regeneration of local communities, then you are moving into programme territory.

### Example

A broadcasting organization initiated a small project to set up a health and safety help desk, the project brief being to install a call-logging system, telephony and minor role changes. The consultant used the vision statement as a tool to define the end game.

The senior management team realized the full implications on their current ways of working and organizational structure, which required a broader realignment to deal with this new customer engagement route. This led to a programme of change affecting a large number of staff.

A standard project-output approach to the requirement would have delivered technology and tools effectively, but not have achieved the change, and the money would have been wasted. MSP techniques are not only applicable to large-scale change.

It is important that organizations which adopt MSP use it in the right context; Table B.2 will help to differentiate a programme from a corporate portfolio or a large project.

## B.3 BUSINESS ALIGNMENT

Programmes do not exist in a void. There will be other initiatives in existence in the business; and to be successful, the adoption of MSP as a means of achieving change must bring together a number of existing elements and deliver coherence.

In developing the programme, particular focus should be given to the following:

- Other influence groups and governance committees will have a vested interest in the programme and may find their sphere of influence in conflict with the fledgling programme (stakeholder identification and engagement).
- The programme vision statement must have relevance to and bring alignment with corporate objectives, mission statements, strategies, policies and any other relevant documents.
- The blueprint can often be missed out of programme definition, as it is a complex document to create. Some organizations use the term 'target operating model' or 'to-be state', which may be used for a similar purpose. Whatever the name given to it, this is a key document for pulling together any information that currently exists to help gain credibility for the programme and the team.
- 'Benefit' is a term often used but rarely understood in the rigorous way as defined by MSP. Involving operational areas early in helping to define benefits will prove rewarding, as in the past they will probably have suffered from not being consulted yet have been expected to deliver the improvement to the products or services. Consider producing a 'lighter' benefit profile, which helps people to understand the concepts before imposing the full rigour.
- Projects will almost certainly already exist, and some will need to be included in the programme. Others will not and may have to be closed prematurely. The selection should be treated sensitively, as there will be stakeholders (in particular, project executives) who will have strong views on what happens to their initiative and may see the new programme environment as threatening their status or control.

**Table B.2 Portfolio, programme and project characteristics**

| Portfolio characteristics | Programme characteristics | Project characteristics |
|---|---|---|
| Focus will be on leadership and alignment with corporate strategy | Focus will be on direction and delivery of strategy | Focus will be on management and coordination |
| Vision and blueprint will be for the entire organization | Vision and blueprint focus will be within the programme boundary | Concentration is on delivering outputs to time, quality and cost constraints |
| Timescales for the portfolio will be vague or even undefined; portfolios tend to be continual | Timescales will be loosely defined, but there will be an end point at which the programme will be focused | Quality will focus on fit-for-purpose outputs meeting clear requirements |
| Risk will be viewed from the strategic and business continuity perspectives | Risk focus will be on aggregation of project risk and operational transition, with escalation routes for strategic and operational risks | Business case will be focused on accurate budgeting for the output delivery |
| Integrity of the entire business performance will be within scope | | Risk will be focused on the costs, quality and timescales of delivery |
| Benefits orientation will be to organizational benefits that affect all areas and linked to organizational goals that are managed at corporate level | Issue orientation will be towards resolving inter-project escalations and benefits delivery | Issue management will have product and fit-for-purpose focus |
| Stakeholder engagement will have a strategic and external focus | Planning will be oriented to delivering outcomes through tranches and managing project interdependencies | Planning will be product- and activities-oriented |
| Governance will be applied through setting policies and standards | Benefit delivery will dominate, with significant focus on the rigour of benefit profiling and realization | Benefit focus will be delivering fit-for-purpose outputs that enable benefits realization |
| Quality will be viewed from the perspective of portfolio alignment and effectiveness | Governance will be applied through programme strategies and application of organizational or portfolio standards where they exist | |
| Issue management will extend beyond programme boundaries and margins | Stakeholder engagement will be focused at all levels in the organization and key external influencers | |
| Planning will be approached from the point of view of outcome dependency and resolving conflicts | Quality focus will be on management processes | |
| There will be a combination of programmes and projects and other activities delivering objectives | Business case will be focused on benefits realization balanced against the project and programme costs | |
| Business case may not exist or may be conceptual | | |

## B.4 GOVERNANCE INTEGRATION

The governance mechanisms in a programme are most effective when integrated with the corporate governance already used in an organization. This enables the programme to be aligned with the business culture and discourages it from attempting to operate in isolation. Examples of how integrated governance can be achieved are as follows:

■ The stakeholder engagement strategy and tools should be developed and integrated with the organization's corporate communications functions.

■ The programme risk management strategy should be derived from, and directly reference, the corporate risk approach (the risk management policy, process guidance and strategy).

■ The quality and assurance strategy should support and enhance the corporate systems. For instance, if the organization is compliant with an ISO standard, the programme should build that into the way it delivers quality.

■ The information management strategy should reflect and integrate with corporate information security policies, templates and storage systems rather than develop its own, and should fit with any appropriate reporting cycles.

- The resource management plan should utilize procurement frameworks and supplier relationships wherever possible and take advantage of the negotiating power of the organization with suppliers. Include any internal expert groups within its schedule.

This approach may take longer to achieve due to the broader stakeholder engagement and flexibility required, but by drawing on this internal expertise the programme will be better established and reduce conflict with the organization within which it will operate.

## B.5 EMBEDDING MSP

For MSP to become fully embedded in the organization it will require a consistent approach across a number of key themes over a period of time. Implementation of MSP can itself be a programme of change for many organizations.

### B.5.1 Culture

The senior management of the organization will need to be seen to be building, promoting and embedding a programme management culture within the organization. To achieve this it will require:

- **Board-level sponsorship and visibility as champions** Board members should be fully engaged with sponsoring groups, programme boards and working parties.
- **Organizational competence** Programme management knowledge and awareness is needed across the entire organization, not just in the professional programme community. Operations managers need to be fully aware of programme and project management procedures and terminology to enable them to contribute effectively to the outcomes. Business change managers need to be identified and fully informed.
- **Induction programme** All staff should be made aware of the organization's commitment to programme management as part of induction, and career paths should be created and promoted via programme offices.
- **Education and awareness** This should not be restricted to programme and project management practitioners; to establish the

programme within the core of the organization all disciplines and functions should be engaged and committed.

- **Organizational fit** Implementing a rigorous, prescriptive, process approach into an organization which is not process-orientated will prove to be very difficult; the level of rigour therefore needs to be appropriate to ensure that the organization can cope with it.

### B.5.2 Roles

The allocation of specialist roles to support the adoption of MSP could include that of a board, and functional and local champions. More specifically:

- Programme and project management champions – a useful technique that works in most organizations is to identify individuals in each business area to promote programme management practice
- Including elements of programme management in staff job descriptions to help develop their awareness
- Including change delivery objectives for key line management staff and links to the achievement of benefits
- Giving appropriate levels of authority to those in programme management positions.

In addition to the standard roles within a programme structure, the following may also require defined roles for nominated individuals:

- Risk
- Benefits
- Planning
- Communications
- Quality
- Change and configuration
- Design authorities to cover:
  - Technology
  - Property and estate
  - Organizational blueprint
  - Occupational risk.

### B.5.3 Process

This includes training, education and awareness. More specifically:

- Developing standard ways of running programmes and projects

■ Gaining commitment to use the processes and methods
■ Using tools and templates, which will enable this consistency and will drive best practice within the business without creating unnecessary bureaucracy
■ Adopting a flexible attitude to delivery to ensure the right approach to each situation, but not at the expense of quality
■ Ensuring that assurance activities take place to maintain focus on process efficiency and improvement.

## B.6 ASSESSMENT USING P3M3

Adopting MSP will take time. The organization will want to plan how it evolves and should set itself improvement targets. Organizations need to improve their overall performance to benefit from experience and lessons learned. An organization at Level 1 maturity may well deliver a great programme, but will inherit little long-term value if it was a one-off.

The P3M3 (Portfolio, Programme and Project Management Maturity Model) identifies five levels of maturity that an organization passes through as it seeks to achieve and then improve on best practice. It addresses the maturity of an organization in its ability to manage portfolios, programmes and projects from a process perspective. Table B.3 shows a simplified version of the model.

Although not all organizations will start at level 1 in their competence, very few will start or even reach level 5 in all aspects of their business. The primary purpose of assessing a level is to use the information gained to plan the changes necessary to improve an organization's competence in these areas of management and hence increase its ability to absorb change effectively.

The P3M3 is available on the official P3M3 website (see 'Further information') and support is available via the APM Group, who accredit organizations ('accredited consultancy organizations') to offer organizational assessments using the maturity toolkit, and 'registered consultants', who undertake the assessments and provide advice.

**Table B.3 Summary of P3M3 (a best-practice maturity model)**

| Maturity level | Project | Programme | Portfolio |
|---|---|---|---|
| 1 Awareness of process | Does the organization recognize projects and run them differently from its ongoing business? (Projects may be run informally with no standard process or tracking system.) | Does the organization recognize programmes and run them differently from projects? (Programmes may be run informally with no standard process or tracking system.) | Does the organization's board recognize programmes and projects and run an informal list of its investments in programmes and projects? (There may be no formal tracking and reporting process.) |
| 2 Repeatable process | Does the organization ensure that each project is run with its own processes and procedures to a minimum specified standard? (There may be limited consistency or coordination between projects.) | Does the organization ensure that each programme is run with its own processes and procedures to a minimum specified standard? (There may be limited consistency or coordination between programmes.) | Does the organization ensure that each programme and/or project in its portfolio is run with its own processes and procedures to a minimum specified standard? (There may be limited consistency or coordination.) |
| 3 Defined process | Does the organization have its own centrally controlled project processes, and can individual projects flex within these processes to suit the particular project? | Does the organization have its own centrally controlled programme processes and can individual programmes flex within these processes to suit the particular programme? | Does the organization have its own centrally controlled programme and project processes and can individual programmes and projects flex within these processes to suit particular programmes and/or projects? And does the organization have its own portfolio management process? |
| 4 Managed process | Does the organization obtain and retain specific measurements on its project management performance and run a quality management organization to better predict future performance? | Does the organization obtain and retain specific measurements on its programme management performance and run a quality management organization to better predict future programme outcomes? | Does the organization obtain and retain specific management metrics on its whole portfolio of programmes and projects as a means of predicting future performance? Does the organization assess its capacity to manage programmes and projects and prioritize them accordingly? |
| 5 Optimized process | Does the organization run continuous process improvement with proactive problem and technology management for projects in order to improve its ability to depict performance over time and optimize processes? | Does the organization run continuous process improvement with proactive problem and technology management for programmes in order to improve its ability to depict performance over time and optimize processes? | Does the organization run continuous process improvement with proactive problem and technology management for the portfolio in order to improve its ability to depict performance over time and optimize processes? |

# Appendix C:
# Programme office

# Appendix C: Programme office

## C.1 WHAT IS A PROGRAMME OFFICE?

To consider this question we need first to examine the environment in which programme management exists, and then to consider what is required to enable efficient and effective delivery.

A programme office provides more than services to the programme. This chapter explores this wider aspect of the programme office role in the context of the programme management environment, as shown in Figure C.1.

Programme and project offices have a variety of important roles, but this does not mean that they must all be located in the same physical area:

- Organizations might need multiple programme offices in multiple locations

- Programme and project offices can be combined or separate
- Offices could be virtual and provided by individuals in separate locations
- Some support can be provided from outside the physical programme office, e.g. part-time help from programme/project managers.

A programme office often acts as the conscience and support body for the senior responsible owner (SRO) and programme board. It can provide advice and challenge on what decisions the SRO and programme board need to take. It can also be a valuable source of intelligence in relation to the health of the constituent elements of the programme.

External drivers shape organization strategy. External changes may change strategy and implementation activities

Strategy provides the organization vision. Strategy reviews don't coincide with programme reviews

Programmes deliver the new capability to change, improve and realize benefits

Project outputs enable the organization to change. Programmes link them to the strategy

Programmes make ready operations to take project outputs, use them and measure the benefits

When the changes to operations are stable, and sufficient benefit measures completed, programme success can be reviewed

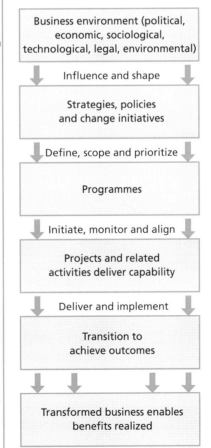

Programmes need to monitor the external environment and assess the impact of any unexpected events

Programmes need to access and interpret strategy information

Programmes manage data/information they create and acquire from other initiatives

Projects manage the data/information they create and acquire from other initiatives, and from their programme

Programmes need access to operational resources, data/information and expertise

Operations preparing for change need help to ensure they get the correct information

*Figure C.1 Programme management environment*

A well-designed and appropriately resourced programme office can provide invaluable services to programmes and projects. It can offer assistance ranging from administration to expertise (such as risk management or finance), and specialist activities such as running programme and project management tools. This leaves the programme team free to focus on the business of running the programme and concentrating their efforts to ensure success. See Figure C.2.

The programme office will often have access to considerable programme and project management expertise and help to coach and mentor less-experienced programme and project personnel. This reduces one aspect of the risk to the programme and helps to develop programme management staff.

## C.2 HOW A PROGRAMME OFFICE PROVIDES SERVICES

### C.2.1 Strategy

MSP programmes exist to implement part of the organization's policy and strategy. A programme office can help with:

- Access to policy and strategic information
- Informing programmes when policy or strategy changes
- Coordinating feedback to the senior management group responsible for strategy, so they understand whether corporate strategic initiatives have been successful
- When strategic initiatives are not as successful as expected, the programme office can help to analyse why, particularly in differentiating between a poor strategic idea and bad implementation of a good strategic idea.

Several programmes will often be needed to implement the whole strategy. A corporate programme office can help to keep track of the full picture for corporate management.

### C.2.2 Programme

Programmes need to be managed with three different perspectives in mind. A programme office can help with each of these perspectives as follows:

- The programme itself:
  - Expertise on programme management

  - Independent audit/assurance
  - Custody of programme information
  - Provision and analysis of programme information
  - Coaching and mentoring
  - Helping with the design and establishment of the programme management infrastructures
  - Custody of the organization's programme management standards, processes etc.
  - Assistance with related techniques
- External perspectives – the organization and its strategies, policies, standards etc.:
  - The programme office can coordinate 'watchers' who spot external events and, together with programme office staff, analyse how these might impact programmes
  - The programme office can maintain relationships with experts inside and outside the organization, to act as a clearing house for demand for analysis expertise
  - The programme office is often best placed to design, establish and maintain information interfaces between programmes and other business systems, for the benefit of all programmes
- Internal perspective – the projects that are part of the programme:
  - The programme office is often best-placed to design, establish and maintain communications between programmes and projects, for the benefit of all programmes
  - The standard of project management is critical to the success of the programme. The programme office can help ensure that projects are aware of and adhere to standards of management required by the programmes.

### C.2.3 Information management

Programmes create and consume large volumes of information. Documents in a programme rarely exist in isolation: they relate to others in that they derive information from them. When programmes use information, they need to ensure that they gain access to the correct versions. The programme office can help as custodians of the repository and via configuration management.

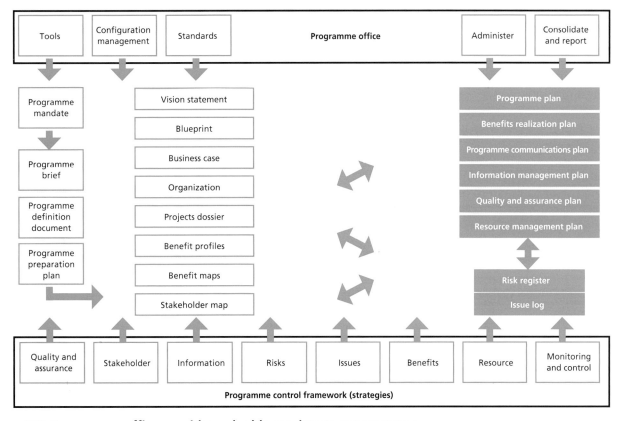

*Figure C.2 Programme office provides valuable services to programmes*

## C.2.4 Resource management

Programmes and their projects require resources – sometimes full time and sometimes part time.

A programme office can assist with resource management in the following ways:

- Maintaining a database of resources, people's skills/attributes, location, availability, contact details and managerial responsibility for the resource
- Providing a view of commitments on other programmes/projects and or on business-as-usual activities, which will impact the ability of a programme to deliver
- Helping with the acquisition of resources by maintaining relationships with external organizations who can supply resources – contract agencies for staff, organizations who rent plant and equipment, agencies who rent/let building space etc.
- In some organizations the programme office actually has responsibility for managing the allocation of resources on programmes and projects.

The permanence of a programme office across the life of the programme can provide a consistent view when other roles are perhaps filled by different people at different times in a programme's life.

## C.3 PROGRAMME OFFICE STRUCTURES

Whilst programme offices must consist of physical entities, people, facilities, tools and equipment, they do not need to exist as one single functional unit. Programme offices can be:

- The corporate portfolio office, which provides a centre of excellence for the whole organization and sets standards for the organization's programmes and projects to comply with
- A single function, more applicable to smaller enterprises, servicing all programmes and projects
- Separate functions for programmes and projects; for example, a programme office at a regional head office, with a project office in each local business unit

- Separate functions in different geographic regions, where it is important that the programme office fully understands the local culture, legislation and business practice
- Separate functions aligned to the organization structure. This is common amongst large global organizations.

## C.4 TOOLS FOR THE PROGRAMME OFFICE

A programme office will often contain expertise on the use of tools which aid programme and project management. Project management tools must also be considered. In any programme there will be large volumes of data/information flowing between the programme and its projects, so tools for programme management which cannot interface to those projects are probably of limited assistance.

### C.4.1 Project management tools

Project management software is about modelling the project. You can model how to put the roof on, how to test the software, when to deliver the printing press. The modelling helps people to see a little way into the future and therefore it helps them to make decisions; these decisions affect the project. It is the people, and the decisions they make, that affect the project – not the tools.

### C.4.2 Programme management tools

In an organization where all work in programmes and projects is planned, resources are allocated and assigned to do work, people find out what they are supposed to be doing for the current period by reference to their computers.

The tools help programmes know what is going on in other parts of the organization, such that each person is kept in touch with plans, changes to programmes and their projects, assignments and all manner of things which are being added to the system by other people. Each person finds out what they should be doing by looking at their part of the plan, and can report back on what they have actually done, thereby affecting other people's plans.

The interaction between people, their work and the purpose of the programmes should be understood and reflected in all plans and documents.

### C.4.3 Programme office tools

These are tools designed specifically for the programme and project office. Inevitably, they often include functionality found on other programme and project management tools. Typically they provide facilities for:

- Risk and issue management
- Requests for information
- Personal expenses
- Change control
- Financial control
- Benefits tracking
- Resource management
- Planning
- Capacity planning.

### C.4.4 Collaboration tools

Programme teams have always needed to share information. Collaboration software tools store and share documents and data, help to manage it (workflow and version control), control access to it (authority and relevance), and they can analyse and transform it to provide easier-to-digest business intelligence.

Programmes should have a workspace which can be structured so that documents can be organized for easy access.

Typical functions are:

- Document storage
- Version control
- Chat rooms
- Forums and discussion threads
- Contact lists
- Resource/equipment tracking.

## C.5 PROGRAMME OFFICE ROLES AND RESPONSIBILITIES

### C.5.1 Overview of the role of the programme office function

The programme office(s) may service a single programme, or may service a number of programmes. The scope of roles for the programme office will vary depending on the size and capabilities of the organization. For example, with appropriate expertise, the programme office may be a centre of excellence for all programmes and projects within the organization, providing specialist skills and facilitation across the programme and its projects. The full complement of roles may be shared across more than one physical programme office, for reasons explained earlier (see section C.3).

The programme office can provide some aspects of assurance for the programme, provided that it is independent from the programme.

The core function of the programme office is to provide an information hub for the programme. This will typically involve the following:

- **Tracking and reporting** – tracking measurements, reporting progress against plans
- **Information management** – holding master copies of all programme information, generating all necessary quality and assurance management documentation, maintaining, controlling and updating programme documentation, establishing and maintaining the index to an electronic library of programme information
- **Financial accounting** – assisting the programme manager with budget control for the programme; maintaining status reports on all projects in the programme
- **Risk and issue tracking**
- Analysing **interfaces** and **critical dependencies** between projects and recommending appropriate actions to the programme manager
- Maintaining the **list of stakeholders** and their interests
- **Quality control** – establishing consistent practices and standards adhering to the programme governance arrangements, including project planning, reporting, change control, analysing risks and maintaining and updating the risk register for the programme
- **Change control** – registering changes for subsequent investigation and resolution, monitoring items identified as requiring action, prompting timely actions and reporting on whether required actions have been carried out.

The programme office may provide additional expertise across the programme, for example:

- Providing a strategic overview of all programmes and interdependencies, and reporting upwards to senior management
- Providing consultancy-style services to project delivery teams at initiation and throughout the lifecycle of the programme, ensuring that a common approach is adopted and good practice is shared
- Carrying out health checks and advising on solutions during the lifetime of the programme and individual projects: for example, facilitating workshops involving project teams, stakeholders and members of the programme team.

## C.5.2 Programme office skillsets

There follows some examples of the core skills required in a programme office.

### C.5.2.1 Planner

- Programme and project-planning techniques
- Use of software tools for scheduling and resource management
- Use of software tools for reporting, analysis and communication of plans
- Process and tools to capture actual progress, such as via timesheets.

### C.5.2.2 Risk and issues

- Techniques for risk and issue analysis
- Procedures to manage risks and issues
- Administration of the associated action plans.

### C.5.2.3 Financial

- Cost estimating
- Cost tracking and analysis such as via earned value
- Understanding of financial methods used for the depreciation and amortization of programme and project costs; for example, appreciation of why the depreciation charges for fixed assets procured by a programme might be allocated to the programme costs, rather than to the acquisition cost.

### C.5.2.4 Programme librarian

- Programme and project-oriented filing systems, both physical and electronic
- Configuration management (see section 11.7)
- Knowledge about how to access relevant information outside the programme office, other systems in the organization, internet resources etc.
- Keeping reference material up to date.

### C.5.2.5 Change control

- Techniques for assessing requests for change
- Procedures to manage requests for change
- Administration of the associated action plans.

### C.5.2.6 Administrator

- General office duties
- Arranging travel
- Booking facilities for programme and project teams.

# Appendix D:
# Health checks

# Appendix D: Health checks

A health check is a quality tool that provides a snapshot of the status of a programme. The purpose of a health check is to gain an objective assessment of how well the programme is performing relative to its objectives and any relevant processes or standards.

What is provided here is a simplified summary of a programme health check. It should be adapted to suit the needs of the organization and programme to which it will be applied. Additional materials for a health check are available from a number of sources – for example, benchmarking against a maturity model such as P3M3, and the OGC Gateway review process, described in guides published by the OGC.

## D.1 HEALTH CHECK PROCESS

### D.1.1 Preparation

- Prepare terms of reference for the health check. It must provide a clear scope for the health check and references to any audit or review standards that are applicable (for example 'OGC Gateway Review 0 – Strategic assessment' or P3M3 maturity level). The terms of reference are similar to a project mandate in that they provide clear instructions and rationale to those who will carry out the health check.
- Determine roles and responsibilities. The programme office will be responsible for administration of all information about the programme. It may be necessary to establish a specific role for the task of information management on large programmes.
- Select review team members and assign specific roles.
- Brief the team and stakeholders who will be involved.
- Confirm understanding for the health check, including any specific focus that the review team should concentrate on.
- Confirm the method of presenting review results.
- Agree on documentation to be supplied to the review team.
- Supply the review team with required documentation.

### D.1.2 Information requirements

- What records and audit trails will be needed? This may relate to management decisions on policy, strategy and tactical approaches, transaction records, process control records or records of system use. Contract documents, for example, may extend over a considerable period of time and may be required for audit well after completion of the programme in the event of disputes.
- How are records to be recovered for scrutiny?
- Where programme records exist only in electronic form, how will their authenticity be demonstrated? It should not be assumed that electronic, as opposed to paper, records will form acceptable evidence.
- Are the programme management framework and processes adequately documented?
- Ensure that any security and confidentiality issues associated with the information are factored in.

### D.1.3 Undertake review

- Review the team, based on pre-reading; identify areas for investigation.
- Interview key programme members as appropriate.
- Investigate specific key areas.
- Conduct review based on the health check framework, adapted appropriately.
- Schedule time for involved staff.
- Hold interviews and/or discussions, as appropriate.

### D.1.4 Analyse review findings

- Prepare draft report, focusing on:
  - Overall health assessment
  - Areas of concern
  - Recommended actions
  - Agreed action plan.
- Establish learning points.

- Present the report for comment and agree actions.
- Collate agreed actions for inclusion in the final report.

### D.1.5 Agree corrective action plan

- Confirm with review team appropriate actions that are needed/recommended.
- Prepare a schedule of actions showing effort and timescales.
- Forward the schedule to the review team for inclusion in final report.
- Confirm agreement to conclusions and learning points.
- Action learning points, as appropriate.

### D.1.6 Follow-up

- Monitor to check that agreed actions are carried out.
- Assess effectiveness of actions.
- Close health check, or recommend that further reviews are needed.

## D.2 HEALTH CHECK FRAMEWORK

The framework provides a checklist to be applied to a programme using MSP. It is not exhaustive, and should be adapted to suit each individual programme. These sample questions should be read in conjunction with Chapter 2 (principles), the governance theme chapters and the transformational flow chapters.

### D.2.1 Governance themes

#### D.2.1.1 Programme organization

- Is there a complete control framework actively used, based on known good practice, adapted to the programme and moderated by previous lessons learned?
- If the programme has completed one or more tranches, has this framework been reviewed, and if necessary was it refined for the remainder of the programme?
- Has everyone engaged in the programme got a clear role description, which has been based on MSP guidelines and suitably adapted to the programme?
- Has everyone engaged in the programme been briefed on their role, and have they understood and accepted their responsibilities?

- Is there evidence in the control framework (the programme's strategy documents) and in the programme's plan that sufficient allowance has been made for audit and assurance activities?

#### D.2.1.2 Leadership and stakeholder engagement

- Is there a common and shared understanding of what is meant by 'stakeholder'?
- Is there a detailed set of stakeholders and are they being targeted in practice?
- Are targets or goals set for each group or set of groups?
- Is there a clear programme communications plan for achieving these targets or goals?
- Are the relevant members of the programme management team strongly motivated to achieve these targets or goals?
- Is there measurement for the effectiveness of engagements and communications?
- Do key stakeholder groups feel sufficiently engaged with the programme, and do they understand the programme's objectives and constraints, and the anticipated benefits that they or the organization will receive?
- Is feedback from stakeholders measured and acted upon, and fed back to the stakeholders?

#### D.2.1.3 Benefits management

- Is it clear from the programme brief what outcomes and benefits are required, and how they relate to the organization's strategy?
- Is there evidence that the benefits required are driving other management activities, such as (but not limited to) the blueprint, projects dossier, programme plan?
- Has adequate attention been given to identifying and minimizing dis-benefits?
- Is it clear how benefits depend on other items and activities, for example project outputs?
- Are the overall management rules for realizing benefits clearly described in the benefits management strategy?
- Have benefits been analysed and mapped so that there are clear links between enablers, intermediate benefits and end benefits?
- Does every benefit (intermediate and end) have a completed benefit profile?
- Has each benefit owner demonstrated adequate commitment?

- Does the benefits realization plan, juxtaposed with other plans, clearly explain what work is needed prior to transition, during transition and after transition to prepare for, transform and realize the required benefits?
- Are benefits reviews clearly planned, in terms of when they are needed, how they will be conducted and how the results will help to judge whether the programme is successful?

### D.2.1.4 Blueprint design and delivery

- From the blueprint document(s) is it clear what the organization is designed to look like at the end of the programme, what it is like today and what it will be like at intermediate states at the end of each tranche?
- Were suitably skilled persons involved in the blueprint preparation: those who have a good understanding of the current organization, and those who have the skills and attributes to produce a good design for the future?
- Have there been adequate iterations in the blueprint design to be confident that the design of the future organization combined with a sound approach to deliver it has a good chance of realizing the benefits and producing an acceptable business case?
- In the programme plan, are there activities showing when consideration needs to be given to refining the blueprint based on lessons learned so far, for example at or following the end of tranches?

### D.2.1.5 Planning and control

- Is there a programme plan that is regularly kept up to date as a result of progress input from the programme's projects and other programme-level activities?
- Was the programme plan validated and re-validated at key points, such as tranche borders, to ensure that it remains aligned with the vision statement, benefits and blueprint?
- Are dependencies clearly shown, each with an explanation as to why a dependency exists?
- Has adequate attention been paid to assessing the realism of the timetable embedded in the programme plan?
- Does the contingency in the plan reflect the degree of risk and uncertainty?
- Is there an acceptable mechanism for managing contingency?

- Is the resource management plan resynchronized with the programme plan when either the programme plan or the resource management plan is updated?
- Has adequate attention been paid to assessing whether resources required are likely to be available when required?
- Has the projects dossier been validated against the blueprint to ensure that all the project outputs (for each tranche) will deliver the future state as defined, no more and no less?
- Are assumptions, deadlines and constraints clearly stated?
- Are monitoring and control activities effective?
- Are priorities clearly stated?
- Are activities that are critical to the high priorities clearly marked and protected?
- Have transition plans been developed in adequate detail and with sufficient rigour to reflect the degree of disruption that is expected to occur when the change to the new operations takes place?
- Do transition plans clearly show the work that has to be done pre-transition, during transition and post-transition?

### D.2.1.6 The business case

- Was the business case developed to be the best optimized mix of benefits, time, cost and risk?
- Is the business case aligned with other key documents such as the blueprint, the benefits realization plan, the risk register, the resource management strategy and plan, and the programme plan?
- Are there clear statements, at an appropriate granularity, about risks and assumptions?
- Are costs clearly stated, together with an investment appraisal if appropriate?
- Is the overall approach clearly stated, with qualifying statements that show that the organization has the ability to deliver?
- Does the overall business case remain aligned to the organization's strategy?
- Is the business case regularly updated and reviewed, at least at the end of each tranche?
- Are key stakeholders satisfied with the business case, both in terms of what has been achieved so far, and predictions about what can still be achieved?
- Does the business case remain valid and viable?

### D.2.1.7 Risk and issue management

- Is there a risk management strategy and an issue management strategy, based on sound principles?
- Do actual activities reflect the contents of these strategies?
- Are risks and issues delegated to projects, escalated from projects to the programme, and from the programme to the sponsoring group, according to the rules in these strategies?
- Are the risk register and issue register properly updated regularly as new risks and issues are identified, and as agreed actions are carried out?
- Does each risk and issue have a committed owner?
- Are regular reviews undertaken, to verify that risk and issue management is working, and to assess the overall risk and issue profiles?
- Do key stakeholders accept the degrees of risk in the programme?
- Does key stakeholder activity support the management of risks and issues?

### D.2.1.8 Quality and assurance management

- Is there a quality and assurance strategy that has been developed in collaboration with appropriate stakeholders?
- Does this strategy reflect the components that are important to quality in a programme: leadership, people, processes, compliance, suppliers, the programme's assets, information (including measurement and analysis)?
- Does the quality and assurance plan clearly show what needs to be done to implement the quality strategy, when audit and reviews will be required, and the resources needed for this work?
- Is this schedule regularly updated to reflect quality activities undertaken and changes in other plans?
- Is programme information under control by configuration management, so that information for audit and reviews is readily available?
- Does configuration management adequately support other programme and project activities?

## D.2.2 Transformational flow

### D.2.2.1 Identifying a Programme

- Is there a common understanding about the programme, between the sponsoring group and the programme team?
- Is there a common understanding and shared belief that the programme is worth doing and sufficiently robust to justify investing resources for the next process, Defining a Programme?
- Is there a clear and acceptable plan for Defining a Programme?
- Is the rationale originally applied by the sponsoring group to justify the investment in the programme when they issued the programme mandate still relevant?
- Are the statements, judgements, estimates and recommendations in the programme brief commensurate with the resources deployed on its preparation?
- Can the sponsoring group have confidence in the programme brief, based on the work carried out to prepare it?

### D.2.2.2 Defining a Programme

- Has sufficient work been done to ensure the accuracy and quality of the programme definition?
- Is there a clear vision statement? Has this been suitably expanded into a blueprint?
- Have people with appropriate skills and experience been involved in analysing the options to discover the best solutions to get to the future state as expressed in the blueprint?
- What evidence is there that a reasonable number of iterations have been carried out to find the best mix of future state, projects, benefits and acceptable risk?
- Were projects designed taking into account both technical aspects and the need for effective team-working?
- Have lessons learned from other initiatives been exploited in the preparation and definition of this programme?
- Was the initial assessment and engagement with stakeholders sufficient to understand their interests and attitudes?
- Does the programme communications plan reflect this understanding?

- How thoroughly has the robustness of programme's plans been assessed?
- In particular, does the pace of change represented in the schedules reflect the abilities of the resources that can be made available?
- Does the design of the tranches reflect the uncertainty and risk, where appropriate, with early tranches focusing on matters such as discovery, research, and proof of concept?
- Have opportunities to exploit early benefits been identified?
- Is there adequate contingency relative to the degree of uncertainty and risk?
- What has been done to assess that the programme framework (namely its management strategy documentation) is adequately robust?
- Can programme staff quickly establish an adequate infrastructure to ensure adequate communication and control from the outset?
- Is the business commitment to the programme adequate to achieve the required benefits?
- Is there a business case in place; has the organization committed to providing the resources and capabilities required?
- Does the balance between cost, time, risk and benefits justifying continuing with the programme when compared with other contender initiatives that have not yet started?

### D.2.2.3 Managing the Tranches
- Does the programme have an adequate infrastructure to ensure good governance?
- Is there adequate monitoring of the external environment and significant internal changes, which might influence the organization to the extent that it could result in a change of policy and/or strategy?
- Is there a clear and compelling vision articulated at all levels in the programme?
- Is there evidence of regular leadership activity in the programme and in its projects with stakeholders?
- How effective is the management control of the schedules, risks and issues, changes, dependencies and benefits management?
- Are there adequate contingency arrangements for dealing with the unexpected and ensuring continuity of business operations?

- Are programme costs being actively managed and input to the business case?
- Is risk management effectively embedded, with the active management of risks to the delivery of benefits?
- Are reviews and measures ensuring that the emerging organization change is being adequately and appropriately assessed to confirm that it is in line with the strategy?
- Do forward-looking reviews take place at key milestones to assess whether the desired benefits are likely to be realized, based on what has been developed in the programme so far?
- Are lessons learned from earlier tranches being exploited to improve the chance of success in later tranches?
- Are lessons learned from other programmes, either within the organization or elsewhere, fully exploited?
- How effective is the management of programme team members, business partnerships and external supplier engagements?
- Are sufficient resources with adequate competence being provided?
- Is sufficient time made available for learning?
- How rigorously does the programme confirm completeness, accuracy and promptness of progress reports?
- Does the programme check that communications with stakeholders comply with the approved programme communications plan and that these communications are effective?
- As the programme progresses through tranche boundaries, does it assess the extent to which it is changing from uncertainty and exploration?
- As uncertainty decreases, does the programme re-assess the suitability of its organization, its forward plans for the remaining tranches and the integrity of the programme?
- Is there adequate monitoring to assess the readiness of operations to start transition?
- Are transition plans sufficiently well prepared to manage and control the transformation with minimum disruption?
- Have all project outputs for the tranches been accepted, and is the organization ready to embed them for operational use?
- Are benefit measurement arrangements in place?

- Have baseline benefit measures been taken?
- What evidence is there that the new operations reached a suitable state before benefit measurement started to assess the new operations?
- Is the benefit measurement process and data collection working well enough to give confidence in the conclusions produced?
- Have the plans, definition, management strategies and business case for the next tranche been refined and developed based on lessons learned so far?
- Where the previous tranche was a proof of concept, feasibility or similar, has sufficient time been allowed for learning and refining, before starting the next tranche?

### D.2.2.4 Delivering the Capability

- Have projects been adequately briefed, do they have a clear understanding about how their outputs will contribute to realizing the desired benefits, and do they understand the dependencies with other projects?
- Test project teams from time to time to assess their understanding of their relationship with the programme, with questions such as:
  - How will your project's outputs contribute to enabling change in the organization?
  - What benefits will the outputs of your project lead to?
  - What is the enabling capability that your project outputs will need to deliver benefits to?
  - What other projects are you dependent on to deliver your outputs?
  - Are other projects dependent on your project to deliver their own outputs?
  - What benefits will the outputs of these other projects lead to?
  - What is the current state of these other projects?
- Is the commitment to provide resources confirmed as each project is started and as each project approaches critical points in its lifecycle?
- Is there clarity about the relationship between the programme and its projects; are reporting lines and levels of authority clear?
- Is there frequent communication between the programme manager, business change managers, project teams and operational staff

– not just about the projects' technical aspects, but also with reference to getting ready for transition?
- Are projects assessed frequently and rigorously enough to confirm that that they are on track to enable the capability improvement in the organization that in turn will lead to realizing the expected benefits?
- Are the interfaces with other programmes or initiatives within the organization effectively managed?
- Do project staff have an up-to-date understanding of the status of other projects on which they are dependent?
- Are projects regularly checked to ensure that their plans, definitions and business case remain aligned to the programme?
- What evidence is there that the projects are being managed to an acceptable standard?

### D.2.2.5 Realizing the Benefits

- Is there adequate engagement with operational management to be sure that they will be ready to use the outputs when delivered?
- Is there good collaboration between the programme, its projects and operational staff to regularly assess that the project outputs being developed are likely to enable the scale of improvement required and lead to the benefits desired?
- Is there still the commitment to measure and track the benefits? Where at least one tranche has completed, are benefits being properly measured and tracked?
- Is the programme regularly checking for barriers that might prevent change taking place effectively enough to realize the desired benefits? When such barriers are identified, how effective is the action taken in overcoming the obstacles?

### D.2.2.6 Closing a Programme

- Is there clarity about the reasons why the programme is closing?
- Have sufficient benefit measures been captured to judge success against the business case?
- Where appropriate, are operational staff ready to take over further benefit measurements?
- Are adequate reviews taking place? Are unambiguous objective conclusions emerging?

- Has responsibility for future benefit reviews been assigned?
- Are benefits self-sustaining?
- Will lessons learned be compiled and distributed?
- Have all remaining resources been re-assigned?
- If the programme is closing before its planned end, have all options been thoroughly investigated to make sure that it cannot continue successfully?
- For programmes closing early, have reviews, audits or health checks produced a clear understanding of the reasons why it should not continue?
- For programmes closing early, will best use be made of what the programme and its projects have produced so far?
- Will the programme be closed in an orderly manner?

Further information

# Further information

The following is a list of useful references, some of which were used by the MSP authors.

## LITERATURE

Bartlett, John. (2002a). *Managing Risk for Projects and Programmes*. Project Manager Today Publications.

Bartlett, John. (2002b). *Managing Programmes of Business Change*. Project Manager Today Publications.

Collins, Jim. (2001). *Good to Great: Why Some Companies Make the Leap and Others Don't*. Harper Business.

Covey, Stephen R. (1990). *Principle-centred Leadership*. Simon & Schuster.

Kotter, John P. (1996). *Leading Change*. Harvard Business School Press.

Office of Government Commerce. (2010). *Management of Risk*: *Guidance for Practitioners*. The Stationery Office, London.

Nanus, Burt. (1992). *Visionary Leadership: Creating a Compelling Sense of Direction for Your Organization*. Jossey-Bass.

Office of Government Commerce (2011). *Management of Portfolios*. The Stationery Office, London.

Office of Government Commerce (2010). *Management of Value*. The Stationery Office, London.

Partington, David; Pellegrinelli, Sergio and Young, Malcolm. (2005). Attributes and levels of programme management competence: An interpretive study. *International Journal of Project Management, 23*, 87–95.

Reiss, Geoff; Anthony, Malcolm; Chapman, John; Leigh, Geof; Pyne, Adrian and Rayner, Paul. (2006). *Gower Handbook of Programme Management*. Gower.

Robinson, Peter P. (2005). *Always Change a Winning Team: Why Reinvention and Change are Prerequisites for Business Success*. Marshall Cavendish.

Senge, Peter M. (1990). T*he Fifth Discipline: The Art and Practice of the Learning Organization*. Century Business.

Ward, John and Daniel, Elizabeth. (2006). *Benefits Management: Delivering Value from IS and IT Investments*. Wiley.

## USEFUL WEBSITES

In addition to those cited below, local government websites can also be useful sources of information.

MSP
www.msp-officialsite.com

Best Management Practice
www.best-management-practice.co.uk

P3M3
www.p3m3-officialsite.com

The Cabinet Office of the UK government
www.cabinetoffice.gov.uk

APMG-International – accredited examination institute
www.apmg-international.com

Association for Project Management
www.apm.org.uk

Project Management Institute
www.pmi.org

Glossary

# Glossary

The following is an explanation of common terms used in the guide. It is drawn from the OGC PPM Common Glossary and includes terms that are relevant to MSP.

Document titles are not included within the glossary, as these are fully explained in Appendix A. Documents that are mentioned in the guide but are not defined in Appendix A are described here, where appropriate.

## accountable

Personally answerable for an activity. Accountability cannot be delegated, unlike responsibility.

## aggregated risk

The overall level of risk to the programme when all the risks are viewed as a totality rather than individually. This could include the outputs of particular scenarios or risk combinations.

## as-is state

The current operating structure and performance of the parts of the business which will be impacted by a programme.

## assumption

A statement that is taken as being true for the purposes of planning, but which could change later. An assumption is made where some facts are not yet known. There is a risk that assumptions are not correct.

## assurance

All the systematic actions necessary to provide confidence that the target (system, process, organization, programme, project, outcome, benefit, capability, product output, deliverable) is appropriate. Appropriateness might be defined subjectively or objectively in different circumstances. The implication is that assurance will have a level of independence from that which is being assured.

## baseline

A reference level against which an entity is monitored and controlled.

## benefit

The measurable improvement resulting from an outcome perceived as an advantage by one or more stakeholders, and which contributes towards one or more organizational objective(s).

## benefits management

The identification, definition, tracking, realization and optimization of benefits within and beyond a programme.

## benefits register

Summary document that contains key information from the benefit profiles.

## best practice

A defined and proven method of managing events effectively.

## border

The time-bound limitations of a tranche, i.e. when end-of-tranche reviews are held and the programme receives endorsement to move into the next tranche.

## boundary

The scope of what a programme will cover; the extent of its influence and authority.

## business as usual (BAU)

The way the business normally achieves its objectives.

## business case management

The manner in which a programme's rationale, objectives, benefits and risks are balanced against the financial investment, and how this balance is maintained, adjusted and assessed during the programme.

### business change authority

An individual who represents a group of business change managers, similar to a senior BCM or business change sponsor.

### business change manager (BCM)

The role responsible for benefits management, from identification through to realization, and for ensuring that the implementation and embedding of the new capabilities are delivered by the projects. Typically allocated to more than one individual and also known as 'change agent'.

### business change team

A group of specialists appointed to support a business change manager in the business change management aspects of benefits realization.

### capability

The completed set of project outputs required to deliver an outcome; this exists prior to transition. It is a service, function or operation that enables the organization to exploit opportunities.

### change manager

Reports to the business change manager (BCM) and may operate at a project level to support benefits realization, namely focus on the realization of a particular benefit.

### configuration

A generic term used to describe a group of products or items that work together to deliver a product or service, or a recognizable part of a product or service. A configuration may be configuration item of a larger configuration.

### configuration item

An asset that is subject to configuration management. The asset may be a component of a product, a product, or a set of products in a release.

### configuration management

Technical and administrative activities concerned with the creation, maintenance and controlled change of configuration throughout the life of a product.

### consult

To give groups or individuals the opportunity to contribute to and make recommendations on an action or document.

### corporate governance

The ongoing activity of maintaining a sound system of internal control by which the directors and officers of an organization ensure that effective management systems, including financial monitoring and control systems, have been put in place to protect assets, earning capacity and the reputation of the organization.

### corporate portfolio

The totality of the change initiatives within an organization; it may comprise a number of programmes, standalone projects and other initiatives that achieve congruence of change.

### corporate portfolio board

One name for the body within the organization that has authority to make decisions about the composition and prioritization of the organization's portfolio of programmes and projects. This may be the corporate board, and in MoP (Management of Portfolios) it is also referred to as the 'portfolio direction group' or 'investment committee'.

### cross-organizational programme

A programme requiring the committed involvement of more than one organization to achieve the desired outcomes; also referred to as a 'cross-cutting' programme.

### dependency

An activity, output or decision that is required to achieve some aspect of the programme. It can be internal or external to the programme.

### dis-benefit

A measurable decline resulting from an outcome perceived as negative by one or more stakeholders, which reduces one of more organizational objective(s).

## emergent programme

A programme that subsumes one or more pre-existing projects into a coherent alignment with corporate policy and strategy.

## end goal

The ultimate objective of a programme – the same as the 'to-be state' or 'future state'.

## feedback log

A document that is used to capture, track and ensure that all stakeholder feedback is dealt with.

## gated review

A structured review of a project, programme or portfolio as part of formal governance arrangements carried out at key decision points in the lifecycle to ensure that the decision to invest as per the agreed business case remains valid.

## governance

The functions, responsibilities, processes and procedures that define how a programme is set up, managed and controlled.

## inform

In the context of a RACI table, to advise a group or individual of a change or a decision. In MSP, this is typically used in the context of something that affects activities or document creation.

## issue

A relevant event that has happened, was not planned and requires management action. It could be a problem, query, concern, change request or risk that has occurred.

## key performance indicator (KPI)

A metric (either financial or non-financial) that is used to set and measure progress towards an organizational objective.

## leadership

The ability to direct, influence and motivate others towards a better outcome.

## margin

The flexibility that a programme has for achieving its blueprint, benefits and business case.

## opportunity

An uncertain event that could have a favourable impact on objectives or benefits.

## outcome

The result of change, normally affecting real-world behaviour or circumstances. Outcomes are desired when a change is conceived. Outcomes are achieved as a result of the activities undertaken to effect the change; they are the manifestation of part or all of the new state conceived in the blueprint.

## output

The tangible or intangible artefact produced, constructed or created as a result of a planned activity.

## P3M3

The Portfolio, Programme and Project Management Maturity Model that provides a framework with which organizations can assess their current performance and put in place improvement plans.

## plan

A detailed proposal for doing or achieving something, detailing the what, when, how and by whom.

## policy

A course of action (or principle) adopted by an organization; a business statement of intent, setting the tone for an organization's culture.

## portfolio

The totality of an organization's investment (or segment thereof) in the changes required to achieve its strategic objectives.

## product

An input or output, whether tangible or intangible, that can be described in advance, created and tested; also known as an output or deliverable.

## programme

A temporary flexible organization structure created to coordinate, direct and oversee the implementation of a set of related projects and activities in order to deliver outcomes and benefits related to an organization's strategic objectives. A programme is likely to have a life that spans several years.

## programme assurance

Independent assessment and confirmation that the programme as a whole or any one of its aspects is on track, that it is applying relevant practices and procedures, and that the projects, activities and business rationale remain aligned to the programme's objectives. *See also* gated review.

## programme board

A group that is established to support an SRO in delivering a programme.

## programme management

The coordinated organization, direction and implementation of a dossier of projects and transformation activities (i.e. the programme) to achieve outcomes and realize benefits of strategic importance.

## programme manager

The role responsible for the set-up, management and delivery of a programme; typically allocated to a single individual.

## programme office

The function providing the information hub and standards custodian for a programme and its delivery objectives; it could provide support for more than one programme.

## programme organization

How a programme will be managed throughout its lifecycle, the roles and responsibilities of individuals involved in the programme, and personnel management or human resources arrangements. Also known as programme organization structure.

## project

A temporary organization that is created for the purpose of delivering one or more business outputs according to a specified business case.

## project register

An alternative term for 'projects dossier' (see Appendix A) – the document that records the list of projects.

## proximity

(Of risk) the time factor and how close an event is; i.e. risks will occur at particular times, and the severity of their impact will vary depending on when they occur.

## quality

The degree to which the features and inherent or assigned characteristics of a product, person, process, service and/or system bear on its ability to show that it meets expectations or stated needs, requirements or specification.

## quality assurance

The planned systematic process that will be used to provide confidence that outputs will match their defined quality criteria.

## quality control

The process of monitoring specific results to determine whether they comply with the relevant standards, and of identifying ways to eliminate causes of unsatisfactory performance.

## quality management system

The complete set of quality standards, procedures and responsibilities for a site or organization.

## register

A formal repository that is managed and requires agreement by the board on its format, composition and use.

## responsible

Used to describe the individual who has the authority and is expected to deliver a task or activity; responsibility can be delegated.

## risk

An uncertain event or set of events that, should it occur, will have an effect on the achievement of objectives. A risk is measured by a combination of the probability of a perceived threat or opportunity occurring and the magnitude of its impact on objectives.

## risk appetite

The amount of risk the organization, or subset of it, is willing to accept.

## risk assessment

The identification and evaluation of risks.

## risk estimation

The estimation of probability and impact of an individual risk, taking into account predetermined standards, target risk levels, interdependencies and other relevant factors.

## risk evaluation

The process of understanding the net effect of identified threats and opportunities on an activity when aggregated together.

## risk identification

The determination of what could pose a risk; a process to describe and list sources of risk (threats and opportunities).

## risk management

The systematic application of principles, approaches and processes to the tasks of identifying and assessing risks, and then planning and implementing risk responses.

## senior responsible owner (SRO)

The single individual with overall responsibility for ensuring that a project or programme meets its objectives and delivers the projected benefits.

## sponsor

The main driving force behind a programme or project. Some organizations use the term sponsor instead of SRO.

## sponsoring group

The driving force behind a programme, which provides the investment decision and top-level endorsement for the rationale and objectives of the programme.

## stakeholder

Any individual, group or organization that can affect, be affected by, or perceives itself to be affected by, a programme.

## stakeholder map

A diagrammatic representation of the stakeholders relevant to an organizational activity and their respective interests.

## stakeholder register

A document that contains a summary of the information in the stakeholder profiles.

## strategy

An approach or line to take, designed to achieve a long-term aim. Strategies can exist at different levels in an organization – in MSP there are corporate strategies for achieving objectives that will give rise to programmes. Programmes then develop strategies aligned with these corporate objectives against particular delivery areas.

## threat

An uncertain event that could have a negative impact on objectives or benefits.

## to-be state

The future planned state of an organization as described by the blueprint.

## tranche

A programme management term describing a group of projects structured around distinct step changes in capability and benefit delivery.

## transformation

A distinct change to the way an organization conducts all or part of its business.

## transition plan

The schedule of activities to cover the 'transition' phase of the benefits realization plan.

## vision

A picture of a better future that will be delivered by the programme.

## workstream

The logical grouping of projects and activities that together enable effective management. Workstreams may delineate projects against a variety of criteria.

Index

# Index